CW01011266

BLIND TRUST

How parents with a sick child can escape the lies, hypocrisy and false promises of researchers and the regulatory authorities

This book is dedicated to our daughter Rebecca, without whom this book would never have been written. Rebecca was our first child, born in 1994 with Sturge-Weber syndrome (SWS – see www.sturge-weber), a complex disease for which only symptomatic treatment is available. Rebecca was moderately mentally and physically handicapped and suffered from epilepsy, among other things. And she was always full of zest for life. Over time her epilepsy had become more stable, but in June 2021 she had an epileptic fit in the night, suffocated, and passed away. Living with a special child shapes the life of parents and siblings and gives you an insight into areas and aspects of society that would otherwise remain closed. Rebecca will always stay alive in our hearts.

BLIND
TRUST

How parents with a
sick child can escape
the lies, hypocrisy
and false promises of
researchers and the
regulatory authorities

Klaus Rose, MD MS

Foreword by Jane M Grant Kels MD, FAAD

Hammersmith Health Books
London, UK

First published in 2022 by Hammersmith Health Books – an imprint of
Hammersmith Books Limited
4/4A Bloomsbury Square, London WC1A 2RP, UK
www.hammersmithbooks.co.uk

© 2022, Klaus Rose

All rights reserved. No part of this publication may be reproduced, stored in
any retrieval system or transmitted in any form or by any means, electronic,
mechanical, photocopying, recording or otherwise, without the prior permission of the publisher and copyright holder.

The information contained in this book is for educational purposes only. It is
the result of the study and the experience of the author. Whilst the information
and advice offered are believed to be true and accurate at the time of going to
press, neither the author nor the publisher can accept any legal responsibility or
liability for any errors or omissions that may have been made or for any adverse
effects which may occur as a result of following the recommendations given
herein. Always consult a qualified medical practitioner if you have any concerns
regarding your health.

British Library Cataloguing in Publication Data: A CIP record of this book is
available from the British Library.

Print ISBN: 978-1-78161-202-6
Ebook ISBN: 978-1-78161-203-3

Commissioning editor: Georgina Bentliff
Designed and typeset by: Evolution Design & Digital Ltd
Cover design by: Madeline Meckiffe
Index: Dr Laurence Errington
Production: Deborah Wehner of Moatvale Press, UK
Printed and bound by: TJ Books, Padstow, Cornwall, UK

Contents

Foreword

It is a great honour to be invited to write a preface for Dr Klaus Rose's new book. He has become one of my heroes in medicine. Dr Rose has taken on the giant regulatory authorities involved in childhood drug trials – the European Medicines Agency (EMA) and US Food and Drug Administration (FDA) – as well as pharmaceutical companies and academic physicians who have advanced their careers by advocating and participating in these trials. The best analogy for this struggle is to compare Dr Rose to a young David trying to defeat the Philistine giant in the Old Testament story in the Book of Samuel. In this analogy, the 'giants' are inappropriately advocating for unnecessary and potentially harmful clinical trials in 'children' for drugs where proof of concept has already been established.

Since 1962, pharmaceutical companies, in an effort to protect themselves from damage lawsuits, have inserted paediatric warnings into drug labels [the literature supporting a pharmaceutical]. These labels warned that the drugs had not been tested on children. As a result, children were referred to by many as 'therapeutic orphans'. Consequently, the American Academy of Pediatricians (AAP) began to support separate paediatric clinical trials and, in collaboration with the FDA, paediatric pharmaceutical legislation was introduced resulting in patent extensions for pharmaceutical companies that undertook clinical trials in 'children'. In Europe, the EU has been even more demanding in that the European Medicines Agency (EMA) has demanded that the company developing a drug submit a draft 'paediatric investigation plan' (PIP) mandating that the company would perform clinical trials in minors. The PIP negotiation with the EMA usually takes one year and must be approved and later performed for the drug ultimately to be approved and available to adults. If the PIP is rejected, the EU approval of the new drug is blocked until a new draft PIP has been submitted and has been successfully negotiated.

This has resulted in delayed availability of new drugs to our vulnerable children and grandchildren despite the fact that proof of concept has already been undertaken. Instead of expensive and lengthy clinical trials, all that is needed are dosing studies for smaller children. The resultant delay is not only unconscionable but the trials often place children in the control group at potential harm.

In this new text, Dr Rose exposes the lies, hypocrisy and false promises made by researchers and regulatory authorities and offers solutions to parents and others who are involved.

Jane M. Grant-Kels MD, FAAD
Professor of Dermatology, Pathology and Pediatrics
Vice Chair, Department of Dermatology
Director of the Cutaneous Oncology Center and Melanoma
    Program
Founding Chair Emeritus, Department of Dermatology
Founding Director Emeritus of the Dermatology Residency and
    Dermatopathology Lab
University of CT (Connecticut) Health Center Dermatology
    Department, Connecticut, USA

About the author

Klaus Rose MD MS is a medical doctor who worked in the pharmaceutical industry for 20 years. He was an enthusiast for pharmaceutical studies in children and became global head of paediatrics first at Novartis and then Genentech/Roche before becoming an independent advisor on paediatric studies for drug approval in 2011. Through this work he came to understand a large proportion of 'investigations' in children are not only unnecessary but also ethically questionable yet these problems are hidden behind the message of 'helping children' that is hard to challenge. His book for scientists and health professionals involved in drug trials – *Considering the Patient in Pediatric Drug Development: How good intentions turned to harm* – was published by Elsevier (Academic Press) in 2020.

Preface

I am a medical doctor. After clinical training I joined the pharmaceutical industry to use my languages in an international job. When in 1997 I came across paediatric clinical studies, I was intrigued, also because our eldest daughter suffered from a rare, complex disease. I became passionate about 'paediatric drug development', became global head of paediatrics at Novartis from 2001 to 2005, and had the same position at Genentech/Roche from 2005 to 2009. Since 2011 I have been independent, advising companies on paediatric studies that are requested/demanded by the European Medicines Agency (EMA) and the US Food and Drug Administration (FDA). From early on, I saw that many paediatric studies required by the regulatory authorities were questionable, but did not investigate this further until recently. Finally, I found the answer to the riddle in historical documents from the American Academy of Pediatrics, the FDA and the EMA. Demanding separate paediatric studies began when drug toxicities were observed in newborns in the 1950s. Real dangers of drugs to babies were exaggerated into alleged risks of all drugs in all 'children', even those who were already physically mature. Justified early concerns for babies have since grown into a worldwide industry of pointless and even harmful 'paediatric' studies as the many cases highlighted in the book will show. But they make perfect sense if you look at who benefits. US lawmakers were persuaded to reward pharmaceutical companies funding 'paediatric' drug studies with patent extensions, allowing those companies to sell their drugs longer at a high price. All of a sudden paediatric researchers were being asked for advice and to conduct studies. 'Paediatric' careers emerged in academic research, the regulatory authorities and pharmaceutical companies.

The catch is that the 18th birthday, an *administrative* milestone, is also used as the milestone for a non-existent physical transformation. The body matures slowly during the process of puberty. A tall 16-year-old athlete is *administratively* still a child, but no longer *physically* immature. Minors do not remain as immature and vulnerable as newborns until they come of age; medicine treats the body, not that body's legal status. This is a new challenge at the interface of medicine and the law in the context of continuing medical progress and blind trust in institutions and regulatory authorities to 'do the right thing' – a new challenge for the 21st century.

I publish in international peer-reviewed medical journals.[1, 2] My first medical textbook, *Considering the Patient in Pediatric Drug Development: How good intentions turned into harm* was released in 2020.[3] More books are in the pipeline. Unexpectedly, I found I had come across the largest abuse in medical research since the unveiling of inhumane studies in the USA in 1966,[4, 5] and the termination of the Tuskegee Study in 1972.[6] *Blind Trust* aims to reveal this abuse, bringing together the many fields of paediatrics to give an overall picture of the ongoing situation, and to help parents to avoid questionable studies that will not help their children and might even harm them.

References

1. Rose K. Published research: https://pubmed.ncbi.nlm.nih. gov/?term=klaus+rose&sort=date&size=100
2. Rose K. Website: www.klausrose.net
3. Rose K. *Considering the Patient in Pediatric Drug Development: How good intentions turned into harm.* Academic Press; 2020.

4. Beecher HK. Ethics and clinical research: From the anaesthesia laboratory of the Harvard Medical School at the Massachusetts General Hospital. *New England Journal of Medicine* 1966; 274: 1354-1360. www.observatoriobioetica.org/wp-content/uploads/2016/09/Beecher_Ethics_and_Clinical_Research_1966. pdf

5. Harkness J, Lederer SE, Wikler D. Laying ethical foundations for clinical research. *Bulletin of the World Health Organization* 2001; 79(4): 365-366. www.who.int/bulletin/archives/79(4)365.pdf

6. Wikipedia: The Tuskegee Syphilis Study. https://en.wikipedia.org/wiki/Tuskegee_Syphilis_Study

Abbreviations

AAP – American Academy of Pediatrics
ACI – autologous chondrocyte implantation
ADHD – attention-deficit hyperactivity disorder
ALL – acute lymphoblastic leukaemia
ANS – autonomic nervous system
ATMPs – advanced therapy medicinal products
CAPS – cryopyrin-associated periodic syndrome
CAR-T – chimeric antigen receptor – T cell
CDC – Centers for Disease Control and Prevention, USA
CFF – Cystic Fibrosis Foundation
CFTR – transmembrane conductance regulator
CINCA – chronic infantile neurologic cutaneous and articular
    syndrome
CNS – central nervous system
CROs – clinical research organisations
DMT – disease-modifying treatment
EC – ethics committee
EMA – European Medicines Agency
Enpr-EMA – European Network of Paediatric Research at the
    European Medicines Agency
EuPFI – European Paediatric Formulation Initiative
FCAS – familial cold auto-inflammatory syndrome
FDA – Food and Drug Administration, USA
FDAMA – FDA Modernization Act
FDARA – FDA Reauthorization Act
FMF – familial Mediterranean fever
GIGO – garbage in, garbage out
IBD – inflammatory bowel disease
ICMJE – International Committee of Medical Journal Editors

IPMSSG – International Paediatric Multiple Sclerosis Study Group
IRBs – institutional review boards
JIA – juvenile idiopathic arthritis
MACI – matrix-assisted autologous chondrocyte implantation
MAS – macrophage activation syndrome
MHRA – Medicines and Healthcare Regulatory Agency, UK
MIS – multi-system inflammatory system
MPH – methylphenidate
NCT number – National Clinical Trials number
NIH – National Institutes of Health, USA
NORD – National Organization for Rare Disorders, USA
NSAID – non-steroidal anti-inflammatory drug
PIP – paediatric investigation plan (required by EMA)
PRCSG – Pediatric Rheumatology Collaborative Study Group
PRINTO – European Paediatric Rheumatology International Trials
    Organisation
T1DM – type 1 diabetes mellitus
T2DM – type 2 diabetes mellitus
TNF – tumour necrosis factor
TRAPS – TNF receptor-associated periodic syndrome

Part I

Introducing the flawed concept of 'paediatric' research

Chapter 1

Introduction

The instinct to protect our children is one of the key drivers that helped mankind to survive hostile conditions during our origins in primaeval times. In those early days, we had to overcome life-threatening dangers like prey animals, wildfires, snowstorms, flooding, hostile tribes, starvation and more. Today's society is far more complex and is differentiated into rich and poor, educated and less educated, the stylish and the homespun, and many different ideologies. We have a government; we have institutions and laws; we have modern medicine. Nevertheless, when it comes to survival, our instincts still kick in – the family against the rest of the world. Modern ideology contends that we all are equal, but this is only correct in theory. Cynically speaking and to quote George Orwell's *Animal Farm*, some people are more equal than others – they have access to more and better resources.

Parents are scared when their child gets sick. Fear is another old and powerful instinct. Many diseases that in the past were merciless child killers can today be prevented, treated, or both. But fear for our children continues to have a deep impact on our lives as parents, grandparents and members of society as a whole.

Today's society is changing and evolving increasingly fast. Families have become smaller. When children grow up, they often move away for education or work. Social mobility has increased. With increased mobility, the immediate support from grandparents and the extended family has become less crucial than it used to be generations ago. Education has become more complex. Children are no longer dressed as little adults as was the case a century ago. In rural areas, young children used to be sent out to play with other children all day long. They returned home when they were hungry, and in the evening to sleep. This may still work somewhere, but not in our cities. And most of us now live in cities.

Healthcare has become more complex along with everything else. The list of diseases against which we can vaccinate our children is constantly growing. Also, for the healthcare of their children parents depend today more on education and modern communication and less on the advice of older generations than in the past. Child mortality has decreased with improved hygiene, housing, nutrition, clothing, education and, of course, healthcare as well as many more factors. We now have specialised healthcare professionals working in many diverse institutions. This includes direct care for the individual by a range of highly trained professionals in specialised, well-equipped hospitals supported by ongoing research at many levels.

It is with this research that this book is concerned and its interface with the medical care of children and young people. Research in both academic institutions and commercial organisations continually improves and expands available technology, drugs and medical devices. However, where this research is carried out simply for the purposes of doing research rather than to improve what is available, we have a problem as this book will show.

Clinical guidelines ensure standard treatment for those diseases where a certain level of accepted practice has been reached. Today, surgery can correct congenital malformations of the heart, the digestive system, the abdominal wall and many other organs; injuries can often be repaired; post-surgical infections can be overcome. This can be done only with the support of modern drugs – such as antibiotics and immune-suppressants – modern surgical tools that allow keyhole surgery, modern imaging techniques, electronic documentation of patient histories, and more.

A flawed concept in paediatric research

Unfortunately, despite all these advances, a flawed concept has slipped into today's paediatric research. As long as a minor can be treated routinely with well-established medications and/or procedures, this should not concern parents, but if their child suffers an accident, or is diagnosed with a serious and/or rare disease, or the parents observe that somehow their child is not developing as s/he should, then they can suddenly be exposed to the consequences of the flawed concept.[1, 2, 3, 4] They may be asked to consent to their child being included in a study for a new drug or device or procedure. This study will be justified by explaining that we do not know if the given intervention works in children. As I will show, parents should listen to their instincts/gut feelings about such requests. They have the right to decide if their child should participate in a study and if this will be in their child's best interests. They can and should refuse experimental treatment if they suspect anything fishy.

Medical treatment should always consider both body and soul. Prayers address the soul. Drugs are physical and treat the body though they can of course also affect the mind and emotions. The flawed concept at the heart of this book relates to the physical body and how it differs between adults and children.

So what is this flawed concept? It is the rigid separation of medical research into 'paediatric' – children aged 0 to 17 – and 'adult' (generally, over 18). The body does not change on the night of the 18th birthday, yet laws in the US, European Union

(EU) and post-Brexit UK insist that individuals administratively classified as 'children' should receive medications that have been examined separately in extensive 'paediatric' clinical studies.[5] This concept of separate 'paediatric' studies and 'paediatric' drug development sets an artificial barrier in the way of the clinical work of paediatricians and general practitioners to provide treatments they know to be useful, because these are subject to separate research coordinated by academic paediatric researchers and demanded by the regulatory authorities.

As we shall see, the different meanings of the term 'child' create an artificial semantic blur. Legally and administratively, a 'child' is a minor who has not reached the age of majority (18 in most countries), but physiologically and bodily, most adolescents mature long before this official age limit.[2, 3, 6] When a young person wants to buy alcohol, they may already look like an adult and may already be physically mature. Nevertheless, they must provide a document (ID) to prove their age.

The semantic blurring of the term 'child', and the clinical studies the conflicting meanings trigger, may still appear to be far away from our everyday concerns. However, it is among the key tasks of research to explore the limits of what we know already and to recognise where new knowledge is needed. On what then should we be focusing 'paediatric' research? So much has been achieved up until now with research that has pushed back the frontiers. Seventy-five years ago, many paediatric wards were filled with children in iron lungs, as polio had taken away their ability to breathe on their own.[7, 8] Without iron lungs, the young patients would have died. Iron lungs became unnecessary when polio was prevented by vaccination. Without research, neither the iron lung nor the polio vaccine would have been developed.

Our concern for our children may mean we are less critical than perhaps we should be of some types of research. As an example, paediatric oncology has marketed its need for research funding very cleverly. To emphasise its importance, cancer is often described as the most frequent cause of death in children 'by disease'.[9] Well, the most frequent cause of death in children is actually accidents, followed by suicide, and only then malignancies.[10] Nevertheless, parents' fears that one day their child might develop cancer, and the overall protective instincts of human beings to help sick children, mean that paediatric oncology studies find it easy to get funding and support, be they worthwhile or not.

The appeal to further improve the healthcare of 'children' always sounds very noble. It is no surprise that children's medical research charities find fund raising relatively easy. However, behind this shiny surface there is an ugly truth. Many of the 'paediatric' studies that are triggered by demands from paediatric researchers and the regulatory authorities are unnecessary. Others may even harm young patients.[3, 4] In the course of this book I aim to show how to distinguish the useful from the useless and the useless from the downright bad.

To understand the flawed concept in paediatric research and its consequences is both easy and difficult. It is difficult if you try to immerse yourself in depth in too many scientific disciplines and details, or if you deeply and blindly believe everything that medical doctors, authorities, and 'experts' tell you. It is easy under three conditions: you must be curious; you must be ready to ask questions; and you need some scepticism about authorities, official doctrines and official rules.

The flawed concept behind 'paediatric' studies has emerged over decades. Overall, drug studies in minors younger than 18 years are called 'paediatric drug research' which are part of 'paediatric drug development'. Many of the researchers and healthcare professionals who were trained in this concept are acting in good faith. Parents with sick children are probably those for whom the absurdities and cruelty of unnecessary 'paediatric' studies are easiest to grasp. As I will show, paediatric drug research has become to a large degree a pseudo-scientific construct. The following chapters will guide you through the transition of drug development from the preserve of academic institutions to the business of for-profit pharmaceutical companies; the myth that 'on-label' treatment is safer than 'off-label' treatment; and the implications of the globalisation of drug development. Part II of this book will show, through many example clinical areas, including cancer, epilepsy, knee surgery and depression, how unnecessary research is harming young patients.

This book is intended not just to bring unnecessary and therefore wasteful research to public attention. It is meant to be of practical use to any parent considering the question 'Should I agree for my child to take part in this research project?' It is my hope that, through specific examples and general guidance, you will know when to say 'Yes' and when, without guilt despite all sorts of pressures, to say 'No'.

Chapter 2

The business of paediatric research

This chapter aims to explain how 'paediatric drug development' has become a huge business worldwide. It outlines the basic processes of drug development and shows how the vast amounts of data collected in minors are driven more by legal compliance and conflicts of interest than the wish to advance knowledge about the best treatments for children. The need for parallel tracks for drug approval in adults and 'children' is, you will see, a misleading construct that has developed a life of its own and blinds public perception and even the perception of many of its protagonists. De-mystifying this situation is long overdue.

Drivers of drug regulation

By today's standards, many of the drugs sold in pharmacies before World War II, though assumed to be helpful to patients at the time, were not. Many contained alcohol, cocaine, and other intoxicants. They were able to improve patients' mood in the short term, or to help them to sleep or to cope with pain, but many were also dangerous. In those days, all products available in pharmacies were sold 'over the counter' (OTC) without a prescription from a medical doctor.

Two major catastrophes have since formed the way drugs are developed today. These involved the antibiotic Elixir Sulfanilamide in the US and the drug thalidomide worldwide.

The sulfanilamide disaster

In 1937 a company developed a liquid form of the antibiotic sulfanilamide, effective against streptococcal infections. The company used, as the solvent, diethylene glycol rather than alcohol (ethanol), but was unaware that this was poisonous for humans. More than 100 people died when Elixir Sulfanilamide was released in the US. No adequate records had been kept by medical doctors or pharmacists as to whom the drug had been dispensed. It required the entire field force of the Food and Drug Administration (FDA) to retrieve all leftover bottles of this product when the company's own recall efforts proved inadequate.[1]

The FDA was empowered to seize Elixir Sulfanilamide bottles only because the drug's name was misbranded. 'Elixir' implies that a product contains alcohol according to the *United States Pharmacopeia – National Formulary (USP-NF)*, but instead this medication had been produced with the highly toxic diethylene glycol.

This first large national drug disaster triggered the US's 1938 Food, Drug, and Cosmetic Act. After this companies had to submit safety data to the FDA for evaluation prior to marketing in the form of a New Drug Application (NDA).[2]

The thalidomide disaster

While the Elixir Sulfanilamide disaster was still local in nature, the next catastrophe was global. Thalidomide was developed and first marketed in Germany in 1957, where it was, from the very beginning, sold OTC – that is, without the need for a prescription. It was promoted as a 'wonder drug' for insomnia, anxiety, morning sickness and more. The promise to help combat morning sickness of course enticed pregnant women specifically. It was soon marketed in many countries.

Thalidomide resulted in a devastating range of limb deformities in the babies of women who had taken thalidomide during a specific time span of their pregnancy. It took until 1962 for the drug to be removed from the last markets worldwide. It was never approved in the US, but had been dispensed in so-called 'clinical studies' in which medical doctors gave the drug to anybody they thought it might help, without any documentation. The number of affected children in the US was very low, but much higher in Canada and many other countries. Worldwide, probably around 10,000 children were affected.[3, 4, 5]

Legislation to prevent further disasters

Prompted by the thalidomide disaster and in contrast to Germany, the US reacted swiftly and decisively. The Drug Efficacy Amendment of 1962 to the Federal Food, Drug, and Cosmetic Act demanded that companies from then onwards had to show efficacy and safety of new drugs before approval, demanded accurate information about side effects in drug advertising, and stopped generic copies of old drugs being sold under new trade names as new 'breakthrough' drugs for high prices. Worldwide, the principle of clinical studies, performed before the application for marketing approval for a new product could be submitted, was gradually introduced.[2]

Thus the thalidomide catastrophe shaped drug development worldwide. Effective drugs cannot now be developed and sold without competent supervision; in the US this is done by the FDA,[6] in the EU by the European Medicines Agency (EMA) as an umbrella organisation over the EU member countries' national regulatory authorities,[7] and in the post-Brexit UK by the MHRA.[8]

A new triangle of power emerged in 20th-century healthcare: traditional professions and institutions; the pharmaceutical (and medical devices) industry; and the regulatory authorities.

Out of this triangle, combined with the general public's trust in the state and in science, emerged the business opportunity for specifically 'paediatric' research. In the US this involved the cooperation between the American Academy of Pediatrics (AAP) and the FDA; US 'paediatric legislation', was then adopted and expanded by the EU.[9, 10, 11]

Children as 'therapeutic orphans'

In the late 1960s, the concept of children as 'therapeutic orphans' – an emotive term in itself – emerged. From 1962 on, following the Drug Efficacy Amendment of 1962 to the Federal Food, Drug, and Cosmetic Act, companies had been including 'paediatric warnings' in information about newly approved drugs to protect themselves from lawsuits in the litigious US legal framework. These warnings were triggered by toxicities that had been observed in premature newborns in the 1950s. Later, additional toxicities had also been observed in mature newborns.

It was the first chairman of the American Academy of Pediatrics (AAP) Committee on Drugs, Dr Shirkey, who claimed these warnings made children 'therapeutic orphans'.[12] His war cry was for all new drugs to be trialled in minors as well as adults and it was very successful. The AAP and the FDA became powerful allies. To cut a long story short, they convinced US lawmakers that separate 'paediatric' studies needed to be performed for all new drugs.[9, 10, 11] The mechanism to do so was to offer pharmaceutical companies the incentive of a six-month extension of the patent protection for any drug requiring such studies: so-called 'paediatric exclusivity'. For pharmaceutical companies, it was very rewarding to earn these patent extensions – it gave them an extra half year in which to sell their own brand drug at a high price before other manufacturers could make and market a generic copy.

Created in 1997 by the US Congress, 'paediatric exclusivity' was intended to incentivise paediatric research. The official story was that pharmaceutical companies typically recruited only adult patients into their regulatory studies, and that for investigation in the 'paediatric population' (under the age of 18) there were no incentives, as the paediatric market was smaller than the adult one.

However, the market for such medications is not in fact as small as was often claimed. In the beginning, the FDA defined 'children' as anybody below 17 years of age. Later, the EU used the age limit of the 18th birthday. Today, both agencies use the 18th birthday. Minors represent roughly a quarter to a fifth of the entire population. In their first years, babies and infants are sick more often than adults. This changes gradually when adults become elderly. A significant proportion of the healthcare costs of patients is spent during their last months of life. Minors represent a significant proportion of the entire population, but babies grow fast, and do not remain babies until they come of age.

Companies tried to bring their new drugs to market cost-effectively. In the early debates about 'paediatric drug development', the researchers wanted as many 'paediatric' studies as possible but, specifically in adolescents, such studies were unnecessary and superfluous. Drug efficacy had already been shown in adults. The paediatric dosing tables and formulas used at the time were, with few exceptions, sufficient for children, only not for newborns and especially preterm and/or under-weight newborns. The importance of changes in the developing body during the first days, weeks and months of life was used to justify 'paediatric' studies in all 'children', blurring two different meanings of the term 'child'. Administratively, everybody is a child until s/he comes of age. But bodily, adolescents' bodies mature much earlier. It was not the market for children's medicines that was too small, but rather the desire of paediatric researchers for funding that was too great.

It would be too easy to blame everything on the desire of paediatric researchers for funding. The shock of the thalidomide catastrophe had a long-lasting effect. Everyone believed that a new, safe chapter had now opened with government supervision of drug development. The reports of toxicities of modern drugs in babies, the new trust in government supervision, and the generally high trust in science led to the belief that only officially approved ('on-label') drugs were safe. Indeed, it was in 1988 that the term 'off-label' first emerged,[13] showing the growing importance of regulatory authorities in healthcare. 'Paediatric drug development' became a movement coordinated through a collaboration between academic science, regulatory agencies and, in the US, the pharmaceutical industry. From that time on, all drugs for 'children', who were now defined administratively, not by their degree of physical maturity, had to be approved specifically in 'children' and for this, separate 'paediatric' studies were required.

The effects of 'paediatric exclusivity'

'Paediatric exclusivity', as described in Chapter 1, holds off competition from generic versions of drugs for six months, allowing the originating company to sell its medicine for the original, higher, patent-protected price for half a year longer than allowed under patent law.

The US's paediatric legislation in 1997 suddenly offered industry the incentive to investigate clinical questions in young patients in a dimension that had never existed before. From then on, companies needed advice as to which studies they should propose to the FDA. To get such advice companies approached leading paediatric academic clinicians, who of course liked this new attention. Once the FDA had issued a 'written request' for paediatric studies and the company had committed to these studies, they needed to be performed. Most diseases in minors are rare. These studies were usually not confined to one or even a few medical centres as these could not provide sufficient 'subjects'. Instead, they were international from the very beginning.[14] Participation in an international study enables many things: international networking beyond the regular academic research conferences; publication in journals of the highest reputation; invitations to give presentations; the hiring of new personnel; assistance with financing research infrastructure; access to journalists; and more. Thus the USA's paediatric legislation was, from 1997 on, a huge business opportunity for individuals and institutions involved in paediatric research.

'Paediatric' clinical trials are estimated to cost two to five times more per patient than adult clinical trials.[15] The costs of FDA-incentivised 'paediatric' studies were analysed in a paper published in 2018: the total costs of 'paediatric' studies into 54 drugs were estimated at \$4.9 billion in 2017.[16] Clinical trial costs may include:

- payments to the clinical research site
- payments for the use of the relevant research centre
- patient enrolment
- administrative trial procedures
- materials
- laboratory use
- imaging
- transport of blood samples, tissue samples and other materials
- data management
- monitoring
- administrative management by the sponsoring company or by a commercial clinical research organisation (CRO)
- the institution's review board (IRB)/ethics committee (EC)
- transportation costs for patients

- insurance
- translation of protocols and other documents into many languages
- and more.

For every unnecessary study that is done, we must bear these costs in mind in addition to the human costs to patients and families and the opportunity costs of meaningful research not carried out.

The official version of events is that the FDA has helped to generate data to guide clinical decision-making for many drugs used in paediatric medicine. Of the 189 drugs granted 'paediatric exclusivity' between 1998 and 2012, more than half received new or extended approval for paediatric use, a quarter resulted in new safety concerns, and an eighth resulted in new dosing information. This sounds convincing and logical, and has been repeated as support for 'paediatric' studies countless times.[17, 18, 19, 20, 21] How true are these claims?

Was the FDA right?

The first paediatric status report by the FDA to Congress in 2001 explained that the FDA expected 'significant advances in pediatric medicine. Superior drug treatment information is expected to permit quicker recoveries from childhood illnesses, with fewer attendant hospital stays, physician visits and parental work days lost'.[19] These were clear clinical expectations. The FDA was committed to advancing child healthcare and believed that regulatory approval of the use of drugs in minors would advance child healthcare. However, in its next paediatric status report to Congress, in 2016, it did not repeat these expectations. Instead, it listed all the studies the paediatric laws had triggered and caused to be funded, and claimed that this activity had improved paediatric healthcare.[22]

Clinical studies in young patients, however, should not be performed for their own sake.

The FDA did not repeat its clinical expectations because there were no real, measurable success stories to be reported. FDA-triggered 'paediatric' studies resulted in more 'paediatric' approvals but were mostly useless or exaggerated, or even harmed patients, as the chapters in Part II will illustrate. They did, however, advance the careers of individuals in paediatric academia, the regulatory authorities, pharmaceutical companies and commercial clinical research organisations that were happy to perform 'paediatric' clinical studies.

The European Union's 'Paediatric Regulation'

The system of 'paediatric' clinical studies was amplified and expanded when the EU introduced its own 'Paediatric Regulation' (Regulation (EC) No 1901/2006), requiring separate 'paediatric' studies in patients younger than 18 years. Paragraph # 2 of the preamble to the 'Paediatric Regulation' is a declaration to combat the market forces that were allegedly unable to provide the necessary studies for the 'paediatric population'.[23]

With the exception of drugs that target diseases officially listed as not existing in 'children' (individuals under the age of 18), companies have had, from 2007 onwards, to submit a draft 'paediatric investigation plan' (PIP) to the EMA for all new drugs. This draft PIP must propose 'paediatric measures', with the three most important elements being:

- juvenile animal studies
- the development of child-friendly formulations (babies cannot swallow tablets)
- clinical studies.

If the EMA does not like the measures proposed by the drug company, it can reject the PIP, and the drug will be blocked from EU approval for adults as well as 'children' until an acceptable PIP has been negotiated. Approval of new products is the life-blood of research-based pharmaceutical companies. In September 2020, the EMA website listed more than 2000 PIP decisions, including accepted, refused, and modified PIPs, and waivers (no PIP required).[24] In 2017, the number of PIPs issued surpassed 1000.[25] Each PIP demands one or several 'paediatric' studies.

PIPs demand studies in 'children' that essentially repeat the regulatory studies for adult approval; often these are placebo-controlled studies to prove efficacy in this population, defined as 1 to 17 years old, 2 to 17 years old, or divided into 'paediatric' sub-groups, such as 6 to 11 years old and 12 to 17 years old.[9, 10, 11]

The costs for all these 'paediatric' studies were estimated in an EU Commission report in 2017. For the industry altogether they were estimated as €2.1 billion per year, based on the evaluation of 85 real PIPs. The total research-and-development costs per PIP were estimated at €18.9 million. On top of this come the company overhead costs of roughly €720,000.[25, 26] Each PIP costs the respective company on average about €20 million. If we multiply the €2.1 billion costs per year by the years since PIPs were introduced (14 x €2.1 billion),[25, 26] the result is €28.14 billion.

The EU also offers a patent extension at the end of patent life, the 'Summary Protection Certificate' (SpC). As there is no EU-wide patent law, companies must file for patent extensions in each individual EU member state, which is feasible for major companies and makes sense in larger countries. Even so, this is barely comparable with the US. In the EU 'paediatric' studies must be negotiated years before it is even known if the compound in question works at all. Be that as it may, these numbers show that the costs are considerable.

Has child health improved in the EU?

The EMA website claims that the EU paediatric legislation is 'designed to better protect the health of children in the EU'.[28] Its 10-year paediatric report issued in 2016 says 'more medicines for children' have been achieved.[25] What this actually *means* is simply that more drugs now have EMA 'paediatric' approval. It concludes that the EU Paediatric Regulation has 'had a very positive impact on paediatric drug development'. Page 14 of the report lists alleged examples of achievements in rheumatology, cardiovascular diseases, infectious diseases and oncology. However, these 'achievements' document only regulatory activism, not clinical improvement.

The EU Commission's 10-year paediatric report, *The State of Paediatric Medicines in the EU*, released in 2017[26] (also published as a brochure with the same text, but additional nice colour photos of young patients and doctors, including an attractive, white female doctor with a brown baby, and some graphics),[27] is based on the the EMA's 2016 report.[25] It likewise outlines alleged achievements and claims that before the EU legislation, drugs in 'children' were administered based on physicians' own experience rather than on the results of clinical research; discusses past challenges like the need to crush tablets for babies and small children; and repeats the EMA position that off-label use of medicines can be dangerous in 'children'.[26, 27]

The EU commission report appears convincing at first glance. To decode it, we need to repeat two basic, common sense questions:

- Was there a crisis in child healthcare before 2006?
- Before the EU Paediatric Regulation had there been an increase in child mortality, that later improved as a consequence of the EU Regulation?

The answer to these questions is 'No'. Despite many more medicines now being 'on-label' (approved) specifically for children, the EU Paediatric Regulation has not fundamentally improved child health. The 'successes' and 'achievements' were regulatory in nature and did not correspond to real clinical improvements.

How the research community benefits

For scientists and medical doctors who want to achieve a position in academic paediatric research, the currency to promote their careers is scientific publications. When you apply for a new position, you have to submit a curriculum vitae (CV) with a list of publications in scientific journals of high reputation. One key factor in the algorithm of journals of high reputation appears to be the complexity and cost of the respective study. The more complex and costly the study, the more likely it is to be published in a journal of the highest reputation.[29, 30, 31]

Financially speaking, paediatric research legislation provided a business opportunity in the new academic discipline of developmental pharmacology. This was also the case for many paediatric researchers who had previously envied their adult counterparts for all the regulatory studies that the pharmaceutical industry had to finance to get new drugs approved. In the US, these paediatric researchers now had strong allies in the AAP and FDA. When the FDA defined 'children' as anybody younger than 18 years, and received the authority to demand funding for 'paediatric' studies irrespective of the stage of maturity of the 'children' involved, performing these studies became a legitimate research objective. To this day, scientific and medical journals of the highest reputation publish studies that prove that drugs already known to be effective in adults also work in 'children'.

Case study: Liraglutide

One such example is a publication in the *New England Journal of Medicine (NEJM)* in 2019 about a study that shows that the drug liraglutide (used for type 2 diabetes) works in 'children' aged 10 to 16 years of age as well as adults.[29] This was a randomised, double-blind, placebo-controlled study (the 'gold standard' in drug research). However, liraglutide had already been approved in adults with diabetes mellitus back in 2010.[32] The justification for the study was: 'Regulatory agencies mandate that new drugs that had been approved for use in adults with type 2 diabetes undergo efficacy and safety trials in youth with the disease'.[29] In 2012, the FDA had offered a patent extension ('paediatric exclusivity') for 'pediatric' use of liraglutide.[33] The EMA had meanwhile issued an early liraglutide PIP for treatment of diabetes, which between then and 2017 was modified eight times, demanding studies in 'children' aged 10 to 17 years.[34] (There is also an EMA liraglutide PIP for the treatment of obesity in 'children' aged 6 to 17 years.[35])

Citing the requirements of the regulatory authorities reported in the *NEJM*[29] is not a scientific justification for research; it is merely a regulatory justification. It contradicts the basic recommendations of the Declaration of Helsinki,[36] adopted in 1964 by the World Medical Association in reaction to the criminal studies done by Nazi doctors in the Third Reich, with the aim of preventing future abuse of patients in medical research. According to the Declaration of Helsinki, the primary purpose of medical research in humans is:

- to understand diseases and
- to improve the prevention, diagnosis and treatment of disease.

At no point does it allow pointless studies in humans for regulatory purposes.

In 2019, based on the 'paediatric' studies reported in the *NEJM*, the FDA approved the use of liraglutide in 'children' as well as adults.[37] The use of liraglutide in minors had, however, already been documented 'off-label' in 2013.[38] The design of the *NEJM* study six years later was scientifically massively exaggerated; it merely confirmed what adult physicians and paediatricians already knew. To formulate it provocatively, all it did was add an official rubber stamp. Furthermore, the *NEJM* liraglutide report did not explain why the sponsoring company had to pay for this study.[29] The company needed this study (and its associated 'data') in order to obtain FDA approval for liraglutide use in 'children'. Furthermore, the age limit of the patients who took part in the study was taken in this publication as a given and not further discussed or scientifically justified.[29] This is not what science should do. Parents expect their medical doctors to be more careful.

If we were to check the study scheme against the usual standard parameters, we would be satisfied: it was double-blind, placebo-controlled and randomised, as demanded by respected regulatory authorities, and performed by renowned clinicians with a high standing in academic research. But the study exposed young patients to placebo (inactive) treatment, although the efficacy of liraglutide was already well known.[29,32,38]

In the wake of the EU Paediatric Regulation, which has now been in force since 2007, the EMA established the European Paediatric Network (the Enpr-EMA), 'a network of research networks, investigators and centres with recognised expertise in performing clinical studies in children'.[39] The Enpr-EMA hosts annual workshops and other events. The 2018 workshop was characterised as a 'holistic approach to paediatric research',[40] which sounds scientific and positive at first glance until we ask the heretical question: 'How are we defining "paediatric"?' The Enpr-EMA is a central coordinating platform that allows networking of the key stakeholders with a material interest in 'paediatric' studies. A key publication describing it was authored by EMA officers and representatives of organisations with a material interest in 'paediatric' research.[41] This publication is not an independent report.

International 'paediatric' research activity has become like a huge machine propelled by the FDA and the EMA, with the EMA in a dominant position. There is no effective supervision of the EMA. The national paediatric professional organisations in the EU member states have never played a decisive role in the emergence of the EU Paediatric Regulation. Instead, this Regulation was based on the US precedent and its development was driven by interaction between the EMA and the EU Commission. Paediatric specialists were invited to comment. All recommended EU-specific paediatric legislation.[42]

We could describe the EU Paediatric Regulation as a childhood disease of the EU, where good will, ruthless exploitation of professional interests, and effective camouflage of conflicts of interest have erected a construct of plausible and attractive ideas.

Case study: EU PIPS for flu vaccines

There are now at least 17 EU PIPs for vaccines against the influenza virus.[11] As you almost certainly know, influenza, mostly referred to as 'the flu', is a contagious viral infection, affecting predominantly the upper respiratory tract, including nose, throat, bronchi and lungs. Its most frequent symptoms are fever, runny nose, sore throat, muscle and joint pain, headache, cough and fatigue. It returns worldwide on a regular basis and causes considerable morbidity and mortality. Annual vaccinations against seasonal influenza are performed routinely. New vaccines are produced annually to match changes in circulating viruses. The selection of influenza antigens for these vaccines is based upon the global surveillance of influenza viruses in circulation and the spread of new strains around the world.[43]

Though the 18th birthday is not a physiologically significant event but merely a legal and administrative one, and influenza affects people of all ages, the EMA has demanded separate paediatric vaccine studies. One example among many is EU PIP EMEA-001782-PIP01-15-M03. This requires two 'paediatric' studies. The first one is a randomised, double-blind, active-controlled, three-arm multi-centre study to evaluate immunogenicity and safety compared with another vaccine in children and adolescents aged from 3 to 17 years. The second one is a randomised, multi-centre study in children between the ages of 6 and 35 months.[44]

There is no good scientific justification for these studies. Medicines and vaccines treat the body, and not the *legal* status.[11, 45, 46]

The process of drug development

The process of drug development is long, complex and expensive. It begins with the identification of new compounds, found in nature or systematically designed in the lab, as having therapeutic potential. Safety testing in the laboratory is followed by testing in animals. Only thereafter can the trial compound be given to humans. After initial safety testing in humans, clinical testing in large numbers can begin. Most compounds are abandoned because they fail these tests and are classified as unsafe or ineffective, but if the pivotal clinical tests (see below) show efficacy and there are no safety concerns, the compound is approved and officially becomes a drug.

Early standard processes aim at preventing later nasty surprises. Pre-clinical laboratory studies assess the potential to trigger malignancies and provide an idea of the mode of action. They are followed by animal studies, but toxicities observed in animals are not good at predicting toxicities in humans.

Limitations of animal testing

Animal testing of new drugs is being increasingly challenged today. Its value in predicting future adverse effects is not much better than tossing a coin.[47]

Animal studies have been required by law in the US since the US Federal Food, Drug and Cosmetic Act of 1938. The fundamental assumption and hope of all studies in test tubes and in animals is to avoid later fatal disasters in humans.[48, 49, 50] However, toxicities have occurred in human volunteers after animal studies had declared compounds 'safe'; one tragedy involved a monoclonal antibody developed by the company TeGenero, which provoked a cytokine storm in human subjects.[51] Furthermore, when animal studies have led to the belief that a compound is unsafe, it is usually abandoned. Many potentially effective drugs have thereby been lost to patients. We will never know how many. Many drugs that were developed before animal testing became obligatory would not have been approved under current regulations. For example, penicillin is lethal in guinea pigs. Paracetamol is toxic in cats and dogs. Aspirin triggers embryo toxicity in rats and rhesus monkeys.[47, 52]

Toxicology is sometimes called the 'science of safety' because it has evolved from studying poisons and chemical exposures to studying safety in general.[53] For all toxicology tests in drug development, there are detailed national and international guidelines.[54, 55] Pharmaceutical companies that develop drugs either have their own toxicology department or outsource these studies to non-clinical contract research organisations.

With the US and EU paediatric research laws, special studies in young animals have become part of the safety evaluation in drug development, covered by national and international guidelines.[54, 55, 56, 57, 58] In theory, juvenile animal studies address safety concerns that cannot be adequately addressed otherwise, including the investigation of potential long-term safety issues. These studies in young animals have become an integral part of modern drug development, but most specialists admit that their medical value has not been established.[11]

When paediatric studies were introduced as additional regulatory requirements, the age of animals in the animal studies was re-investigated. Many animal studies had been performed on animals that were regarded as adult at the time but that today would be regarded as juvenile.

As I have said, the degree to which animal studies can predict toxicities in humans is limited, if it exists at all,[47, 52] but modern biomedical research would be impossible without animal models. Many advances in surgery, cancer treatment and other specialties would not have been possible without animal models.[59, 60] There are processes in the human body for which there is no counterpart in the body of other animals – for example, in the formation of keloid scars in humans at the site of a healed skin injury. However, our current thinking prohibits hurting healthy human subjects to explore improvements in scar treatment. This is an example where very special animal models had to be developed in order to mimic the characteristics of wound healing in humans.[59, 60]

The discussion of animal studies and the rights of animals involves strong emotions.[61, 62, 63] Studies in young animals at least do not harm humans, which clinical studies in young patients often do.[9, 10, 11] Studies in young animals are also less expensive than studies in young patients, though of course this has no bearing on the ethics or usefulness of such work.

Academic discussion of the value of studies in young animals will probably continue until the concept of 'paediatric drug development' in general is critically discussed in the public arena, and until patient and parent advocacy groups participate more in this discussion. Once paediatric drug development is examined critically as a whole, the lack of sense of most additional juvenile animal studies will also come to light.

Randomised clinical trials

Studies to support drug approval and registration are designed to show that a new drug or a new treatment works at all, or better than a comparison treatment or 'placebo' using the double-blind, randomised, controlled-trial methodology.

Clinical studies are classified into four phases:

- In phase 1 studies, the first in-human studies, healthy volunteers swallow the new compound or have it injected to check initial safety in humans.
- Phase 2 studies investigate efficacy and safety in a limited number of patients who have the target disease; these studies help to get an initial idea of the efficacy of the new medication.
- Phase 3 studies are the pivotal safety and efficacy studies that will decide eventual approval. These involve large numbers of patients. Classically, the regulatory authorities demand two such studies as the basis for submitting an application for approval.
- Phase 4 studies test further questions after approval.

In randomised clinical studies the treatment the individual patient receives is decided by chance (randomly), usually by a computer-generated allocation to one of the treatment groups.

This procedure prevents any bias of the personnel involved in the study influencing the allocation of patients into a treatment or placebo group with a new therapy that is assumed to be superior. 'Blinded' study design means that the physician does not know which treatment each patient then receives. This excludes other factors, such as the physician's liking for (or dislike of) certain individuals or entire groups of people. In 'double-blind' studies, neither the physician nor the patient knows which treatment has been assigned.

Placebo tablets or pills do not contain any active ingredient, but look the same as the active treatment.

When penicillin was used for the first time, it was given to patients who were at death's door as the result of infections and would die without treatment so its effectiveness was easy to judge. In other diseases, proof of efficacy is less clear-cut. Antiepileptic drugs do not prevent all epileptic seizures, but do prevent some, many, or even most of them. If in a double-blind study patients receiving the placebo have many more epileptic seizures than those receiving the active ingredient, this is accepted as proof of efficacy of the active ingredient.

Early clinical studies aim at establishing a basic understanding of a given drug's absorption, distribution, metabolism and excretion (ADME). Pharmacodynamics investigates how a drug affects the body; pharmacokinetics looks at how the body processes the drug, if and how the drug is absorbed, transported, metabolised and excreted. Combined pharmacodynamics and pharmacokinetics (PD/PK) are key parameters often demanded by regulatory authorities.

Clinical studies were initially organised by pharmaceutical companies. In the last decades, the operational tasks of clinical studies have been increasingly outsourced to independent clinical research organisations (CROs) that have become an industry in their own right.

Limitations of clinical studies and evidence-based medicine

In theory, data-based evidence and evidence-based medicine mean that everything should be transparent and replicable, and not be influenced by the personal preferences of the observers and participants involved in the study.

'Evidence-based medicine' began as a movement in the 1990s. Its initial focus was on educating clinicians in the understanding and use of published literature to optimise bedside treatment. It also aimed at producing clinical practice guidelines. 'Evidence-based medicine' claims to place the practice of medicine on a solid scientific footing, to develop sophisticated hierarchies of evidence, to recognise the crucial role of patient values and preferences in clinical decision-making, and to develop a methodology for creating trustworthy recommendations.[64, 65]

However, 'data' are only as good as the assumptions on which they are based and the framework in which they are collected. In computer science, the term 'garbage in, garbage out' (GIGO) recognises that: flawed, or nonsense input produces nonsense output – garbage.[66] This challenge also applies to medicine. Clinical studies are not organised by disinterested researchers who live, teach and research in ivory towers. Instead, they are organised for concrete goals: to decide if a specific compound is effective enough to be approved by the regulatory authority, which in 1962 was predominantly the FDA. Today, the EMA also plays a major part. Key publications of the advocates of 'evidence-based medicine' ignore many of these confounding forces.[67, 68] The Cochrane Organisation has a major role in analysing research data to support allegedly evidence-based healthcare interventions.[69] These movements have accompanied the development of clinical guidelines, but they also have the tendency to ignore huge blind spots regarding their own position in society, and disregard the many other factors that influence medical treatment decisions.

Studies with true therapeutic intentions

How can we judge if a study has true therapeutic intentions? Chapter 4 explains how to distinguish the useful from the unnecessary. What can be achieved with a study that looks at true therapeutic benefits is illustrated by the story of Emily Whitehead and her contribution to improved leukaemia treatment for young people.[70, 71, 72, 73]

Case study: Emily Whitehead and experimental use of tisagenlecleucel

In most types of leukaemia today young patients survive thanks to appropriate treatment and generally more young patients now survive than adults.

In acute lymphoblastic leukaemia (ALL), the most frequent malignant disease in young people, until 2000 roughly 90% of patients could be healed with the combination of chemotherapy, bone marrow transplantation and modern effective intensive care, but it was not possible to predict which patients would survive. The diagnosis of ALL, the side effects of chemotherapy, and the unpredictability of the outcomes were a nightmare for the entire family. Fine-tuning chemotherapy had reached a ceiling. The next successful breakthrough was done by engaging the patient's own immune system. In chimeric antigen receptor (CAR) T cell therapy, blood is taken from the patient. The T cells are re-programmed to recognise, attack and destroy malignant ALL cells.

CAR T-cell therapy has potential side effects, includes a cytokine storm, an extreme response of the immune system that can be fatal to the patient. The immune system goes into overdrive, releases too many cytokines and immune cells. High fever develops. Untreated, a cytokine storm can kill.

The patients who participated in the pivotal study of this new treatment, tisagenleceucel, had no further chance of surviving if given standard treatment, because either they had relapsed after chemotherapy, or chemotherapy had not been successful in the first place. One of these patients was 6-year-old Emily Whitehead, who had contracted ALL when she was 5 years old and had relapsed after chemotherapy.

She was moribund and her parents had to make a tough decision: hospice to accompany her with tender loving care into her death, or a cutting-edge experimental therapy. They went for the cutting-edge experimental therapy. Emily and her parents were lucky.

As I explain in greater depth in Chapter 5, the EMA now forces companies that develop new anticancer drugs to perform studies in patients aged 0-17 years with various cancer types, on the assumption that cancer in 'children' is fundamentally different from cancer in adults. Two international 'paediatric' studies in melanoma had to be terminated because the EMA-required treatment (one drug) was below the standard-of-care.[74, 75] There are 'paediatric' researchers who demand such 'paediatric' cancer studies, but these studies have no true therapeutic intention. Instead, their main purpose is to promote the career of 'paediatric' cancer researchers. Many pointless, EMA-required 'paediatric' cancer studies recruit worldwide.[11] Had Emily Whitehead's parents fallen into the hands of a 'specialist' who was participating in one of the innumerable oncology trials required by EU PIPs, Emily would probably be dead today. Instead, Emily and her parents were lucky in being referred to a study with true therapeutic intentions. Her doctor was prepared to try something new that might be of benefit. Blood was taken, her leukocytes (T cells) were re-programmed to attack malignant leukaemia cells, and were re-infused. Her T cells did their job and attacked the malignant leukaemia cells.

The next challenge was the above-mentioned cytokine storm which gave Emily a high fever. Cytokines are messenger substances in immune responses, inflammation, and other processes. Emily was lucky again. A new drug, a compound against a specific interleukin, was available. The treating physician in charge knew that if he did nothing, Emily would die, so she was given the interleukin antagonist. It worked. Emily survived. Today she is a healthy teenager.

In the tisagenlecleucel pivotal study over 80% of the participants responded to treatment. The cytokine storms could be managed. The FDA approved this new drug very fast. Today, tisagenlecleucel is approved in patients up to 25 years of age in both the US and the EU. The regulatory authorities did not demand a second efficacy study.

Until now, the British Medicines and Healthcare Regulatory Agency (MHRA) has not developed any critical distance from the EU PIP system. Indeed, it has published several guidance documents and sets of guidelines that completely mirror and accept the EMA PIP logic.[76, 77, 78]

Conclusion

Double-blind placebo-controlled studies are seen as the gold standard in clinical research, but they are not the answer if they lack medical and scientific sense. We know today that some drugs work differently in men and women, or in people of different ethnicities, but it would not make sense to demand clinical studies of every drug in blond vs. dark-haired individuals, or separately for each age group – let us say, antibiotics in 25- to 26-year-olds only, and so on.

The methodology of clinical studies and drug development in general is complex. It is natural to assume that the specialists know what they are doing, but there always remains the need to apply one's own common sense. Separate proof of efficacy in 'children' defined by an administrative rather than a significant physiological age limit does not make sense. It has become a justification for research that advances 'paediatric' careers in academia, regulatory authorities, for-profit clinical research, and pharmaceutical companies. The specialists that advocate these studies are not free from conflicts of interest. Parents that have a child with a medical need should be aware of this, or they are in danger of exposing their child to useless or even harmful treatments and procedures – a new type of danger for young patients in the 21st century.

Chapter 3

Can 'children' receive 'adult' medicines?

Everybody has an idea of what children are, but how should we define them? We think of them as small, vulnerable individuals who are highly dependent on their parents. Different age limits for different administrative purposes define the status of a minor as opposed to the age of majority when a person becomes responsible for the consequences of their own actions.

The specialty of 'children's' medicine is known as 'paediatrics' from the Greek παιδί (*paidi*) for child and ἰατρός (*iatros*) for doctor or healer. Of all the medical specialties, it is one of the most recent to emerge, with neonatology (care of preterm and low-weight infants) being even newer. The American Academy of Pediatrics (AAP) was established in 1930. It is the largest national professional representative body of paediatricians in the world. The AAP defines its patients as being up to 21 years old, and even older in the case of patients with special medical needs, provided the patient, their parent(s) and the treating paediatrician agree.[1] However, this age limit is used for administrative purposes. It defines who can be treated by paediatricians. It does not claim that patients under 21 years of age are children, nor that people over 21 are necessarily adults.

The term 'paediatric clinical studies' blurs different meanings of the terms 'paediatric' and 'child'. At 15 years a young person can be taller and stronger than their parents. They are *legally* still minors ('children'), but no longer *physically* so. Their body is already mature after the process of puberty. Furthermore, the beginning and end of puberty vary greatly between individuals. Young people in developed countries go through puberty much earlier now than a century ago.[2]

Before the advent of separate drug approval for 'children', paediatricians had always been aware that young people needed different dosages of drugs compared with adults. As more effective drugs were developed, paediatricians and general practitioners learned to give the right doses to children.[3, 4] A rule of the thumb was to give school children half an adult dose, and smaller children maybe a quarter dose. For dosing in minors, different formulas and tables were used in different countries, and by and large this worked well. Child mortality continued to go down.

The traditional formulas and tables lost their role with the insistence of regulatory authorities on separate 'paediatric' drug trials with separate 'paediatric' dosing recommendations. In fact, such dosing recommendations in adolescents are unnecessary. A young person with a mature body needs adult drug doses. In 95% of the drugs that have achieved FDA-approved dosing recommendations in adolescents, based on separate 'paediatric' studies, the adolescent doses have been determined as identical to those in adults.[5] You do not need to have studied medicine to understand that. Common sense is sufficient.

Drugs treat the body, not the legal status of a patient. As ever, there always are confusing issues. What about an adolescent who weighs 250 kg? If the drug dose is calculated blindly on the basis of the bodyweight, a dose that is too high will result. Dosing recommendations should include a maximum. What about an anorexic adolescent who weighs only 25 kg? If the drug dose is calculated blindly on the basis of bodyweight, a dose that is too low will result. However, these are not 'paediatric' challenges.

Birthdays do not change the body and physicians should not blindly use formulas without common sense.

The emphasis of the FDA and EMA on separate 'paediatric' dosing recommendations is also part of a power struggle between the medical profession and the regulatory authorities. Paediatric medicine developed 'off-label' (without specific 'paediatric' approval) decades before the term 'off-label' emerged in 1988.[6]

To develop dosing recommendations for younger children, it is gross overkill to insist on separate 'paediatric' safety and efficacy studies and/or multi-centre international dose-finding studies. There is no reason to suggest that antibiotics, monoclonal antibodies, or antiepileptic drugs should not work in younger humans if they work in adults. They work, with the exception of those few that are toxic in very young babies. The key question is the dose.[7]

As we saw in the previous chapter, 'paediatric' drug studies did not emerge due to any real crisis in the medical treatment of children, although the thalidomide disaster had been a wake-up call. The requirement for 'paediatric' studies emerged instead because paediatric researchers *alleged* that there were dangers with all drugs if used in 'children'. The formulas and dosing recommendations that paediatricians had used for decades were not totally useless, but they were mechanistic and did not reflect the rapid changes in the developing body during the first days, weeks and months of life. That premature babies showed toxic reactions when treated with antibiotics did not mean that all minors of any age were in danger when they received these medications.

The emerging new understanding of how the bodies of very young children rapidly mature after birth (and some months longer if the baby is born prematurely) was transformed into an exaggerated warning that all drugs could be dangerous to all 'children', using the semantic blurring of that word to appeal to everybody's protective instincts towards young people. This also occurred at a time when the role of children in society was going through profound change. In 1959, the United Nations General Assembly adopted the Declaration of the Rights of the Child, defining children's rights to protection, education, healthcare, shelter and good nutrition.[8] Materially, this declaration was rather empty, but it reflected the spirit of the time, and when paediatric researchers advocated 'paediatric' studies to protect 'children' against the side effects of drugs, the fact that 'children' were defined administratively and legally, not scientifically regarding their bodies' maturity, was discretely obscured.

The most adamant advocates of separate 'paediatric drug development' also demand double-blind randomised clinical trials in newborn babies. They argue that such trials are the gold-standard of scientific exploration, but this argument is flawed. Where there is concern about potential toxicities, treatment must be cautious. Well, treatment should always be cautious. However, today's neonatology could not have emerged without the use of effective anti-infectives, antiepileptics, and a myriad of other effective modern drugs experimentally in individual cases, as need and risk dictated.[9]

The process of human development

As we know, the development of the human body starts when a male sperm cell enters a female egg cell and they fuse into a new cell, the one-cell embryo. The fusion usually happens as the egg makes its way down from the ovaries to the uterus. The fertilised egg needs approximately a week to reach the uterus, where it implants itself. Again as we all know, the one-cell embryo divides into more cells that then differentiate into different layers and tissues and later into the many organs of the body.[10] Some organs develop fully only after birth; the lungs are not used for breathing as long as the child lives in the mother.

During pregnancy, the baby is exposed to drugs and medications the mother takes. Some drugs do not pose a risk to the baby, but others are very dangerous, such as thalidomide. Morphine, street drugs, smoking and alcohol can damage the growing baby.

The mother might need medication during pregnancy. Today, the dangers and risk profiles of most drugs are well understood. It is very important that the mother informs the physician, midwife, pharmacist or other healthcare professional about everything she is taking, including over-the-counter drugs, homeopathic remedies, and potentially harmful substances. It might be necessary to give medication to the mother in order to treat the baby, such as corticosteroids to accelerate the production of lung surfactant (see page 42) if the baby is likely to be born prematurely. As we can increasingly diagnose disorders in the baby during pregnancy, fetal therapy in the mother's womb is becoming generally available.

The moment the baby comes out of the mother, it inhales and uses its lungs for the first time. Immediately after birth, the umbilical cord is severed, which interrupts the supply of nutrition and oxygen from the mother's blood through the placenta to her child.

All the baby's organs must now adapt to the external world. The liver and the enzymes it uses to process food and drugs still reflect, immediately after birth, life within the womb. They undergo rapid change during the first weeks and months.[11] The liver enzymes of newborn babies, and more so of preterm newborns, are partially different from those of adults. This is one of the main reasons why in very young babies drugs must be used with extreme care. Some drugs, including antibiotics, can be toxic to a preterm newborn. The liver and kidneys undergo fast maturation after birth.

Maturation is a complex process. All tissues, organs and systems mature at different times and different speeds.

Assessment of biological maturity varies with the body system being considered. The more commonly used systems to assess maturity are the skeletal, sexual and somatic (conscious) nervous systems.[12]

Puberty is the transitional period between childhood and adulthood. During this, the reproductive organs mature. A significant growth spurt takes place. Major psychological, behavioural, cognitive, emotional and hormonal changes accompany the process of puberty. It begins at about 8 to 10 years in girls and 10 to 12 years in boys in Europe and North America. Roughly two years later the speed of growth reaches its peak. Secondary characterics follow. Boys, now becoming young men, usually reach physical maturity a bit later than girls. However, there is considerable variation. Puberty has accelerated considerably in Europe and North America over the last 100 years, but has more or less come to a standstill over the last decades.

In very early societies, coming of age often corresponded to the body's maturity. This has changed in modern society where administrative and legal factors carry increasing weight. Until the beginning of WWI, most people did not have or need any sort of identity document. Children were entered into the family's passport if needed. In early societies, adulthood was defined by young men becoming strong enough to kill an enemy; young women, when their capability to bear children began. In modern society, however, this close relationship between physical maturity and legal status has to some extent become disconnected.

As we have seen, in very young children, medication must be given with extreme caution, especially in the first few weeks. In preterm newborns, this period lasts longer. But the extreme vulnerability of newborns does not last until that person becomes administratively and legally adult.

Chapter 3

Neonatology – the science of treating preterm and newborn children

Neonatology is the subspecialty of clinical medicine that takes care of premature newborns, newborns with low birth weight and newborns with birth defects and/or other problems.[13] Over the past century, the outlook for newborn babies with a birth weight of 1 kg has changed from 95% mortality to 95% survival.[9, 14] Most major advances in the treatment of preterm and sick newborns were achieved by empirical and applied health research, and not by regulatory clinical studies.[15] Comparably to other pioneer disciplines, early neonatologists were not focused on meeting regulatory requirements, but simply tried to help their patients. They used whatever was available. Naturally, mistakes were made at times. For a while, too much and too pure oxygen was given to neonates to support their respiration, but this led to eye damage. Oxygen-induced eye damage for a while became the commonest single cause of infant blindness, exceeding in the US all other causes of blindness in childhood. It took a while to find that out. Eventually, the level of oxygen used was corrected, and the number of babies that became blind went down.[16] Altogether, the work of neonatology and the neonatal intensive care units (NICUs) was and is highly successful.

Neonatology is probably the youngest paediatric sub-discipline to be recognised. It is carried out in hospitals in specialised neonatal intensive care units and has always used whatever was available and known to be effective to help the tiny patients, including equipment, drugs, and more. Important factors were the miniaturisation of blood samples to measure blood gases and other markers; the ability to provide nutrition intravenously; and the ability to maintain a normal body temperature. The management of respiratory distress syndrome improved with intravenous glucose, assisted ventilation, giving corticosteroids to the mother to trigger the production of lung surfactant by the unborn baby, as mentioned above, and the introduction of surfactant into the lungs of newborns.[9]

Lung surfactant is a fluid that prevents the collapse of the tiny final bubbles in the lungs where gas exchange takes place. Preterm newborns who do not yet produce their own surfactant develop respiratory distress syndrome and are in danger of dying. The term 'surfactant' was created by merging the three words 'surface', 'active' and 'agent'. The first generation of surfactants used were animal-derived, followed by the production of synthetic versions. Initially, surfactant was (and still is) introduced by intubation but better ways of doing this continue to be under research, such as applying it by aerosol.[17, 18] Lung surfactant is a treatment that cannot be tested in healthy adults; the first studies that led to massive improvements in neonatal survival were triggered by clinical need, not regulatory requirements. Regulatory considerations reached neonatology only over the last decades.

Many scientific publications complain about a lack of 'paediatric' drug studies in general,[19, 20, 21, 22] and specifically studies in neonates,[23, 24] but there is a logical flaw in this often repeated lament. If we were facing alarming death rates in NICUs, such complaints might be justified, but neonatology is a successful paediatric sub-discipline.[9, 14] Asking for more specifically neonatal drug/produced approvals is a regulatory, not a clinical, demand. Those who demand more such approvals pretend that they do so to improve neonatal and paediatric healthcare, but we only have to use our common sense to assess this demand. Reviews of the history of neonatology do not even mention the role of the regulatory authorities.[9, 14] Neonatology developed 'off-label' decades before the term 'off-label' even existed.[6]

Without antibiotics and other anti-infectives, many newborns would have died. Furthermore, today's neonatal population is very different from the one in the 1960s. Neonates with much lower body weight survive today. Calling for more studies in neonates is an easy way for researchers to ask for funding. For industry employees such calls help to maintain and advance 'paediatric' industry careers.[19, 20, 21, 22] Behind the demand for separate regulatory studies in neonatology lurk the same conflicts of interest as in 'paediatric drug development' in general.[19, 20, 21] Regulatory authorities also continue to demand 'paediatric' studies in 'children' of all ages.[19] However, the demand for more 'paediatric' approvals and more regulatory studies in neonatology assumes that such studies will further advance clinical care without any factual support for such an assumption. This is flawed. The treatment of young patients in general and of babies in particular did not improve through better drug trials, but through better medicines, better training for neonatologists and nurses, improved guidelines and dosing recommendations, and improved child-friendly formulations. The role of regulatory approval in neonatology is limited.

There is always room for improvement. As we have seen with lung surfactant, it would be even better to administer it as an aerosol instead of via intubation. Clinicians have been trying this for more than half a century, but have so far failed. Eventually, somebody or a company will find a way.

Regulatory studies investigate if a new drug works better than a placebo or a comparison treatment. With the exception of compounds that are toxic to neonates, antibiotics, antifungals, antivirals and antiparasitic drugs work just as well in term and premature newborns as in older people. Of course, they must be administered with extreme care. Neonatologists have learned this over the past decades by careful testing. Very young neonates can develop so fast that a dose given in the morning might already be too low by the evening.

Anti-infective medicine in newborns

Today, antifungals are used in premature and very-low-birth weight babies as these infants are known to be particularly vulnerable to invasive fungal infections. Antifungals prevent such invasive infections that otherwise could kill.[25] Several groups of effective antifungal drugs exist.[26] Not all are officially approved in neonates and even fewer in very-low-birth weight babies.

The International Council for Harmonisation of Technical Requirements for Pharmaceuticals for Human Use (ICH) brings together the regulatory authorities and pharmaceutical industry to discuss scientific and technical aspects of drug development.[27] Its guidelines are used worldwide and are published on the websites of all major regulatory authorities. This group has also produced a key document on drug development in the 'paediatric' population, defined as from birth to adolescence (12 to 16 or 18 years, depending on region); this has recently been amended,[28] yet its definition of babies' age groups does not yet even acknowledge the existence of very-low-birth weight neonates. It only acknowledges 'preterm newborn infants' as a group. It will probably take one or two more decades before this huge, inert machine processes the progress that real-life neonatology has made in the meantime.

To license anti-infective agents in neonates would require large international multi-centre studies with many similar patients, half of whom would be randomly allocated to receive a less good treatment, or even no treatment (a placebo). Such studies have been tried, supported by EU money. One such was performed with the antibiotic meropenem on neonatal late-onset sepsis. It could not recruit the planned number of patients. Many clinicians stopped treatment outside of the rigid schedule of the study protocol because they put the clinical needs of their young patients first. The authors of the study explained this was 'due to the clinicians' decision to stop antibiotics earlier than the pre-defined duration, presumably because they felt that clinically the sepsis episode had resolved and the infant had recovered'.[29] In other words, the demands of a large international randomised clinical trial conflicted with the individual conscience of the clinicians taking part and the parents' wishes for the best care for their child. The mantras of 'paediatric drug development' and 'evidence-based medicine' conflicted with real-life neonatology.

Advocates of these mantras can see the practical problems of 'paediatric' studies with antibiotics also.[30, 31] They conclude that more studies are needed. Of course, this will also require more funding.

Parents who are asked to let their newborn baby participate in a clinical study should be extremely cautious and should enquire in depth who is funding this study, and why. If it is a study funded by a pharmaceutical company due to a request from the US Food and Drug Administration (FDA), and/or a demand from the European Medicines Agency (EMA) as a condition for drug approval, this alone should be warning enough to steer clear. Parents of preterm babies should also be aware that studies might simply be marketing studies to keep the relevant head of the medical department happy.

Publications in learned journals are the life blood of clinical academic careers, as I have said. If you want to move forward in your career, you have to provide an impressive list of research publications. In so far as this research truly advances healthcare, this is a good thing, but if publications are merely the result of following FDA/EMA demands for pointless neonatal studies, parents should refuse to have their children involved.

Child-friendly dosing and formulations

Children do not have teeth at birth, and cannot chew and swallow solid food. At the beginning they depend on their mother's milk and then increasingly on food processed into porridge/purée. Up to the age of about 6 years, most cannot swallow tablets/pills. Medicines administered orally to young and very young patients are given as liquids or in a quick-dissolving form that disperses rapidly in the mouth. These are called 'paediatric' or 'child-friendly' formulations, although they can also be used by adults with swallowing problems. Young children are also not yet able to override the reflex of spitting out everything that does not taste good.[32, 33, 34, 35] Taste masking is important in the development of child-friendly formulations.

In former times, pharmacists ground tablets and reconstituted them as a liquid. Many mothers are used to making liquid antibiotic syrup from powder and water. The technical development of child-friendly formulations is the most reasonable part of the entire 'paediatric drug development'. Furthermore, it does not expose young people to clinical studies. However, the term 'paediatric formulation' is also misleading. Only a fraction of young people (below the official age of becoming an adult) need special pharmaceutical formulations such as liquids or quick-dissolving pills.

Today, companies must develop new drugs also as liquids or in other forms that can be administered to young patients.[33, 34, 35] The American Association of Pharmaceutical Scientists formed a Pediatric Formulations Task Force, consisting of members with a variety of expertise, including paediatric medicine, formulation development, clinical pharmacology and regulatory science, to identify clinical, manufacturing and regulatory issues and topics. Dosage, form, palatability standards and more are important to provide appropriate oral formulations.[4] The European Paediatric Formulation Initiative (EuPFI) was established in 2007 when the EU Paediatric Regulation came into force.[36, 37]

Several EMA documents describe the requirements for child-friendly formulations.[38, 39, 40] There are also many textbooks on this subject. As these address predominantly healthcare professionals who see only young patients, the blurring between the different meanings of the word 'child' is less crucial for them.

Many medicines also include other ingredients for added stability, to mask the flavour or for other functions. These additional ingredients are known as 'excipients'. Some excipients can harm young and very young children and babies. Alcohol, for example, can cause neurotoxicity. Preservatives may lead to allergic reactions. The EMA guidelines demand a safety assessment of all excipients used.[38, 39, 40] Over recent years, technical development has rapidly advanced. New technologies include mini-tablets, tablets that dissolve immediately in the mucosa (lining) of the mouth, and three-dimensional (3D) printing.[41] The FDA has approved 3D-printed levetiracetam tablets for oral suspension to treat patients with epilepsy older than 4 years, or weighing more than 20 kg.[41, 42]

Which excipients are safe for younger patients is one of the key topics of discussion between drug developer and regulatory authorities.[33, 34]

Although the obligation to develop child-friendly formulations is probably the most reasonable aspect of 'paediatric drug development', conflicts of interest remain. Overviews given by specialists in paediatric formulation characterise 'paediatric drug development' as positive overall,[35, 36, 37] which is not appropriate. Though regulatory demands for paediatric formulations may be mostly reasonable, this does not make the entire 'paediatric drug development' machinery reasonable, nor does it make all 'paediatric' clinical studies or studies in young animals demanded by the regulatory authorities reasonable. EuPFI is supported by several pharmaceutical companies.[37] Of course, academic researchers have welcomed that funding.

Chapter 4

Finding good and identifying bad studies

There are three major possible reasons for reading this chapter: out of general interest, because you want to learn more about ongoing clinical studies that might help your child, or because you are considering whether to allow your child to participate in a specific study that has been proposed to you.

Finding worthwhile studies and identifying bad ones that either lack medical sense or might even harm have both demanding and relatively easy elements. You need a combination of common sense, curiosity, background knowledge, experience and at least one person, but better several, with whom you can discuss your thoughts. On the one hand, parents who are raising children could not survive without some common sense. On the other hand, not everyone can be a specialist in the many disciplines involved in clinical studies with minors. However, it is not by chance that the law gives parents the ultimate authority to decide whether their child should participate in a clinical study or not. With the exception of extreme cases where the courts can rule against their authority, parents are usually clear-sighted as to what is best for their children, and they know them best.

There are several types of information to which the public in general and parents of children with special medical needs specifically are exposed when considering involving their child in a research study:

- Explanations, justifications and reports about 'paediatric' studies on the websites of the US Food and Drug Administration (FDA), the EU's European Medicines Agency (EMA), and the UK's MHRA from 2021 on.[1]
- Justifications for 'paediatric' studies in scientific journals.[2, 3, 4, 5]
- Scientific publications of individual studies or of groups of studies in learned journals.
- The oral explanation of a particular study, face-to-face, by the treating physician within the procedure that documents parents' consent.

Many justifications and reports are freely available on the internet. However, the documentation that parents have to sign if they agree to their child's participation in a study is usually not online. Parents who want to do their own research are advised first to go through explanations and publications in the public domain. This will help them to understand specific studies and read them critically.

Using the <u>clinicaltrials.gov</u> database

There are several approaches parents can take to finding out more. If a specific study has been proposed, an easy first step is to look for the study on the US clinical studies database www.clinicaltrials.gov. Today, all clinical studies are listed in a publicly accessible clinical trials registry. There are several, but www.clinicaltrials.gov is the largest and the most user-friendly. It covers all studies worldwide with a few exceptions.

With the study title and the name of the medication being investigated it is easy to find a specific study. Either open www.clinicaltrials.gov and enter the study title and the drug name on the first page, or, if you are not at ease with that, you can use any search engine, including Google. Usually, you will be linked directly to a specific study listed on www.clinicaltrials.gov.

The study design (e.g. randomised controlled) is usually included in the title, or immediately after the study title. To read about the design, you click on the study title, which will lead you to the next level of information. In order always to be able to return to a specific study, it is important that you write down the National Clinical Trials (NCT) number. If you enter an NCT number directly into any search machine, it will lead you directly to the study information stored in www.clinicaltrials.gov.

In the study description you will find a description of the study type (open-label, randomised, double-blind, placebo-controlled, active-controlled, etc.), and the status of the study (recruiting, not yet recruiting, unknown, terminated, and more). Scrolling further down, you will find the planned number of patients to be included, the study's start and planned end dates, the inclusion and exclusion criteria, and the age of patients to be recruited. Some studies will already have results, some will have a link to related publications, and in most cases you can have a look at all study sites that are recruiting.

This book's focus is on 'paediatric' studies (studies in patients below 18 years of age) that are funded by pharmaceutical companies and are incentivised and/or required by the FDA or the EMA. If you are looking for a specific study and you find an overwhelming number of possibilities in response to your search, maybe because the medication concerned is being investigated in several dozen studies, you may go to 'advanced search' and choose the funder type, e.g. the National Institutes of Health (NIH), or industry, to narrow your search down. If you are looking for an industry-funded study, click 'industry'. Once you have your list of studies, you will be able to go through them one by one, looking for key information.

To get an overview of which studies are currently recruiting in a specific disease, or with a specific new drug, or both, you should first decide if you want to know about ongoing studies only, or all studies. The field for 'status' is the top one on the www.clinicaltrials.gov website. You can choose either 'recruiting and not yet recruiting studies', or 'all studies'. Then enter the condition or disease, followed by 'additional information' – for example, the drug you are looking for. On the start page, the next information you might enter is the country you are looking for, or you can leave this open. With these pieces of information entered, you can choose to click on 'advanced search'. This takes you to a second search page that offers the choice of several statuses for recruiting participants and for expanded access, together with the age of the patients, the phase of the study, the funder type ('sponsor') and the type of documents you are looking for. Once you have entered these items, you can click on return and take a look at what you have found.

What is the age of participants?

As discussed in the previous chapters, studies that recruit minors only – i.e. patients aged 12 to 17 years or 2 to 18 years – should immediately trigger a red flag in your heart and mind. The 12th, 17th, 18th and 21st birthdays do not represent a biological transition. They are administrative age limits only.

Age limits need not always be seen as a warning signal. The study in which Emily Whitehead was cured from relapsed acute lymphoblastic leukaemia (ALL) included patients up to 25 years of age (page 30).[6, 7, 8, 9] Of course, this age limit is arbitrary too, but the rationale behind it was that the researchers knew that young patients' immune systems are more flexible. Probably, they could also have used 26 or 24 years as the cut-off limit, but we will not discuss this further here. The company that performed the pivotal studies in the topical ointment crisaborole for treating atopic dermatitis recruited patients aged 2 to 79 years.[10] Probably the FDA would not have accepted younger patients. However, there is no fundamental medical reason not to treat a 22-month-old baby with atopic dermatitis with crisaborole.

Is the medication approved in adults?

If a specific study claims to be investigating if a medication works in 'children' (efficacy), your next question should be whether the medication is already FDA-approved in adults. Usually, the FDA is faster at giving first approval than the EMA. As described above, you can use any search engine, enter the name of the medication and the search terms 'FDA label' or 'FDA prescribing information'. If the drug is already approved in adults, the prescribing information pops up, and you can open and download it for later use. If the drug is FDA-approved in adults and the 'paediatric' study you are considering is placebo-controlled, then it probably lacks medical sense. As discussed throughout this book, the FDA and the EMA demand separate, repeated 'paediatric' proof of efficacy for drugs whose efficacy has already been shown in adults for reasons that have nothing to do with improving the outcome for patients. There is no medical sense in demanding repeated proof of efficacy when a drug is already known to be effective in humans. Now you know whether the proposed study makes medical sense; if it doesn't, don't allow your child to participate.

Comparing treatments

Another piece of information you might find is that the study is designed to compare one treatment against another. You will then need to find out more about the comparator treatment. PubMed is useful for this (https://pubmed.ncbi.nlm.nih.gov/).[11] PubMed is a search engine, free of charge, that lists publications on life science and biomedical issues, maintained by the US National Library of Medicine (NLM) at the US National Institutes of Health (NIH).[12] Usually, the key information concerning each article ('paper') is in the 'abstract' (opening summary). If you want to learn more, you have to read the entire article. Many papers today are open source, which means that you can access them directly without payment. Such papers are marked with 'free article' in red. You click on the paper's title, then on the link to the full paper. Sometimes you need to click once more for the PDF version. If it appears to have important information, download and store it. If it is not open source, you can write an email to the corresponding author and ask for a PDF file. The likelihood of their sending it is about 50:50. Of course, this also depends on how much time you have. Or you can buy the article, but you might first look if you cannot find the relevant information free of charge in other papers.

If you want to learn about a treatment on the basis of free-of-charge ('open access') papers first, you can narrow your search in PubMed by clicking on 'free full text' on the left side of the screen. If you want review articles (these look at the results of many papers) only, click on 'review'. If you want papers that are one or maybe up to five years old at most, click on '1 year' or '5 years'. There are more search options. You will learn with time and experience.

If the new drug under investigation is being compared with an old one, you should check if the comparison treatment is current or if it is outdated. You can use Google and/or PubMed to get a picture of the comparison treatment, including how long it has been in clinical use, its efficacy, its side effects, and more. Once you have read about it, discuss it with your treating physician and with the person who has proposed your child participate in the study. If you have the gut feeling that something they are saying is not quite right, or if they avoid clear answers, ask for more time and search on your own in more depth.

Finding clinical specialists and textbooks

Another, completely different, avenue is to look for clinical specialists who you might consult. For this you can use either PubMed or Google to look for published research papers. Once you have entered a search term, PubMed will provide you with papers in the selected clinical area, e.g. 'leukaemia'. Again, you can select only papers that are open source If you think a paper might be useful, download and save it.

Yet another avenue is to look for textbooks to explain the context and background. Amazon is a good way to see what is available, but it can take a long time to publish a textbook so sometimes they do not represent the most up-to-date information. On the other hand, they do include only well established information, which can be helpful, and a textbook author is usually a long-term authority on their subject.

Parent advocacy groups

There are many more avenues to investigate. Parents of children with the same disease as your child can be of help. Sometimes, in patient and parent advocacy groups, there are healthcare specialists with advanced training. This is not a guarantee that whatever they say will be right, but you might get useful information.

Remember, there are no stupid questions, only stupid answers. If you never discuss medical issues in your daily life, the initial discussions will not be easy. But who says that life must be easy? Once you have started to talk to other parents of children with specific medical needs, you will see that everybody has to go through the initial phases of learning. You may feel like an idiot, but don't worry. The more you push your brain to process the necessary information, the more it will adapt.

Reading critically

In contemporary understanding, fraud in science is the secret falsification of research results by individual researchers, or invention of non-existent patients, in the hope of never getting caught.[13, 14, 15] Such fraud is openly criminal.[16] In the past there have been pharmaceutical companies that attempted to falsify study results. Given the extent to which the data submitted by pharmaceutical companies is now controlled, this type of fraud takes place more in the minds of bitter opponents of 'Big Pharma' than in reality.[17, 18, 19]

Today, we are confronted with a new, 'modern' type of deceit practised on patients, parents and the public. The justification for 'paediatric' studies exploits the high public trust in science, the state, and institutions to make these studies appear science-driven. The real challenge is that relevant parts of academic science are deeply involved in this fraud. This new challenge is something that parents should be aware of if they want to protect their loved ones against abuse in clinical studies. As you will see in Part II of this book, many of these studies are at best 'only' pointless, but in serious and lethal diseases they can harm the patients by withholding effective treatments, and they deceive patients and parents into thinking such studies will genuinely help other patients. When parents realise how they have been deceived, they should get angry and think about potential consequences.

Examples of flawed research studies

There is no way around parents' informed consent. Parents are today the last barrier against 'paediatric' studies that at best are unnecessary but often expose young patients to treatment below the standard of care. Here are some key examples to be aware of many of which are covered in greater detail in Part II:

- Flawed studies are a potentially lethal risk in cancer treatment. Two 'paediatric' studies in melanoma have had to be terminated because medical doctors would no longer refer their patients to a study that used a single drug when the state-of-the-art treatment was already known to require two drugs[20] (see Chapter 5, Cancer).
- Maybe one of the most pernicious ongoing studies is one in which young (under 18) mothers are recruited into an allegedly 'paediatric' study that tests brexanolone (an antidepressant) against placebo in depression after child birth.[21] Mothers receiving the placebo (half those taking part in the study) thereby receive no active treatment at all (see Chapter 10).
- Maybe even more pernicious is the 'paediatric' study that tested an effective anti-emetic that accompanies chemotherapy against placebo in patients younger than 18.[22] Again, half of those taking part in the study received no treatment at all (only a placebo) for their nausea.
- Maybe an ongoing 'paediatric' orthopaedic study is even worse. It compares an effective bio-engineered product with a procedure 'microfracture' after a knee injury.[23] Microfracture has its place, but it is for the surgeon to decide in the individual case what is appropriate depending on his/her experience and expertise and the patient's injury, not for random allocation to one treatment or the other (see Chapter 9).[24]
- Then there are the five-year 'paediatric' studies required by the EMA in patients with allergic hay fever, comparing effective allergen-specific immunotherapy (ASIT) with placebo.[25] When you withhold effective treatment from young allergic patients, there is an increased risk of disease progression towards asthma while the ongoing allergic symptoms will negatively affect academic and sporting achievement and overall quality of life.

- Maybe the most pernicious of all are placebo-controlled 'paediatric' studies of painkillers required by the EMA that seek to recruit minors in pain because allegedly the efficacy of pain treatment in young patients has not yet been proven in clinical studies (see Chapter 11).[26]

There are the many other 'paediatric' studies required by the EMA. Most will never recruit enough patients because there are not enough young patients on the entire planet with the often rare conditions involved for all these studies to be completed.[27, 28]

Conclusion

Parents should be aware that there are two types of clinical study in young patients – those that are based on regulatory dogmatism, in which I recommend you do not allow your child to participate, and those with real clinical purpose. These try to save children's lives when previously there would have been no hope,[29, 30] or offer the chance of improved quality of life to the participating patients.

In the second part of this book I explore many different specific instances where 'paediatric' trials have, or are, fulfilling administrative requirements without benefiting patients in any way, or even causing harm.

Part II

How the flawed concept of 'paediatric' research affects the treatment of specific conditions

Chapter 5

Cancer, leukaemia and other malignancies

The background

When in 1939 the first ward for children with cancer in the US was opened, there were no effective treatments. The patients did not stay for long. The ward offered comfort to parents and patients, could give medicines to help with sleeping and to alleviate pain, and could offer other symptomatic help. Little more could be done, and the young patients died. Why were these wards opened at all? They signalled that the challenge of cancer in young patients had been recognised. Five thousand, 500 or even 50 years earlier, most women bore many children, but few reached adulthood. Child mortality was high. The death of a child was dreadful for the parents, but not a surprise. Life went on. Most mothers had more children.[1, 2]

Malignancies in children have always existed, but were not recognised as a specific challenge until very recently. The symptoms of weakness, lack of appetite, fever, cold, dehydration and pain were similar to those associated with infectious diseases. You could pray for the child, which people did a lot in those days. Often the little patient did recover, but sometimes not.

Cancer is not one single disease but cancer cells have key characteristics in common; they cease to follow the common rules of cell behaviour: to arise, to grow, to cooperate with other cells, to die and to be removed. Cancer cells grow without control. They live longer and/or divide more than normal cells. They do not respect tissue boundaries. They can invade adjacent tissue, spread and form metastases – new distant tumours. If they invade a blood vessel, they cause rupture and internal bleeding. If they invade the gullet (oesophagus), they block food intake. They can perforate the walls of the intestines, allowing the contents to invade the abdominal cavity and cause inflammation, pain and finally death. Cancer can originate from solid tissue (so-called 'solid tumours') and from cells that are mobile in the body – leukaemia if they come from white blood cells, lymphoma if from the lymphatic system. Other 'exotic' malignancies originate from other cells. 'Cancer' and 'malignancy' are thus umbrella terms for a range of very different diseases.[2, 3] Some occur almost only in adults, others almost only in children; many, such as leukaemia, can occur at any age. Overall, cancer in children is still very rare.[4]

There are many causes for cells to become malignant. One is exposing them to irritation over a long period of time by smoking (lung cancer), irradiation (many cancers) and/or modern foods (colonic and rectal cancer). Obviously, this is different in young patients who have not yet lived for decades.

We are just beginning to understand the interplay between cells turning malignant and the control, suppression and removal of malignant cells by our immune system. Probably cells get into the initial malignant state often, but are detected and removed by the immune system very early on. We see cancer developing once control and repair have broken down. In earlier days, the surgical removal of a solid tumour was thought to be sufficient. Today we know of 'micro-metastases' circulating in the blood and have various methods to assess the degree to which the body's defences have broken down.

Medicine is more than the interaction between the individual healthcare professionals and the patient. Into this interaction flow the healthcare professionals' training, the patient's thoughts and feelings, the parents' thoughts and feelings (if the patient is a child), and those of the entire family. In the past when nothing could be done, thoughts went into prayers, and the parents had to live with their grief. However, once infectious diseases had been pushed back and cancer in minors had become a distinct challenge, attempts to do something began. The first paediatric cancer wards provided the best professional help that existed. They could not assist with much more than symptoms, as I have said, but the challenge was recognised. Newspapers and radio reported. Money was collected. Parents brought their children with cancer long distances to the specialist wards, and medical doctors referred their young patients to these wards. Step by step, people became aware that cancer occurred in young patients as well as adults.[5] Paediatric oncology was from the very beginning a specialty that extended beyond small geographical areas.

First successes occurred but not with brand new drugs. On the contrary, adult cancer treatment had advanced with surgery, chemotherapy and radiation. Now chemotherapy was also given to minors, extrapolating from effectiveness in adults. It took time before routine protocols were established but cancer in minors was no longer an automatic death sentence.[6, 7]

Progress in treatment

Today, worldwide pharmaceutical research flows into local treatment of all conditions. This book focuses on the consequences of the transition from largely unsupervised pharmaceutical company drug development to drug development massively controlled by regulatory authorities. This began when the US responded to the thalidomide debacle; as described in Part I, to prevent such a disaster happening again the Food and Drug Administration (FDA's) power was hugely increased. This book's central thesis is that when minors came increasingly into the focus of research, in the interaction between the FDA and the organisations that represented paediatric healthcare and research, something went wrong. Instead of research being driven by what young patients needed, it became driven by rules that supported a massive industry of unnecessary studies. The problem became worse when flaws in the US system were copied, augmented and expanded by the European Union (EU) and its European Medicines Agency (EMA). Things got even worse with the US FDA Reauthorisation Act (FDARA) of 2017, which authorised the FDA to demand studies in young people of modern anticancer drugs already in use in adults, inspired by the EU approach.[8, 9, 10]

In its early days, paediatric oncology was a clinical challenge only, as described. Young patients were admitted to the specialist wards in the hope that help would be found. Eventually, this happened, but not as a result of brand new paediatric drugs. The oncology drugs that worked had been available for decades and were approved for use in adults, but nobody had used them before in minors. At this time, physicians did not care about the approval status of the drugs they used. Their studies were regional, national and soon international and done in the interests of the patients, not because they were required by regulators.

In its first decades, paediatric oncology focused on studies showing what could be achieved with effective drugs that were already available – a unique historical situation. Paediatric oncology was initially not touched by the regulatory discussions affecting general drug development.

These early studies were so successful that study participation became standard-of-care in the treatment of minors with cancer.[10, 11] Sadly, later on, this precedent was used to justify studies that did not offer serious hope, but pretended to try to help;[12] their focus was on regulatory approval only so the drugs concerned could become 'on-label' (see below) for younger patients.[13] In those days, there was a common belief that paediatric healthcare would improve if the drugs used for treating young patients got specific paediatric approval.

In the decades following the thalidomide catastrophe, the world got used to drugs being approved by regulatory authorities.[14] In 1988, the term 'off-label' emerged.[15] As we have seen, paediatric oncology emerged 'off-label' long before this term even existed.

After the thalidomide disaster, several developments took place. The administrative side of medical services gained weight.[10] Initially, the prescription of chemotherapeutics was accepted and funded by healthcare institutions. Gradually, the insistence on being 'on-label' (approved for this specific use) increased. The power of the FDA grew. It had (and has) no legal authority to tell medical doctors which drugs to prescribe, but it has the authority to challenge pharmaceutical companies' promotional activities, which of course affect doctors' prescribing decisions.

'On-label' and 'off-label' in adults and 'children'

'Off-label' prescription is very common. It is an essential part of modern medicine. Medical doctors are not an appendix to the regulatory authorities. They decide to prescribe drugs on the basis of their training, professional experience, learnings from conferences, discussions with colleagues, clinical guidelines and – last but not least – exposure to medical advertising. The FDA sued many companies for promoting off-label use and this resulted in multi-million dollar fines.[16] The prohibition on discussing reasonable off-label medical use of drugs of course limits doctors' right to exercise their clinical judgement freely. On the other hand, allowing off-label use in general could mean pharmaceutical companies getting drug approval for a niche indication, and then promoting the drug for different uses.

This is a complex issue that requires balance – the debate will probably never end, but that is another story.

There is a fundamental difference between approval/non-approval of a drug in general, and approval/non-approval for use in 'children'. Thalidomide was never approved for nausea in pregnancy in the US, but it is today FDA-approved for treating leprosy and multiple myeloma. Non-approval of a drug in 'children' means that that drug is approved for patients after their 18th birthday, but not before. Approval/non-approval in general is based on science and data, such as supports the approval of thalidomide for leprosy and multiple myeloma. However, the non-approval in 'children' is based on the administrative definition of what a child is which lacks scientific foundation. The difference of one year is pretty negligible in adolescents though it is clear the difference of one month in babies is not.[8, 10, 17]

The entry of paediatric oncology into 'paediatric' drug development occurred when the specialty had by and large exhausted the advantage of its unique situation in there already being effective drugs available which needed 'only' to be explored in minors with cancer. Advances in paediatric oncology had reached a plateau. In the most common cancer in children, acute lymphoblastic leukaemia (ALL), about 90% now survived. A new era had begun.

It was thought that investing more in research would be enough to save the remaining 10% of minors with ALL and the more than 10% non-survivors with other types of cancer. We are back at the beginning of our adventure: human instincts. Where large funds are offered, few will resist. Investing billions in flawed research without achieving anything practical will nevertheless build the careers of researchers who claim to be near the next breakthrough. The key challenge is not to invest blindly, but to seek real breakthroughs. Research needs a supportive framework that rewards good outcomes.

In paediatric oncology the opposite occurred with the first US paediatric legislation in 1997. The first step was the FDA incentivising flawed studies, followed by the expansion of this system by the EU, followed by the FDARA copying the EU precedent back into the US.[13]

Oscar Wilde once said that he could resist anything except temptation – a nice way to say that few will resist when really tempted. When US paediatric legislation was introduced, paediatric oncology was at the peak of its historical path to success, but it had, as I have said, reached a plateau.[6] The new regulatory framework, rather than leading to successful new treatments, became an obstacle to further progress.

Chemotherapy and more

Chemotherapy agents are not specific. They are toxic to humans (and animals) of any age. However, when their use was transferred from adult cancer to cancer in minors, young patients proved to have more reserves, provided they were given the chance to use them. Without treatment, they died, but minors with leukaemia survived better than adults when treated with chemotherapy. They can survive higher doses and are more resilient.

This led to the assumption that a comparable transfer from adults to 'children' would also work with modern anticancer agents, which are more targeted. Rather than being toxic to all cells, they target specific genes, proteins, or signals that are involved in the growth and survival of cells that have become malignant. They can affect malignant cells directly, the environment that supports the malignant cells, or other structures or signals that are involved in the growth of malignancies. They include monoclonal antibodies, growth blockers of specific tissues, e.g. blood vessels, inhibitors of specific enzymes, and more. The assumption that using these new targeted drugs would help treat cancer in 'children' as well as adults (given such a transfer worked well with cytotoxics in the past) has been sold to scientists and the public as a promising way to treat 'paediatric' cancer. Great in theory, but it turns out, of limited value. If it were so easy, then the EU would already, after 14 years of paediatric studies required by the EMA, have achieved serious breakthroughs. None has occurred. But many careers in 'paediatric' oncology are based on this concept. The US FDARA was backed by more than 100 institutions engaged in paediatric cancer research.[18] These institutions have a vital interest in studies funded by pharmaceutical companies. There is no scientific substance to the promises that by administratively ordered 'paediatric' studies paediatric oncology will further advance. The hopes of parents, relatives and patients are abused.

'Something' appears to be being done, but it is pointless. Not only is this a waste of funds and energy, but it jeopardises public trust in science, research, education and the authorities.

How therapeutically-oriented research can save lives

The story of Emily Whitehead illustrates how willingness to try effective drugs in new ways, off-label, can lead to breakthroughs. Emily contracted ALL when she was 5 years old. She went through routine chemotherapy but relapsed. Her parents then had to decide between palliative care and trying a treatment never before used in a child. They opted for treatment – what did they and Emily have to lose?

Emily participated in a study with CAR T-cell therapy. Blood was taken, her T cells were re-programmed to attack the malignant ALL cells and then infused back into her bloodstream. They did their job successfully, but triggered a cytokine storm. Cytokines are messenger substances that control complex processes like inflammation. Emily developed a high fever.

The cytokine storm was treated with an antibody against an interleukin. This use was off-label, but it worked. The treating physician later described how he had never in his life seen a fever go down so fast. Emily recovered. Today, she is a healthy, cancer-free teenager.[19, 20]

Emily and her parents were lucky. Her doctor referred her to a study with therapeutic intention – there was strong existing evidence that suggested CAR T-cell therapy might work. Had she been recruited into one of the countless 'paediatric' studies of modern anticancer drugs demanded by the EMA she would now probably be dead.[10, 11, 13] EMA PIPs demand 'paediatric' cancer studies (many in adolescents who are physically no longer children) in almost all targeted anticancer drugs. These studies are justified by the claim that, like the successful switching of targets in chemotherapy in the past, switching the target from adult malignancies to malignancies in young people before their 18th birthday will improve cancer treatment in minors. Companies are forced to commit to these studies and to finance them. But they are based on empty promises.

The EMA demands a draft 'paediatric investigation plan' (PIP) early in the development process of any drug. In the course of a one-year-process, a final PIP is negotiated. If the EMA is not satisfied, it rejects the proposed PIP and the new drug is blocked from later approval, until a new draft PIP has been submitted and finally accepted. For research-based companies, the approval of new drugs is their life blood. They have no choice but to come to terms with the EMA, as long as the EMA position is covered and supported by the mainstream clinical doctrine and EU politics, and as long as the European Court of Justice is not prepared to intervene. 'Children' are defined as being younger than 18 years. A PIP is required for all new drugs, unless the targeted disease is listed as a disease that officially does not exist in 'children'. This list has been reduced repeatedly since 2008, with even malignancies that only occasionally occur in adolescents, such as melanoma and liver cancer, no longer being on that list.[21]

A blatant example: melanoma

Melanoma, also called malignant melanoma, is a skin cancer that develops from pigment-producing skin cells. Melanos (μέλανος) means 'black' in Greek. Most melanomas occur in the skin, rarely also in the mouth, intestines or eye. Once metastasised, melanoma in adults is very aggressive and might be considered as the most dangerous type of skin cancer.[22] The vast majority of melanomas develop in adulthood, but 1-2% do occur before the age of 20.[23] To complicate matters, additional very rare type of melanoma do occur in minors.

Melanoma in adults (and rarely also in adolescents) is called 'conventional' melanoma, in contrast to the really rare melanoma types that can also occur in childhood. Melanomas in childhood are a science in their own right. We distinguish 'Spitz naevi', which are mostly relatively harmless, atypical 'Spitzoid naevi', which can become malignant, and melanomas arising in large congenital naevi.[23, 24] Truly paediatric melanomas are different in nature from conventional melanomas.

This excursion into these rare cancers is necessary because the EMA decided in 2008 in its limitless wisdom that enough melanomas existed in patients before their 18th birthday to justify 'paediatric' melanoma studies. This decision was based on a misinterpretation of US statistics. If a conventional melanoma is surgically removed in good time before it has metastasised, then the patient will be cured and no longer need any treatment. This applies to adults and young people. The EMA, citing the absolute number of US patients diagnosed before their 18th birthday, claimed that this was sufficient to justify 'paediatric' studies; they had however overlooked that in most adolescents the melanoma is removed early. These patients do not require any further treatment. This is not the case in older patients. Melanoma is so common in adults, especially at an advanced age, that the pharmaceutical industry has developed a number of drugs which allow at least a limited extension of lifespan. Two 'paediatric' melanoma studies that the EMA had insisted upon (one was also incentivised by the FDA, by the way) had to be terminated. In the meantime, a combination of two drugs had emerged as the therapeutic standard. The EMA-required studies in 'children' offered only one drug. In the end, doctors stopped referring any more patients to these studies and both had to be terminated.[25, 26]

Nowhere did the EMA mention the types of melanoma that are specific to children, yet because it had the power to refuse approval for adult melanoma drugs, companies had to conduct the aforementioned 'paediatric' melanoma studies. The academic reports are now available for both studies.[27, 28] It is clear both served the relevant academic researchers and authorities well by showing that they were doing all they could to fight 'childhood cancer', yet these studies denied combination therapy to young patients at a time when these drugs were already on the market – a clear example of how the combination of best intentions and blind zeal can harm young patients.

Today, the FDA recommends the inclusion of adolescents in promising adult cancer studies. Not the EMA, though. In 2019, it issued a PIP for the new anti-melanoma drug bempegaldesleukin, which is currently in development; this requires a 'paediatric' melanoma study of this drug's efficacy in combination with two other anti-melanoma drugs.[29] In doing so, the EMA has ignored the overwhelming scientific evidence and the numerous scientific publications that have long since proved the senselessness and harmfulness of the 'paediatric' studies it has requested.

Two 'schools' in 'paediatric' cancer research

Cancer research in young patients is today divided into two 'schools'. One represents true clinically-driven research, as in the case of Emily Whitehead. The outcome of true research is not predictable. Every researcher and every company will claim that it has *the* approach that will bring breakthrough results but clinical studies may show otherwise. This is competition, and there is nothing wrong with it. It is the fate of research that most projects fail. This is dreadful for the individual patient, the parents, the entire family, and for the respective company and/ or institution, but it is unavoidable.

The other school has specialised in 'paediatric' studies of new anticancer compounds that are incentivised, or even required, by the regulatory authorities but have no solid scientific foundation. Before the passing of the FDARA, the FDA did not have the authority to demand such studies. Now, though these studies offer nothing more than empty promises, this approach is supported by the law. It is an extraordinary and historically unique situation that laws justify clinical studies that are useless and may even harm patients. As the laws are different in the US and EU, they trigger different studies, but all these studies recruit patients worldwide. US-triggered studies recruit in the US, Europe and worldwide; EU-triggered studies recruit in Europe, the US and worldwide. Parents who want to protect their children against such studies need to be aware of the key problems involved.

Key issues with 'paediatric' cancer studies

1. Problems with the definition of 'paediatric'

The term 'paediatric oncology' is not based on science. It is an *administrative* definition. When a 15-year-old patient with cancer is admitted to hospital, there are administrative rules as to which type of ward should take them, but the cancer is not 'paediatric' if they end up on a paediatric ward, nor 'adult' if they are admitted to an adult ward. However, the term 'paediatric oncology' has come to mean simply 'what paediatric oncologists treat'. The cancer is not defined by transparent, reproducible criteria, but by the administrative processes of the institution in which the oncologists work.

2. Focused on regulatory approval rather than clinical benefit

When the first paediatric law was introduced in the US in 1997, there was no effective therapy for cancer beyond chemotherapy and surgical removal of early cancers that were still localised and without metastases. Chemotherapy involved using combinations ('cocktails') of known-to-be-effective drugs. These combinations had been developed clinically in the treatment of young patients with cancer, leukaemia and other types of malignancy – successes which pushed forward the boundaries of what could be achieved. From 1997 on, two types of 'paediatric' cancer study emerged: those aiming at clinical benefit, and those aiming at achieving spurious 'paediatric' labels (approval) for chemotherapy agents that had already been in clinical use for decades, and were used in combination treatments in paediatric cancer that had in the meantime become standard thanks to decades of hard work by paediatric oncologists. There was no reason to doubt the efficacy of the individual components of such cocktails, but the second type of FDA-incentivised study nevertheless aimed at achieving 'paediatric' labels for these individual components. Young patients who had relapsed after chemotherapy, and their parents, were talked into participating in such studies, believing these would offer a final hope. This hope was in vain; the promise of a last chance was empty when clinically it was already known that the single agents being 'trialled' worked best when used in combinations. Around the year 2000, young patients who had relapsed after chemotherapy had no chance of surviving a new round with just one chemotherapy agent.[11, 13, 25, 30]

Another example of FDA-incentivised research without clinical benefit is a 'paediatric' study looking at nasopharyngeal carcinoma (cancer of the nose and/or throat) in 'paediatric' patients aged up to 21 years. It compared standard chemotherapy treatment with standard chemotherapy plus docetaxel, another chemotherapy agent. The research paper from this study claimed that nasopharyngeal carcinoma was a 'paediatric' disease of children and adolescents.[31] As it happens, nasopharyngeal carcinoma occurs in all age groups, including children and adolescents, adults and very senior patients.[32] The real reason for this study was simple: a patent extension for the company producing docetaxel. This study had several winners: the pharmaceutical company funding the research, the participating researchers, the clinical research organisation (CRO) that organised the study and the FDA, which could show how it was doing everything possible to fight against 'paediatric' cancer. But the losers in this study were the patients and their parents.

3. The most up-to-date treatments may not be offered

There are more effective treatments today beyond chemotherapy. These new treatments are collectively known as 'targeted therapy'. There is now competition for patients between studies that test advanced effective treatments and the questionable studies described above that follow regulatory automatism. Beware of any study that follows regulatory automatism and check what treatment is already approved in adults.

4. Treatments found to be effective in adults do not need testing again in adolescents

Many types of cancer that occur more often in adults than children occasionally affect patients before their 18th birthday. Melanoma in a 15-year-old patient is not 'paediatric' because this patient is *legally* still a child. It is melanoma and should be treated accordingly. There are many EU PIPs that demand 'paediatric' studies in various allegedly 'paediatric' cancer types, including melanoma as described above.[25] Such studies are questionable. Not all of them will be organised, but those that do go ahead will recruit patients worldwide. Likewise, leukaemia in a 25-year-old is not fundamentally different from leukaemia in a 15-year-old. Even so, there are many EU-triggered PIPs that demand additional studies in 'paediatric' leukaemia, testing for effectiveness that has already been confirmed.

5. Regulatory 'paediatric' studies do not bring about progress in treatment

Cancer treatment changed profoundly with the introduction of targeted therapies. The first targeted therapy was imatinib (Gleevec) against chronic myelogenous leukaemia (CML). The next breakthrough was CAR T-cell therapy (tisagenleceucel) against relapsed or refractory acute lymphoblastic leukaemia (ALL), i.e. against types of ALL that resisted chemotherapy or that returned after initially successful chemotherapy.[19, 20, 33, 34] These advances did not arise from regulatory 'paediatric' studies but from innovative research with a truly therapeutic intention, as shown in the case of Emily Whitehead.

The central approval process for anticancer drugs has not resulted in an immediate leap forward in cancer treatment for young people. However, it has changed the perception of paediatric oncology from being a niche area of clinical practice to an area of key importance – a voice to be heard. The immediate effect of paediatric laws was not *clinical*, but *political*, first in the US and then in the EU.

The increased political weight of paediatric oncology was initially perceived as a step forward, but it did not produce any breakthrough improvements in treatment. It has instead become an obstacle to further progress. It blocks patients from potentially helpful studies and it wastes the contribution of patients aged over 12 years in studies dictated by political dogma rather than clinical need. However, the deepest tragedy is that it blocks therapeutic progress. Therapeutic progress is not only a medical issue. The USA and Europe are technically very advanced regions, but with the paediatric legislation now in place both support structures, institutions and traditions that feel comfortable with the current situation. The obstacle to progress in paediatric cancer treatment also has economic consequences. Worldwide, there are many wealthy parents who would give away their last farthing to save their children from a horrifying death. Innovative effective treatment would attract such parents, which would result in new jobs and new institutions. We just need to overcome the institutional obstacles.

The FDA has partially stepped back from the dogma of 'paediatric' cancer and 'paediatric' cancer studies and now recommends recruiting adolescents into adult cancer studies.[35] In other words, it now accepts that all 'paediatric' cancer studies in patients aged 12-21 years were questionable. The FDARA gives the FDA the authority to mandate paediatric cancer studies with new anticancer compounds in patients aged up to 11 years.

Conclusion

Clinical oncology, the regulatory authorities and industry have not yet addressed the tension between the administrative classification of young people as 'children', which is necessary in any complex modern society, and therapy that should be based on the body's degree of maturity. Administratively, 'paediatric' cancer is currently not defined by transparent scientific terms but as the cancer that is treated by paediatric oncologists, which is a circular argument. Leading scientific journals report on 'paediatric' cancer. If you look carefully, you will see that the tissue examined is from patients aged up to 21 or even 25 years old.[36, 37] How 'paediatric' is that?

Parents need to be aware of the hidden conflicts of interest in paediatric oncology.[8, 9, 10, 11, 13, 25] Blind trust is always dangerous.

Chapter 6

Suicide and depression in young people

It is natural for parents to be constantly concerned about the health of their children. Even if our brain tells us that today most diseases can be prevented or, if necessary, treated, our heart speaks a different language – we are often more concerned than logic tells us we need to be. And our heart is not always wrong. Children are often still in danger, and children do die. Statistically, this happens rarely, but statistics will not help a family whose child has bad luck. The most frequent cause of death in childhood after the first year of life is accidents.[1] Many accidents that used to occur are prevented today by safety measures such as buckling children into special car seats, getting them to wear a helmet when they ride a bicycle or later a motorcycle, and/or by getting them to wear protective clothing appropriate for skiing, snowboarding, inline skating, soccer, football, rugby, or whatever else they do to release their energy. Accidents at home can be prevented by making the furniture childproof, especially when children are still young. The good news is that the accidents that do occur are not always lethal. If something happens, it can often be repaired by surgery.

A basic awareness of childhood cancer is in most parents' minds, but this is no longer the most common cause of death in children, after accidents. That award goes to an unexpected and completely different challenge: suicide. Suicides occur at all ages, from pre-puberty onwards, but are a particular challenge in young people. Modern society is increasingly complex, and the rules for navigating it have to be learned. Some of these rules are official. Others are not written down. If a child is lucky, their parents will explain this. And if not? Some areas are covered by taboos, including how to deal with sexual advances from relatives or from authority figures in school, the work place, sports and elsewhere. Again, as long as parents are able to explain things, and are prepared to defend their child, dangers exist but are low. It is different if the parents for whatever reason do not intervene and hope that somehow things will work out by themselves. Even more challenging are situations where young people are confronted with criminal behaviour by somebody who in theory should be a role model. The parents may assume that it is too dangerous for them to oppose such behaviour openly or there may be taboos involved that put too strong an obstacle in the way of addressing such challenges.

As we grow up, we learn how to deal with difficult situations. Over time, we get battle-hardened and learn to differentiate between surface appearance and reality. If there is no direct solution to a challenge, we learn to find ways around it. Young people, however, often lack the experience to handle challenges that later on may appear banal. For them, they are dramatic, and they can trigger dramatic reactions, including suicide.

Mental disorders, including depression, are risk factors for suicide. Suicide can be an impulsive act, triggered by relationship problems, such as a break up or harassment and/or bullying, but may equally be the result of long-term depression and/or anxiety, or increasing substance abuse. After a first suicide attempt, further attempts may be made.[2] Treating underlying mental disorders is therefore one of the main ways to prevent suicide.

Depression and other mental disorders occur in childhood as well as in adulthood. Today we understand this, but in the past, the official medical dogma was that depression did not exist in childhood. Only gradually did this change.[3] Today it is acknowledged that mental problems in minors include emotional and behavioural disorders. Disruptive behaviour such as tantrums, attention-deficit hyperactivity disorder (ADHD), and conduct disorders are common problems in pre-school and school-age minors. Occasional low-intensity naughty, defiant or impulsive behaviour, including angry outbursts or stealing, are regarded as normal in pre-school children. We all have to learn. However, extremely difficult and challenging behaviours outside the norm for age and level of development are regarded as behaviour disorders.[2] Suicide can occur as a consequence of severe mental illness, but it can also be caused by improper treatment of an underlying mental problem.[4, 5] Among the treatments available for depression generally, which may be used properly or improperly, are 'talking therapies' such as cognitive behaviour therapy, and medicines such as antidepressants. Here it is we come to the impact of the regulatory authorities once they started to require separate approval for antidepressants specifically in 'children'.

At the beginning of the 20th century, depression was called 'melancholia'. The current scientific framework for understanding and classifying mental illnesses had yet to be developed. Melancholia was regarded as a manifestation of internal personality conflicts. Most psychiatrists assumed that patients should discover, address and resolve the roots of their internal conflicts. Psychoanalysis – a set of theories and therapeutic techniques based on the concept that the unconscious mind has a key role in mental disorders – was famously established in the late 19th century by the Austrian neurologist Sigmund Freud, followed by many others, who often established new, slightly different schools of thought. Psychoanalysis interprets most mental challenges and disorders as signs of unconscious conflicts that interfere with daily functioning and can cause many different symptoms, including phobias, anxiety, depression and compulsions. Psychoanalytic therapy tries to make these unconscious conflicts so accessible to conscious thinking that the underlying tension can be reduced.[6] There is, however, no scientific basis for the various claims of the different psychoanalytic theories. Furthermore, psychoanalytic therapy takes several years and is extremely expensive.

In the 1950s, a revolution took place with the introduction of psychoactive drugs. This introduction has been described as one of the great medical advances of the last century, comparable with the discovery of antibiotics and vaccines.[7] Several groups of effective antidepressants gradually emerged.[4,7] One important task in the development of antidepressants and other drugs for mental disorders was to define measurable endpoints for clinical studies to test drugs and to adapt the framework of clinical testing to mental disorders. Antidepressants help many, but not all, depressed patients. New types and classes of antidepressants are continually being developed.[8]

An essential, although uncomfortable, part of today's complex world is the existence of confusing theories about almost everything. On a regular basis, new theories tell us that depression does not need professional treatment and medicines do not help. Antidepressants are characterised either as quackery or as being sold by the greedy pharmaceutical industry merely to increase their profits.[5,9]

During the time when melancholia/depression was thought not to occur in minors,[3] this mattered little from a treatment point of view as effective antidepressant drugs did not exist. Then, as mainstream medicine gradually accepted that young people could be depressed, the need for effective drugs collided with the emerging mantra that in 'children', defined as anybody younger than 17 or 18 years, all diseases are completely different from those in adults.[10, 11, 12, 13] However, depression, schizophrenia and other mental illnesses in young humans are not different diseases before and after the 17th or 18th birthday. Adolescents, and indeed pre-adolescent children, are less prepared for the complexity and contradictoriness of today's society – everybody must find their own way to cope with it – but the mental health problems that arise from this are the same. Does this then mean that if an antidepressant is effective in an 18-year-old it will also be effective in a 17- or 16-year-old? Or does that effectiveness need to be established again from scratch in separate 'paediatric' studies?

As described in Chapter 1, in the US pharmaceutical companies that undertook such 'paediatric' studies were (and still are) rewarded by the FDA with patent extensions that allow(ed) them to sell their products for half a year longer at patent-protected higher prices, before generic competition begins. Meanwhile, for researchers, these studies provided research funding, the opportunity to publish in learned journals, invitations to conferences to report on their 'paediatric' research findings and other opportunities to network. The FDA could meanwhile demonstrate how it was protecting the most vulnerable in our society, the 'paediatric population'.

The American Academy of Pediatrics (AAP) declared that separate studies in children were a 'moral imperative'.[14, 15] This 'moral imperative', however, blurred the two overlapping meanings of the term 'child': young, vulnerable babies and infants, and those young humans who were legally not yet of age but were physically mature.[11, 12, 13] With the exception of those who are most in need of help – young people with depression or other mental health problems, and their families – all the other main players benefited from the extra studies.

Most regulatory 'paediatric' studies of antidepressants have been scientifically questionable from the start. Depression in young people is relatively rare. Clinical research in young people with depression and other mental challenges is not in itself questionable, but these studies have artificially separated out a young population defined initially by their 17th birthday. (In the early 'paediatric' FDA-incentivised studies the FDA used the 17th birthday to define 'children'.) It then subjected them to double-blind, randomised, multi-centre, placebo-controlled studies quite unnecessarily. This has meant they have not received drugs already known to be effective and potentially life-saving. In the case of placebo-controlled trials, indeed, a relevant proportion of the young people in any study were given a placebo rather than a drug that had already been proven to be helpful in over-17s. In this way, young people have been denied effective treatment and placed at unnecessarily greater risk of suicide.

'Black box' warnings of suicidality

In addition to the general problem of 'paediatric' studies denying effective treatments to minors, a further challenge emerged that has led to great confusion for physicians wanting to provide the best treatment for patients and their families needing help with depression.

Triggered by the incentive of a six-month patent extension, many 'paediatric' studies were performed with a number of established antidepressant drugs. Incidentally to the focus of their research, one pharmaceutical company reported that several young patients in one of these studies talked about wanting to commit suicide.[16] The expression of such thoughts was given the label 'suicidality' and the FDA convened a conference of specialists to discuss this in depth. The result was a so-called 'black box warning' against the use of antidepressants in young patients from then on. This is included in the information sheets that accompany all such medicines. The conference also decided not to approve the prescription of antidepressants in 'children'. Later it expanded these warnings from 'children' to young adults. Worldwide, regulatory authorities took up the warnings about 'suicidality' in slightly different ways, but none took issue with the FDA's black-box warning.[3]

The studies mentioned here were based on the underlying assumption, which is now well known to the reader, that in 'children' (defined as under 17 years) all diseases are fundamentally different. Over the years, the FDA also started defining 'children' as under 18 years of age. The incentive of six months' patent extension triggered many 'paediatric' studies, but as the key criterion for taking part was administrative, the studies were flawed from the start.

It should be noted that some antidepressants are known to be associated with suicidality in the first few weeks of taking them. This question was not, however, what the studies were designed to look for. To investigate the question of whether this risk of suicidality was higher in younger than in older patients might have been a reasonable study objective. Instead, these studies investigated nothing new; they were *regulatory* studies that re-tested the respective compounds for their efficacy and came up with answers that surprised no one.[17, 18]

Several psychiatric professional groups spoke up against the black-box warnings and warned that these would probably do more harm than good,[3,5,19,20] but at that time, shortly after the turn of the millennium, the FDA was at the peak of its public esteem. It preferred to ignore these warnings. Just then it could afford to.

Clinical studies prove the efficacy of a treatment compared with another treatment or placebo in a decidedly artificial framework. Such studies help the regulatory authority to decide about drug approval. Physicians and the public trust that the data collection and the authority's drug approval based on the collected clinical data will be done correctly, but if essential elements of a study are flawed, its results will be worthless. Clinical studies have their merits, especially in comparison to earlier approaches that relied more on the eminence of opinion leaders than on reproducible methodology, but we should not trust blindly. As discussed in relation to studies in 'paediatric' cancer, in computer science we speak of 'garbage in, garbage out' (GIGO) when flawed basic assumptions lead to flawed conclusions.[21] This is also true of many 'paediatric' studies of antidepressants that have investigated a sub-population (under 17s) artificially created by an administrative age limit without scientific foundation. To this day, in the psychiatric literature there is no solution to the dilemma that we should not leave young depressed patients untreated but cannot use antidepressants.

To crack that key challenge requires us to address the indefensible weak point in these studies: they were indeed randomised, double-blind and placebo-controlled, but investigated an artificially selected population, based on the assumption that in 'children' all diseases are different from those in adults. The black-box warning continues to appear on drug information sheets and produces confusion for both patients and their physicians.[5, 22]

The black-box warning does not prohibit the prescription of antidepressants for young patients, but if you are a general practitioner or psychiatrist in the US where being sued for damages is one of the major risks of your job, you will think twice before you do so. Although in general the literature agrees that young patients with depression should be treated, in the medical literature discussing the issue of antidepressants in young patients, you will find positions that criticise the black-box warnings as well as those that defend them. The weak point of this discussion is the belief that this is only about the interpretation of 'data'. The core of the matter lies deeper. It is not a question of data, but of seeing this as one of the many consequences of the confusion at the interface between drugs and their approval.

As we have seen, the EU demands that every new drug that is proposed for approval must come with a 'paediatric investigation plan' (PIP) unless the targeted disease is officially not found in under 18s. Many such EU PIPs have been issued for new drugs that aim to treat depression and other mood disorders. As such new drugs are continually being developed, the EU and its European Medicines Agency (EMA) are continually demanding new 'paediatric' studies. There are not enough young patients on this planet for all these EMA-required studies.[11, 13] Will these drugs ever be available to young people who need them?

There is no miracle approach that would help young people with self-doubts, bad experiences or serious mental challenges. If parents are willing and able to talk to their children, and if their children listen at all, this is already a good base for a solution. However, if the predominant form of communication in the family is violence, young people are unlikely to trust their parents. Friends may be able to help, as may social services, religious institutions, colleagues in sport and many more. Medical doctors and other health professional groups are just one of many options.

Antidepressants and other psychiatric drugs do not perform miracles. We can compare them to a crutch. It is better if you don't need crutches, but with an injured leg, they are indispensable for a while. In the same way, antidepressants help to some degree, but they are just one tool among many others that can provide support.

These drugs have now come with 'paediatric' warnings for over two decades. The FDA and EMA have staked their reputations on supporting their 'paediatric' warnings about antidepressants in young patients; as a result they have manoeuvred themselves into a difficult position. They will hesitate to admit in public that they were wrong. The warning that antidepressants can lead to 'suicidality' has made medical doctors hesitant to prescribe these drugs to young patients even though they may be a desperately needed part of treatment.[5, 19, 20, 23] Many suicides arising from lack of treatment could have been avoided.[22]

A recent paper reports how a young depressed woman, who had read the warnings that came with her prescribed medication, was scared and did not take it. Finally, she tried to jump out of the window. Fortunately her husband caught her just in time and prevented a tragedy. Following this, the medical doctors and her husband were able to convince her she should take her antidepressants. However, even the authors of this paper accepted the danger of the alleged risk of suicidality as a 'fact'.[5] It was not. It was a pseudo-fact, created by garbage-in-garbage-out research,[21] and by the flawed concept of separate 'paediatric' studies in an administratively and artificially created separate 'paediatric' population.[11, 12, 13, 22]

Conclusion

Antidepressant drugs are just one of a range of treatments that may help young patients with depression and it is important they are available for psychiatrists and family doctors to use, with care, where they think such a 'crutch' will be useful, especially where a patient is potentially suicidal. Unnecessary regulatory studies have not only wasted resources and patients' confidence but have led to spurious 'black-box' warnings on all antidepressants for under 18s, leading to treatment being withheld and/or rejected when it is most needed. The judgement of individual clinicians should not be overridden by 'regulatory' findings while under 18s should not take part in studies testing the efficacy of drugs that are already known to work.

Chapter 7

Diabetes

Diabetes mellitus, commonly known as diabetes, is characterised by high levels of blood sugar over long periods of time because the body's normal mechanisms to control blood sugar no longer work well. Diabetes initially might not cause any symptoms, but it can sometimes be caught early with a routine blood test before a person develops symptoms.

The immediate consequences of higher levels of blood sugar are more frequent urination, increased thirst and increased appetite. Long-term consequences include cardiovascular disease, damage to the nervous system including eye damage and stroke, damaged kidneys and foot ulcers, possibly leading to amputation.[1]

The main mechanism to control blood sugar is the hormone insulin. There are two types of diabetes. In type 1 diabetes mellitus (T1DM) the body no longer produces insulin because the immune system has attacked and destroyed the insulin-producing cells in the pancreas for reasons we do not yet understand completely.[2] T1DM was in the past called 'juvenile diabetes mellitus' because it occurred in young patients as well as adults.

Type 2 diabetes mellitus (T2DM) was in the past also called 'adult-onset diabetes', because it develops mostly in adulthood. T2DM diabetes occurs when the cells become less responsive to insulin. As a result, glucose starts to build up in the blood.[1]

T2DM is mostly caused by a mismatch between the amount of food ingested and the calories consumed by physical activity – that is, by eating too much and using the body too little. When T1DM begins, its symptoms usually develop fast within weeks or months, while T2DM usually develops slowly and symptoms may for a long time be subtle or even absent. Most diabetes patients have T2DM, making it part of today's general challenge of increasing obesity.

The role of insulin was discovered 100 years ago. Its clinical use began when it became commercially available by means of its extraction from animal pancreases. It had to be injected several times a day. Subsequently, it was chemically modified, and insulin analogues were developed that allowed better control of blood sugar levels over 24 hours. Today, insulin is industrially produced using recombinant technology in a cell-based fermentation process.[3] (This involves altering genetic material outside an organism.)

Before insulin was produced industrially, T1DM was a lethal disease. Today, it has become a chronic condition treatment of which allows a good quality of life, if managed well. In contrast, T2DM is a chronic condition with multiple long-term consequences that seriously reduce the quality of life. While mostly a disease of adults, T2DM can affect young people as well and is associated with overweight/obesity. Childhood obesity has increased dramatically in the past few decades, disproportionally in young people of low societal status and income, and ethnic minorities.[4]

Treatment of diabetes

The focus of treatment is to keep the level of blood sugar close to normal.

The predominant treatment for T1DM is insulin or synthetic insulin analogues. The US Food and Drug Administration (FDA) classifies today's insulin types into rapid-acting, short-acting, intermediate-acting and long-acting insulins, and pre-mixed combinations.[5]

Treatment for T2DM includes eating food that contains more fibre and less fat and sugar, exercise, weight loss, and finally drug treatment. Today there are several classes of drug that help to lower glucose production in the liver, help the pancreas to release insulin and help the body to use insulin more effectively. These classes of drug include sulfonylureas, biguanides and thiazolidinediones. There are now first-generation, second-generation and third-generation sulfonylureas. Glyburide is a second-generation sulfonylurea, glimepiride third-generation. Metformin, a biguanide, was US-approved, withdrawn, and re-approved in 1995 after having been used in Europe for 20 years. Rosiglitazone is a thiazolidinedione.[6] Further new drugs are continually being developed,[7] as the market for such is constantly growing, with an increasing number of people becoming 'insulin resistant' and the growing challenge of worldwide obesity.

'Paediatric' development of anti-diabetic drugs

As with all other drugs, the FDA in the US approved anti-diabetic drugs for use in adults only. When the first US paediatric legislation was introduced in 1997, the FDA issued requests for 'paediatric studies' of the insulins asparat and glargine to confirm their efficacy and safety in the 'paediatric population'.[8] Today, insulin glargine is FDA-approved for T1DM in 'children' aged 6-15 years, but not for T2DM.[9] Insulin aspartat is FDA-approved for T2DM in 'children' down to the age of 2 years, but not in younger patients.[10] Liraglutide is FDA-approved in T2DM down to 10 years of age.[11]

In T2DM, the FDA offered patent prolongation in return for 'paediatric' studies in four oral drugs: metformin, glimepiride, rosiglitazone and the combination of metformin with glyburide.

All these drugs and drug combinations were already approved in adults. In under 18s (or under 17s in some cases), they were all found to reduce levels of blood sugar, but three did not reach statistical significance. Only metformin was approved in 'children'.

The key characteristic of the patients who participated in these 'paediatric' studies was not their chronological age – they all were minors (some studies used 18 years and others 17 as the cut off) – but the fact that they were all massively overweight.[12] T2DM does not develop in young people on its own or for reasons unknown, as do leukaemia, the flu, or T1DM. Instead, we know precisely why it can develop before the 17th or 18th birthday: these young peopls eat too much and exercise too little. It is not a 'paediatric' challenge, but a challenge that is based on an unhealthy lifestyle. There is no adult vs. 'paediatric' T2DM. Instead, T2DM can develop due to excessive consumption of calories at any age from early adolescence on.

The non-approval of several antidiabetic drugs in T2DM is one of the most frequently cited examples in discussions about the need for separate 'paediatric' drug development, together with the non-approval of antidepressants in 'children' and young adults (see Chapter 6).[13] But T2DM does not have different dynamics in 'children'. Its key dynamic (over-consumption of calories) is the same before and after the 18th birthday.

Becoming an adult today includes learning to withstand the multiple temptations of modern life and to acquire a healthy lifestyle. Obesity in young (and older) people is a complex challenge. There is no easy explanation, and no easy solution,[14] but separate regulatory studies for both major types of diabetes over more than two decades have offered merely a pseudo-solution for 'paediatric' diabetes, giving the impression that 'something' is being done. It has triggered funds for countless studies while cases of diabetes have soared.

The FDA's written request for 'paediatric' studies in the case of the drug liraglutide asked for such in patients aged 10 to 17 years,[15] but a first report on the successful 'off-label' use of liraglutide in a 16-year-old patient had been published in 2013.[16] Placebo treatment in the FDA-incentivised liraglutide study denied effective treatment to half the participants and systematically deceived the young patients and their parents as to the need for their participation.[17, 18, 19, 20, 21]

The EU steps in

The entire 'paediatric drug development' concept was expanded when, as we have discussed, the EU Paediatric Regulation came into force in 2007.[22] The EMA demands that every single new insulin type and oral antidiabetic agent undergoes a separate 'paediatric' development programme spelt out in a 'paediatric investigation plan' (PIP). There are currently at least six PIPs for T1DM, six for both T1DM and T2DM, and at least 39 for T2DM.[21] All T2DM PIPs demand a double-blind randomised placebo-controlled superiority study in 'children', variably from 6 to 17, 8 to 17, or 10 to 17 years of age. ('Superiority' means that the respective drug must be superior to placebo with statistical significance.) Some demand even more 'paediatric' studies.

Clinical studies that compare effective drugs with placebo result in withholding effective treatment from half of all participants if the respective drug is already known to work in humans. They do not add new understanding or knowledge. They merely satisfy regulatory dogmatism and offer funds for the paediatric researchers and commercial organisations that organise these studies. Such studies are in breach of the Declaration of Helsinki that explicitly limits experimental treatment in humans to improvement of treatment, diagnosis or understanding of a disease. There are no exceptions in the Declaration of Helsinki for pointless studies that satisfy regulatory dogmatism.[23, 24]

To establish the necessary dosages in young patients, an 'opportunistic' study approach would be sufficient.[25, 26] In such an approach, young patients who need treatment anyway, here for diabetes, are treated according to the best knowledge available to the treating physicians, but additional blood samples are taken to confirm the appropriate dose of the medications given. Such an approach allows confirmation of dosage assumptions without the need to organise complex, multi-centre, often international, studies.

Not enough patients for all FDA/EMA-required 'paediatric' diabetes studies

Paediatric clinical researchers, representatives from the pharmaceutical industry, and representatives from both the FDA and the EMA have admitted openly that for the many 'paediatric' diabetes studies there are not enough young patients on this earth.[27, 28, 29] A tirzepatide study would recruit young patients until 2030.[30] One PIP demands a 'paediatric' study of evacetrapib in patients with familial hypercholesterolaemia, diabetes mellitus, or solid organ transplant. Why should parents with a child that has familial hypercholesterolaemia or diabetes mellitus, or has undergone solid organ transplantation, consent to their child's participation when the efficacy of trizepatide is already known?[31]

The course of T2DM in young people is not identical to that in older people,[32] but patients deserve the same treatment before and after their 18th birthday. These 'paediatric' studies lack medical sense and withhold effective treatment. To establish appropriate doses, the 'opportunistic' approach described above is feasible.[25, 26]

FDA-incentivised and EMA-required studies expose pharmaceutical companies to a new, additional risk which in the future they will have to consider increasingly. They can continue to obey FDA and EMA demands, but they might find themselves in a US lawsuit asking for billions of US$ in damages and even more in punitive damages. These 'paediatric' studies do not just harm those patients who are treated in a placebo group. They pretend to investigate if the given antidiabetic drug works in minors at all, pretending that the 18th birthday has physiological significance, but as we have seen in Part I of this book, birthdays are legal and/or administrative limits only. In this context, the children-are-not-small-adults mantra is flawed. Insulin and other antidiabetic drugs work in the same way before and after the 18th birthday. All young patients and their parents are misled as to the value of these studies and consequently harmed.

Conclusion

'Paediatric drug development' in diabetes does not aim at helping patients or developing better treatments for young people. Instead, it uses flawed mantras to justify clinically unnecessary 'paediatric' studies that do not have the potential to improve healthcare. These studies result in 'paediatric' drug approval without producing any new medical understanding. As we have seen, they result in pseudo-scientific publications that advance 'paediatric' careers in academic research, the regulatory authorities, the pharmaceutical industry and commercial clinical research organisations.[21] T1DM can occur at any age, while T2DM occurs in those young patients who are massively overweight. The challenge of T2DM in minors is not 'paediatric', but part of the general challenge posed by overweight and obesity in modern western society.

Chapter 8

Epilepsy

Epileptic seizures vary from being brief and barely detectable to long periods of vigorous shaking. The most common seizure type is convulsion, but there are others, such as so-called 'absence seizures'. Seizures can be provoked by external stimuli including stress, alcohol, lack of sleep and flashing lights but are mostly not due to external circumstances.

The normal electrical activity of the brain, where nerve cells send their signals to other nerve cells, is non-synchronous. During epileptic seizures, the nerve cells fire in an abnormal, excessive and synchronised way. This synchronised activity can be monitored as electrical spikes and waves on an electroencephalogram (EEG).[1] Epileptic seizures are not a disease in themselves, but are events that can be caused by different underlying problems, including head trauma, stroke, brain tumours, infections, birth trauma and genetic abnormalities. Most seizures involve a loss of consciousness.[2, 3]

In the past, seizures often occurred in public. They are unpredictable, sudden events. In all early cultures, the separation between the material world and the supernatural forces that were believed to govern it – gods, magic and religion – was not as precise as we feel it is today. In all early written records, seizures were described as something where gods or other supernatural forces took control. This gave epilepsy a prominent position compared with other diseases. It was called the 'falling sickness', 'holy disease' (*morbus sacer* in Latin), and other stigmatising names. As long as there was no effective treatment, dealing with epilepsy, and especially epilepsy in children, was associated with superstition in the form of amulets hung around the neck, and further symbols, rituals and objects to please the gods and mitigate the symptoms.

Today, antiepileptic drugs (AEDs) prevent many, but not all, epileptic attacks. Many challenges remain, including drug resistance and side effects. Although epilepsy is more treatable and preventable than ever, it has to this day also maintained a degree of eeriness, despite the Enlightenment and the Scientific Revolution, and partially even because of them. Without them, modern drugs would not exist at all. For epilepsy, these movements have exacerbated the contrast between technically manageable health challenges and the helplessness relatives and observers are confronted with during seizures.

A single seizure does not always require the commencement of antiepileptic treatment. Instead, the risk of recurrent seizures needs to be taken into consideration. In adults, key factors to consider include two unprovoked seizures more than 24 hours apart, abnormalities in the EEG recording and a syndrome associated with seizures. In children, key risk factors include abnormal EEG results, a syndrome associated with seizures and severe head trauma. Beginning AED treatment is a serious decision. AEDs can have severe side effects, including potential cognitive and behavioural changes.[4]

Between the introduction of the drug phenytoin in 1938 and 1969, over 20 new AEDs were introduced. At this time, the methodology of clinical studies was also still in its infancy. Over the following 20 years, no major new AEDs were introduced, but the way available drugs worked was better understood. Concurrently, there were also advances in the methodology of clinical studies. The last 30 years has seen the introduction of a second-generation of drugs, and further evolution in the design of clinical studies. Our ability to tailor drug treatment to the individual has considerably improved. However, there are still many gaps, specifically in the treatment of young patients.[5] Around one-third of epileptic patients are still resistant to two or more AEDs and are thus be considered to have 'refractory epilepsy'.[6]

Ambulance services are often called for epileptic seizures by concerned citizens who want to help but are unaware of the basics of the condition. Ambulances may then transport patients to hospital Accident & Emergency centres not because there are good medical reasons to do so, but because they fear litigation, because of public expectations, or because of limited access to relevant patient information.[7, 8] In fact, most seizures resolve on their own within a few minutes. However, status epilepticus is an emergency that requires fast treatment. In a status epilepticus, the convulsions do not resolve on their own but continue for more than five minutes without the person returning to normal.[9, 10] Greater public knowledge of the basics of epilepsy would be desirable and could save resources. It could also spare patients being taken to hospital after a seizure when there was no need to do so, saving precious time as well as healthcare costs. Epilepsy is not only a medical, but also a social and societal, challenge.

Antiepileptic drugs (AEDs) in under 18s

Epileptic seizures can occur at any age, even in children who are still in their mother's womb. They do not require a minimal degree of maturation of the central nervous system before they can happen, unlike multiple sclerosis, Parkinson's disease or many other neurological conditions (see Chapter 15).

When the concept of 'paediatric drug development' emerged (see Part I), there were no real-world clinical challenges in the treatment of epilepsy in young people specifically. Nonetheless, there were calls for studies of epileptic drugs in minors ('children'). As with other health problems discussed in this book, these calls were based on *potential* risks in the treatment of young patients, but these risks did, to a large degree, not exist. There were no real *clinical* dangers. Instead, there were *regulatory* concerns. These concerns were a flawed interpretation of the paediatric warnings in drug labels that pharmaceutical companies had introduced from 1962 on.[6, 11, 12, 13, 14] The only patients in whom real pharmaceutical-related danger existed were newborns, where absorption, distribution, metabolism and excretion (ADME) of food and drugs still reflect the baby's life within the mother and need to be adapted to the outside world from birth on.

Treatment of epilepsy improved with the increasing availability of AEDs. The contrast between perceived AED dangers and what was known by clinicians with real-world experience became obvious when the US National Institute of Health (NIH) organised a conference in 1994 to discuss the use of AEDs in minors. The US's NIH emphasised that most AEDs used did not have separate 'paediatric' approval, and that separate pharmacokinetic (how the body processes a drug) and safety data were missing. The clinicians who treated the patients objected. At the end of the conference, a clear division of opinion was documented: the 'non-government' workshop participants opined that: 'If a drug is shown to be effective for partial seizures in adults, this is sufficient to justify approval for use in partial seizures in children provided that safety and pharmacokinetic considerations are appropriate'.[15] The conference report documents what Shirkey had already observed in 1968: most clinicians ignored the paediatric warnings,[16] but instead used their common sense that told them that the 17/18th birthday is not a physiological barrier but an administrative age limit.

In the following decades, the FDA incentivised numerous randomised double-blind placebo-controlled 'paediatric' studies to prove again and again that AEDs also worked in 'children', but these trials lacked medical sense. As stated, there are specific dangers in preterm newborns and to a lesser degree in term newborns, but no general danger of drug treatment in the administratively defined 'paediatric' population. All drugs and even salt are dangerous if we take too much; we have to get the dose right. Their potential danger is the reason why they must be prescribed and are not sold over-the-counter, but as we have seen this danger does not change with the 18th birthday.

Twenty-five years later, the FDA gave in and accepted that in partial onset seizures (POS), the efficacy of AEDs could be 'extrapolated' from adults to 'children' down to the age of 4 years and then 2 years.[17] In general terms, 'extrapolation' is defined by FDA authors as 'to infer unknown data from known data'.[18] In the context of 'paediatric drug development', the EMA defines extrapolation as 'Extending information and conclusions available from studies in one or more subgroups of the patient population (source population), or in related conditions or with related medicinal products, to make inferences for another subgroup of the population (target population), or condition or product, thus reducing the need to generate additional information (types of studies, design modifications, number of patients required) to reach conclusions for the target population, or condition or medicinal product. ... Extrapolation from adults to children is a typical example but extrapolation may be applied in many other areas ...'.[19]

In the context of 'paediatric drug development', the basic assumption underlying the need for 'extrapolation' is that adults and 'children' are fundamentally different. As we discuss throughout this book, this basic assumption is flawed. Administratively defined 'children' are not fundamentally different from adults. Babies' bodies, and more so prematurely born babies, are rather different from adults, but this difference does not continue until they come of age. The mantra that children-are-not-small-adults is flawed, as we have seen. Therefore, the assumption that a drug that works in adults might not work in 'children' is incorrect as well.

In the context of epilepsy, the term 'extrapolation' is therefore misleading. Young humans are not another species in which the efficacy of drugs needs to be extrapolated. AEDs simply work in adolescents and young adult patients. In this regard, the use of the term 'extrapolation of efficacy' is purely an attempt to save face. On the other hand, extrapolation of dosing is necessary in children who are physically not yet mature, but small studies in a limited number of centres with patients who need the medication anyway are sufficient to confirm the necessary doses, after the dose has already been calculated on the basis of modern methodology. Parents must be asked for permission to take additional blood samples for pharmacodynamics (PD) and pharmacokinetic (PK) measurements. Large multi-centre international dose-finding studies are a massive exaggeration of what is clinically needed.[20, 21]

The FDA reassessment of AEDs was not voluntary. Times had changed, and something had changed too in the public perception and in the minds of parents, who had become increasingly reluctant to allow their children to participate in 'paediatric' AED studies.[15, 22] Furthermore, neurologists had gone through all the studies that included administratively defined 'children' and had concluded that they showed that AEDs that worked in adults also worked in 'children' down to the age of 2 years.[23, 24] One group even asked the heretical question, is the 'children-are-not-small-adults' mantra correct and rejected it.[25] The FDA recommendations today show that medically and scientifically unnecessary 'paediatric' studies were performed for more than 25 years, between 1994[15] and the FDA's retreat from insisting on separate 'paediatric' studies in 2019.[17, 26]

The EMA has reluctantly followed the FDA in accepting 'extrapolation of efficacy' from adults down to children of 4 years of age.[27] There is no longer any reasonable justification for the EMA's former insistence.

Parent opinion

Parents had become increasingly reluctant to allow their children to take part in AED studies. Similar observations are reported in other fields, e.g. in parents' resistance to pain studies.[28] We cannot finally answer the question why such reluctance developed more with AEDs than in other areas. We could speculate that epilepsy is a chronic disease where parents had and have more time to reflect, while in oncology (Chapter 5) the situation is usually much more a life-or-death scenario. Furthermore, the reluctance of parents is an indirect observation that can be extracted from medical publications.

What we observe here is not only a shift in public opinion. It is a veritable paradigm shift regarding the place of children in our society and in the basic attitude of parents away from being obedient subjects towards having the right to decide about the treatment of their children.[29] Parents had for many years accepted 'paediatric' studies because they believed these would help their children and others, and had faith in science and medicine in general. This trust is wearing out. Parents no longer trust blindly. It is a paradigm shift where an old framework is replaced by a new one, such as the move away from the mediaeval geocentric view of the world, which assumed that the sun and the universe orbit around the earth. Today, we know that our earth orbits around the sun, together with the other planets of our solar system – a heliocentric view.[30] We also know that 'the authorities' are not necessarily to be trusted and that we must investigate and judge for ourselves.

Chapter 9

Knee surgery

Separate drug approval in adults and 'children' by the US Food and Drug Administration (FDA) and the European Medicines Agency (EMA) described in Part I of this book also triggers studies in areas we would not immediately associate with drugs. Knee surgery is a glaring example of how counter-productive this can be.

Part of growing is the lengthening of the long bones. Bones are alive. Maintenance remodelling occurs throughout the entire bone tissue throughout life, but the two growth plates at each end of the long bones are the places where the bone grows. The growth plates are found only in children and adolescents. Once we stop growing, the two sides of each growth plate fuse and form the 'epiphyseal line' which can be seen on X-ray. Complete fusion occurs most commonly in girls at 15-16 years old, and a bit later in boys.[1] One way of showing the end of puberty is to check if the growth plates have already fused. When we see an epiphyseal line only, growth is largely complete and the body has become mature.

In all joints, including the knee, the ends of the bones that form the joint are covered with cartilage. The joint capsule, together with its ligaments, menisci and muscles, ensures its stability. The fluid within the capsule keeps the surfaces lubricated. The cartilage is elastic, absorbs shocks and enables pain-free movement. Once humans are through puberty, the joint cartilage no longer has its own blood vessels; its nutrition is instead accomplished by diffusion from the joint fluid, which is a less potent means of delivery than through direct blood supply. Therefore, joint cartilage has reduced regenerative potential after the closure of the growth plate.[2] In adults, injured knee cartilage is less likely to heal, if at all. Possible consequences are pain, swelling, inflammation, or a locked knee,[3] which can seriously impair performance in sports. Such problems often persist over time and become worse, with the risk of developing arthrosis.[4, 5, 6]

Injuries to the knee cartilage are common, often arising from sports. As young people increasingly participate in physically demanding sports, numbers of injuries are increasing, including in girls and young women.

In young people before puberty, blood vessels supply the cartilage in the knee. Therefore, cartilage injuries in young people usually heal much better. Conservative treatment – rest and abstinence from demanding physical activities for a while – is often successful, and the joint damage can disappear. However, if conservative treatment is not successful, surgery should be considered at a young age also.

There is also another type of damage to cartilage and bone, called 'osteochondrosis dissecans', which occurs mostly in adolescents, both before and after the growth plates close. Its causes are not yet well understood. It may be caused by repetitive micro-trauma, but it also occurs in minors who are not active in sports.[2, 7]

Modern knee surgery

Today there are several surgical methods to treat cartilage lesions of the knee. They all involve 'keyhole' – that is, minimally invasive – surgery. The knee is inspected through a small incision into which an arthroscope is inserted to assess the damage.

Scissors, small pliers and other instruments can be attached to the end of the arthroscope to deliver treatment, leaving only a small scar on the skin.[8] Sometimes, one or two additional incisions are required.

One surgical method currently used is 'microfracture'. In this procedure, the damaged area is cleaned of remaining unstable cartilage. With an arthroscopic awl, multiple perforations (microfractures) are then pushed into the exposed bone, which would normally be covered by cartilage. The holes are placed 3-4 mm apart. When the blood flow from the bone marrow seems to be adequate in all areas of the defect, the procedure is terminated.[9] The perforations in the bone surface cause the release of blood and stem cells from the bone marrow. They form a clot on the surface of the bone, which then builds up a new layer of cartilage.[10]

Another approach is 'autologous chondrocyte implantation' (ACI), which can also be used in other joints. In cases of major cartilage injury, cartilage cells (chondrocytes) are removed from an area where the joint is less stressed. They are sent to a company that will grow them. The cultured chondrocytes are transformed into a patch which is returned to the hospital. In a follow-up operation, this patch is inserted into the damaged area.

Today's state of the art is a third-generation ACI product with a three-dimensional structure ('matrix'), allowing easier implantation, better replication of the normal cartilage architecture, and improved healing and recovery. Usually, the cartilage damage is completely repaired, the knee heals and patients can carry on until the next injury or until they grow too old for demanding physical activities. This two-part operation is now a routine procedure.[4]

There are other operative methods too, but at present ACI and microfracture are the ones that are used most often.[11] In general, younger patients tend to heal better.

Approval for ACI products

Microfracture is a surgical method that does not introduce foreign bodies, so it does not need regulatory approval. In contrast, ACI products do need approval. Both the FDA and the EMA approve ACI products in adults only, using the administrative age limit of 18 years to distinguish adults from 'children'. It will be clear immediately that this disadvantages those 16-17-year olds who have mature bones and cartilage and who need ACI treatment.

While in the US the FDA has approved ACI products only in adults, it has not made 'paediatric' studies a condition for *adult* approval. Surgeons can decide on their own about the 'off-label' use of ACI products in minors. However, for official 'paediatric' approval of ACI products, the FDA requires 'paediatric' studies.

The EU classified ACI products as 'advanced therapy medicinal products' (ATMPs) in 2007.[12] Before this, companies had already developed ACI products that were routinely used in surgery. A manufacturing licence had been sufficient. With the new ATMP classification this was no longer enough. Companies had to apply for approval of ACI products as drugs by submitting clinical study data on safety and efficacy, even if their products had been used successfully for many years. We will not discuss here if this was justified; our focus in this book is that for the approval of ACI products *for any age group* companies now had also to submit a paediatric investigation plan (PIP) proposal and to negotiate it with the EMA, thus committing to separate efficacy studies in under 18s.

This was in 2008 when the EU Paediatric Regulation requiring PIPs had already been in force for a year.[13, 14, 15, 16, 17] Since that time, only one ACI product (spherox) has been EMA-approved, and even spherox is not approved in 'children'.[18, 19, 20] Several companies are still allowed to continue to produce and market their ACI products in individual EU member states as they did before their classification as ATMPs.[12, 20]

A study in the US compares MACI (autologous cultured chondrocytes on a porcine collagen membrane) against microfracture in knee defects in patients aged 10 to 17 years.[21] MACI is already FDA-approved in adults.[22] Obviously, the manufacturer wishes to get 'paediatric' FDA approval as well. Commercially, this is logical. Medically, however, the requirement for a separate 'paediatric' study lacks sense, yet this study is currently recruiting patients in 10 US medical centres. Young patients are randomly assigned to either MACI or microfracture. Both methods are effective, but it should be for the surgeon to decide what is appropriate for the individual. There is no reason the efficacy should be influenced by the patient being older or younger than 18. This is a *regulatory* study that lacks *medical* sense. When my child is operated on, I want the surgeon to use the method he thinks is best in the particular case and not a method that is randomly assigned.

In the EU, five companies that produce ACI products have so far gone through the PIP process. All ACI PIPs demand separate clinical studies in minors *before* their 18th birthday but *after* their growth plates are already closed. These minors are *legally* still 'children', but are already *physically* mature, as defined by the closed growth plates. The studies that are required are listed at the end of each published PIP decision.[23, 24, 25, 26, 27]

Two of these PIPs demand multi-centre safety and efficacy studies of ACI against microfracture, the first in patients aged 16-17 years, the second in 'children' from the closure of the epiphyses (physical maturity) until their 18th birthday.[23, 26]

Many publications compare ACI with microfracture, with contradictory conclusions.[2, 4, 6, 9, 11, 28, 29] Both work, and both work better in younger patients. It should be up to the surgeon to determine which procedure is most suitable, and not the lottery of a randomised trial.

To demand repetition of proof of efficacy in 'children' for compounds and/or surgical procedures whose efficacy in humans is already known lacks medical sense. The comparison of microfracture with ACI in 'children' is based on the assumption that for people younger than 18 efficacy must be shown again. Their body is assumed to be fundamentally different, which is clearly untrue.[30, 31] Adolescent athletes already have mature bodies. On the night of their 18th birthday their legal status changes, not their body.[15, 16, 17, 20]

The FDA will not approve an ACI product for use in the 'paediatric population' without 'paediatric' data. The EMA goes even further and threatens non-approval of products in adults if the company does not commit to separate 'paediatric' studies. For such studies, surgeons must tell patients and parents that it is not yet known if ACI works in 'children' – a flawed claim which every surgeon either knows to be untrue, or prefers not even to think about.

The PIP-required ACI knee studies are not just fantasy outputs of EMA bureaucracy. They translate into real-world studies affecting real patients. An ongoing study documents safety and efficacy of ACI for knee cartilage defects in 'paediatric' patients with closed epiphyses aged 13 to 17 years.[32] The study title describes the research as a 'non-interventional' study. It corresponds to one of the studies required by an ACI PIP.[26] To call this study 'non-interventional' is ridiculous. The description in www.clinicaltrials.gov explains that the patients are operated on within the framework of routine operations in Germany. This study is as unnecessary as the other microfracture study mentioned above.[21]

The same EMA PIP also requires a comparison of ACI with microfracture.[26] At the time of writing, this study has not yet started. It is not listed in www.clinicaltrials.gov. Hopefully, it will never begin.

The ACI PIPs have the dubious honour of documenting concisely the blurring between the legal and the physiological meanings of the term 'child'. As we have seen, 'paediatric' patients from closure of the epiphyses to less than 18 years are physically no longer children. The EU demands questionable research in its crusade for as many 'paediatric' studies as possible. Its demands are based on the executive power the EU Paediatric Law has given to the EMA, and on the carelessness with which these studies are demanded despite their obvious absurdity and potential harm. The newest ACI PIP was issued in 2019.[26]

In 2000, EU leaders declared the EU would, by 2010, become 'the most dynamic and competitive knowledge-based economy in the world capable of sustainable economic growth with more and better jobs and greater social cohesion, and respect for the environment', a promise that became known as the 'Lisbon Strategy'.[33] How can this come about if development is constantly frustrated by bureaucracy and resources are squandered without creating new knowledge?

ACI products are not the most important challenge in surgery and medical care. However, the FDA's insistence on separate approval in adults and minors, and the EU's PIPs for ACI products are striking examples of the damage bureaucracy can cause. The regulatory demands and decisions negatively affect the lives of young patients.

The EU's Lisbon Strategy has turned into a nightmare of regulatory demands that are hostile to science, disguised by pseudo-scientific wording. From Europe, modern science and technology once expanded throughout the world. This leading role has since vanished to a considerable degree.

The EU does need a regulatory framework to advance scientific and medical progress, but the current regulatory demand for 'paediatric' studies does the opposite. It prevents the establishment and growth of innovative companies and of new jobs. Instead, it funds and backs backwards-oriented academic researchers with pseudo-scientific 'paediatric' projects that must be financed by business.

Conclusion

By insisting on the comparison of ACI with microfracture, both the FDA and the EMA are exceeding the limits that should separate the authority of licensing authorities from medical decisions made by surgeons. Both ACI and microfracture are well-established methods. By ascribing an apparent, but non-existent physiological characteristic to the 18th birthday, the FDA and EMA interfere directly in medical practice. It is their job to approve safe medicines and to block unsafe ones. With the administrative division of mankind into two populations, children and adults, they trigger studies where the surgeons must *pretend* not to know the outcome of microfracture or ACI in 'children'. Both work but will be more or less appropriate in individual circumstances – in minors, the decision as to the most appropriate surgical treatment should be personalised. It depends on the size of the lesion, the degree of sports activity of the patient, and many other factors. Studies that compare ACI with microfracture in 'paediatric' patients abuse these patients to answer an irrelevant question, defined by non-medical inclusion criteria.

Chapter 10

Perinatal depression

How come perinatal depression is a topic in a book on 'paediatric' drug research?

Shortly before and after childbirth, a mother can become depressed. 'Postpartum' or 'postnatal depression', now re-named 'perinatal depression' in the US Academy of Psychiatrists' *Diagnostic and Statistical Manual of Mental Disorders, Fifth Edition* (DSM-5), is one of the most common complications in the period before and after childbirth and has potentially significant negative consequences for the mothers themselves and for their entire family.[1, 2] It can be a risk for both the mother, as untreated it may lead to suicide, and the child; children of mothers with perinatal depression have a higher than normal risk of developmental delay and behavioural problems. In extreme cases, children can even be killed by their mother. Thus, it is a problem to be taken very seriously. It occurs typically in the period shortly before to after giving birth and is defined as an episode of major depression associated with childbirth. It affects up to 15% of mothers. In the US, it is the most common obstetric complication among new mothers.[2] For the majority of women with perinatal depression, this is the first experience of depression in their life.

Pregnancy and the period after birth are a life-changing experience. During pregnancy, the female body performs an intricate, physiologically challenging dance, together with the newly formed placenta, to ensure the survival and healthy development of the child. The placenta itself is complex and demanding, as it produces massive levels of hormones only seen during pregnancy. The dramatic fluctuations in hormones after birth then contribute to the potential onset of depression.[3] Symptoms can include extreme sadness, low energy, anxiety, bouts of crying, mood swings, mild elation, irritability, fatigue, confusion and more. Perinatal depression usually does not require intervention, but midwives, paediatricians, gynaecologists, general practitioners and family members should be aware of it, as its occurrence is a risk for both mother and child as explained above. It is also a risk factor for recurring perinatal depression in and after the next pregnancy. If intervention is required, psychotherapy is regarded as the first-line option for treating mild-to-moderate forms; antidepressants in combination with therapy are indicated for moderate-to-severe forms.[1, 2, 3, 4, 5]

All humans who survive childhood go through puberty, beginning physically as a child and finishing physically as a young adult. The entire body matures, including the organs of speech, the reproductive system, the hormonal system, hair growth and more. Major psychological, cognitive and emotional changes accompany this process but generally take longer to complete.[6, 7] Puberty typically ends at 15-16 years in women. At this stage they are physically 'adult' but not necessarily emotionally or cognitively mature. Legally, they are still 'children' and for the purposes of pharmaceutical approval they are still children even when they are doing something as physically mature as having a baby.

Given this contradiction, separate 'paediatric' drug trials for perinatal depression treatment in mothers under 18 are more clearly absurd and pointless than in any other condition. The following two such 'paediatric' studies are among the most ridiculous and openly unethical included in this book.

Two unethical drug trials

Study NCT03665038 is a 'paediatric' multi-centre, 'open-label', safety, tolerability and pharmacokinetics (PK) study of the antidepressant drug brexanolone (also called: allopregnanolone) in females aged 15 to 17 years with perinatal depression.[11, 12] This study, which is currently recruiting patients in 17 research centres in the US, was triggered by an FDA written request for such a 'paediatric' drug trial.[13] Allopregnanolone/brexanolone is a naturally produced steroid that acts on the brain. As a medication, it is FDA-approved to treat perinatal depression in over-18s.[12, 14, 15] Its safety, tolerability and pharmacokinetics (how it is processed by the body) are already known.

The EMA PIP EMEA-002051-PIP02-16 for allopregnanolone/brexanolone goes even further and demands a 'paediatric' double-blind, randomised, placebo-controlled trial of the drug's pharmacokinetics, safety, tolerability and *efficacy* in 'post-pubertal adolescent girls' with perinatal depression,[16] even though its efficacy is well established and non-approval in 'children' means denying effective treatment to mothers under the age of 18.

Physically and biologically, there is very little difference between mothers of 16, 17, 18, 19, 20, 21 or 22 years' old who have perinatal depression. They are all physically capable of bearing a child. Emotionally, the older they are the greater the resilience they may have acquired, but not necessarily. They all have the potential to develop perinatal depression. However, here again we find drugs that are known to be effective in 'adults' are denied to mothers under the age of 18.

To describe these two studies as 'paediatric' is completely misleading and to describe the participants as 'girls' is an insult that belittles their situation.[16] Given the seriousness of perinatal depression and the risks for both mother and child, requiring sufferers to take part in a placebo-controlled study in which half the participants would receive no active treatment, is a particularly inhumane and unethical decision by the EMA. Both studies reflect a patriarchal attitude towards young mothers, not considering them as human beings who first and foremost need medical treatment for their perinatal depression but as objects of administration.[17, 18, 19, 20] Why should brexanolone (also known as allopregnanolone) not work before a mother's 18th birthday? And who will profit from these studies? The authors of the scientific publications, the advocates of 'paediatric drug development' in academia, the regulatory authorities, the pharmaceutical industry and the commercial clinical research organisations (CROs) – never the patients.[17,18,19,20,21] Peer-reviewed journals should refuse to accept such studies for publication and these two studies should be terminated immediately by the institutional review boards and ethics committees responsible. Meanwhile, the company producing pregnanolone/brexanolone and the medical research centres involved should be aware that they might be sued for damages, and indeed punitive damages, by patients, parents and their lawyers.

Most importantly, young mothers and their parents should not agree to participate in either of these studies and should look very carefully at any invitation to take part in research.

Chapter 11

Pain relief

Pain generally has an obvious cause, such as a wound or as a symptom of an underlying problem, such as a general infection, local inflammation, cancer or another serious disease. When it occurs, like love, it is all-consuming – not much else matters.[1] In developed countries, pain is the most common reason for seeking medical help. It can seriously impair quality of life and general functioning. Analgesics ('painkillers') may help, at least for a while, but are seen as only part of the answer; addressing psychological factors, providing social support, hypnosis and/or distraction are among other approaches that can help.[2]

Pain in children is even more complex and demanding because it affects not only the young patient but the entire family, with the mother most often in the frontline.[3,4] Effective treatments exist, but before we look at these we need first to review the different types of pain in children and adults and whether there are differences that might dictate differences in treatment.

Different types of pain

Acute pain occurs if we hit our finger with a hammer, cut ourselves with a sharp knife, are stung by an insect, walk into a patch of nettles with bare feet, or have a toothache. There is pain after a sports injury; after a tiny burn (not serious, but very unpleasant); or after a major burn (life-threatening and extremely unpleasant). Chronic pain can have very different causes, including ongoing inflammation in a joint, the abdomen, the throat, or elsewhere. It can be caused by childhood cancer or alternatively be classed as 'functional pain' – that is, no reason can be found despite intensive diagnostics.

Pain is reported to the brain by the nerves. All nerves and nervous systems within the body are interlinked. Humans have a central nervous system (CNS), consisting of the brain and spinal cord, and a peripheral nervous system (all nerve cells outside the CNS). The latter then is sub-divided into the conscious and the 'autonomic' nervous systems; the autonomic nervous system supplies the muscles of the heart and other internal organs (the 'smooth muscles'), and the glands, and is not under our conscious control. We can tell our hands to open and close, but we cannot tell our gut to work faster. The gut runs its business automatically, coordinated by the autonomic nervous system.

The CNS plays a key part in reporting pain, and even more so when acute pain becomes chronic and is no longer directly linked to a clear lesion or other cause; such chronic pain is thought to arise from nerve pathways that have been set up and continue to be activated despite the original problem having resolved.

The treatment of pain has very different dimensions depending on the type of pain being addressed; these include the relief and suppression of pain during surgical interventions, and the management of acute and chronic pain in general.

Pain experienced by babies

As unborn babies grow within their mother, their organs develop. Long before they are born, their nervous systems are functional – evidence tells us this is from the 26th week of pregnancy,[3] the point after which premature babies can survive. Children feel pain as much as adults do, but their brains are not yet adult; they often process and report it differently, particularly before they can speak and describe what is going on.

Anaesthesia for newborns

The develoment of anaesthesia in the 19th century transformed the experience of pain in individuals and expanded the capacities of healthcare in relieving pain. While children commonly received anaesthesia for surgery from the beginning, they were also perceived to have more problems resulting from anaesthesia, including nausea, vomiting, respiratory depression and cardiac arrest, especially with chloroform. Paediatric pain management during surgery progressed with the increasing availability of anaesthetic agents, the better management of their side effects, improved training of physicians in the use of anaesthetics, and the development of anaesthetic equipment appropriate for use in children and infants. The increasingly improved relief of pain during surgery allowed increasingly more complicated and invasive operations.

For a while, there was the belief that infants were relatively insensitive to pain. In the 1950s, this view provided an accepted position for the use of minimal anaesthesia for surgery in infants. During the second half of the last century, however, it became widely accepted that paediatric pain was an important issue. Studies showed that pain in neonates resulted in high stress. In the 1980s there was a hot debate about minimal anaesthesia in neonates, followed by a dramatic increase in professional and scientific interest in pain in children.[5, 6, 7] The American Academy of Pediatrics (AAP) published two position statements, in 1987 and in 2000, emphasising that newborns experienced the same pain sensation as adults; and that newborns required the same level of pain suppression as adults when they had to undergo surgical procedures.[8, 9]

The history of analgesics

For the relief of acute and/or chronic pain outside of surgery, there were few options in the past. Opioids based on the opium poppy – grown in India – were regarded as relative wonder drugs. By the 18th century, the term 'laudanum' was used for any combination of opium and alcohol. Opium and, after 1820, morphine were mixed with mercury, hashish, cayenne pepper, ether, chloroform, belladonna, whiskey, wine and brandy.[10]

Opioid solution extracted from poppy flowers was brought to North America by the European settlers. They used this for diarrhoea and all types of pain. Opioid addiction was common, but also poorly understood. The hypodermic needle was invented around the time of the US Civil War. Opium administered as morphine by injection offered fast pain relief for injured soldiers, leading to the first epidemic of morphine addiction during the American civil war in the 1860s.

Morphine was regarded as a 'cure all'. Its use was not restricted to the military. Opioids were also mixed into many patent medications, and used to treat all sorts of pain when few effective drugs existed. Many medicines given to children also contained opioids.[11]

Today, we have many more options for pain treatment in adults and children. Paracetamol (acetaminophen) and non-steroidal anti-inflammatory drugs (NSAIDs – such as ibuprofen) are among the analgesics most commonly given to children to control mild to moderate pain. Opioids are indicated in combination with non-opioid analgesics for moderate to severe pain, including cancer pain, acute and chronic pain syndromes, and post-surgical pain.[3] Paracetamol and NSAIDs are okay for banal, but unpleasant pain, such as toothache until the dentist fixes the problem, or headache, or pain after spraining an ankle. Modern opioids are a diverse class of painkillers, ranging from moderately strong, including oxycodone, to very strong, such as fentanyl, which resembles other opiates such as morphine and heroin.

Opioids are good for acute pain, but less good for chronic pain, where various risks, including addiction, can outweigh the benefits.[12, 13] Due to their sedative effects on the part of the brain which regulates breathing – the respiratory centre – opioids in high doses present the potential for respiratory depression and even failure and death. Because of this, traditionally, physicians were reluctant to prescribe opioids heavily. Furthermore, doctors have long been aware of the dangers of drug addiction. During the Vietnam War, many soldiers became addicted to opioids and following that there was a tendency to under-treat. That all changed in the US in the late 1990s.

The 1980s and 90s saw a much reduced reliance on opioid analgesics and it was claimed that this resulted in under-treatment of pain in Europe and North America. In 1995, the American Pain Society launched a 'pain as the fifth vital sign' campaign to encourage proper, standardised evaluation and treatment of pain. However, the rapid institution of strict standards for pain management in healthcare resulted in several unintended consequences. To provide adequate pain control, physicians now relied more on opioid medications. Since 2013, deaths from drug overdose have surpassed deaths from motor vehicle accidents, making overdose the leading cause of preventable death in the USA.[14, 15] In 2017, the US Government declared the opioid epidemic to be a public health emergency.[16]

The opioid epidemic is a good example of the need for balance: it is correct to want an appropriate treatment for acute and chronic pain, but continuous balancing is required.

Approval for painkillers in 'children'

As with many other classes of drug, new analgesics are routinely first approved in adults. For approval in 'children', defined as being younger than 18 years old, separate 'paediatric' studies are required by the regulatory authorities.[17, 18, 19]

In 2009, the US's Food and Drug Administration (FDA) organised a scientific workshop of recognised specialists in pain, clinical research methods, ethics and drug development to look at drugs for pain relief in children. The reason for organising this conference was that parents were refusing to allow their children to participate in pain studies to such an extent that not enough 'children' could be recruited into the pain studies requested by the FDA. The conference's aim was to discuss 'extrapolating' efficacy findings for analgesics in adults to 'children'. In general terms, extrapolation is defined by FDA authors as 'to infer unknown data from known data'.[20] Parents and patient advocacy groups were not invited.

The report from the workshop said that in an ideal world, the efficacy of all new drugs would be established in every single paediatric age group, separately. However, this would unacceptably delay availability and 'paediatric' approval because of the impracticality of completing such efficacy studies in a timely fashion.[21] Parents' objections to such studies had in fact torpedoed the dreams of such an 'ideal world'. They did not want an 'ideal world'; they wanted treatment for their children.

Because of parental refusal to participate in pain studies pharmaceutical companies had been unable to deliver the FDA-requested/demanded data from randomised, double-blind, placebo-controlled studies.[22] The real problem, of course, was that these data were, and are, unnecessary. Children do feel pain, analgesics do work in children,[22] and there is no justifiable reason to expose them to studies that reproduce what we already know.

In a presentation in 2016, the FDA listed the drugs for which 'paediatric' study data were still missing. These drugs were paracetamol; the NSAIDs buprenorphine, ibuprofen, diclofenac and indomethacin; the opioids hydromorphone, hydrocodone, morphine, tapentadol, oxymorphone and tramadol; and a combination of paracetamol and oxycodone.[22] Several of these drugs are no longer patent-protected and are sold under different brand names. Experience shows they work before and after the 18th birthday. Nevertheless, as long as 'paediatric' data for these compounds have not been submitted to the FDA, the prescribing information must contain the phrase, 'Paediatric use: safety and effectiveness not established in patients under 18 years of age'. This is not based on science,[23, 24] yet you can check this is the wording used by searching on the internet for the name of any of these compounds plus 'FDA label'.

The EU's European Medicines Agency (EMA) also demands 'paediatric' studies for analgesics, including open-label and randomised double-blind placebo-controlled studies in 'children' aged 2 to 17 years with various sorts of pain.[25] PIPs (paediatric investigation plans) require studies in 'children' aged 6 to 17 years with migraine,[26, 27] and in 'children' with opioid-induced constipation.[28] As stated above, parents are increasingly reluctant to allow their children to participate, with the consequence that these studies recruit patients extremely slowly. Tapentadol, for which the PIP agreed between the pharma company and the EMA requires six studies in 'children' from birth to 17 years of age, has (at the time of writing) the sad record of so far having had to be modified 14 times (EMEA-000018-PIP01-07-M14).[29] As described in Chapter 2, the first PIP negotiation between the drug developer and the EMA takes about one year; the negotiation for a PIP modification takes 'only' half a year. Thus, for tapentadol the pharmaceutical company has so far had to negotiate with the EMA for a total of eight years.

The original PIP for fentanyl, EMEA-000712-PIP01-09, required two pain studies in newborn children and one in children aged 1 month to 2 years old. In the PIP modification of 2019 the requirement for all these 'paediatric' studies was replaced by a complete waiver.[30] One would expect responsible decision-making from a medical agency such as the EMA in demanding clinical studies. Switching from asking for complex studies in newborns and babies to waiving them completely suggests that, for the EMA, young patients are purely an administrative matter.

Treatment of pain has a number of aspects, as I have said. Medical doctors and parents are scared of overdosing, which might result in toxic effects for young patients; but under-dosing can result in less than effective drug levels and expose young patients to unnecessary pain when effective treatment exists. These, however, are concerns about dosage, not about efficacy. Balance and caution, with careful monitoring, are as ever the key.

Conclusion

For young patients, the insistence of the regulatory authorities on separate 'paediatric' studies of efficacy withholds, or at the very least confuses, effective pain treatment. Placebo-controlled studies deny young patients in the placebo group (often half of all patients in the study) any effective treatment at all. Medically, these studies lack sense as well as humanity. Parents should refuse to let their children participate in such studies and research should be focused on appropriate dosage and the balance between effective pain relief and the dangers of side effects, including addiction.

Chapter 12

Attention-deficit hyperactivity disorder (ADHD)

Restless and undisciplined children have been described since ancient times. However, such children started to be mentioned in a scientific and medical context only after the end of the 18th century. Compared with other mental disorders, the history of ADHD is thus relatively short. For a long time, it was thought that young people would eventually grow out of their disruptive behaviour. More extensive monitoring and examination of children with ADHD showed that their parents often also had comparable behavioural challenges. In consequence, the idea that ADHD also existed in adults began to arise.[1] ADHD in adults is acknowledged today; its diagnosis is usually more difficult than in young people due to multiple additional diseases, disorders and troubles that can affect adult patients on top of their ADHD.[2, 3]

Mainstream medical science today recognises ADHD as the most common behavioural and neurodevelopmental disorder of childhood, affecting about 5% of young people and about 2.5% of adults in most cultures.[4, 5] It is acknowledged as a significant public health issue. At the same time, several structural and functional brain anomalies have been linked with ADHD. The current view of the condition has evolved in parallel with the field of psychiatry, acknowledging a shift from psychological and environmental explanations of behaviour towards a biological framework, based on learnings in neuroimaging and genetic research.[2]

ADHD is usually diagnosed during the school years. It is one of the most common diagnoses in educational and paediatric mental health settings. Many young people diagnosed with ADHD early on, later have problems related to education, social functioning and/or other mental illnesses.

No single risk factor explains ADHD. Both inherited and non-inherited factors contribute. It is, to a relevant degree, familial and inheritable, but research into the contributions made by heredity and molecular genetics suggest no more than an overlap with other neurodevelopmental problems, notably autism spectrum disorders. Further risk factors are: having a biological relative with ADHD; several gene variants; exposure to lead before and after birth; low birth weight; and/or premature birth. However, all known risk factors are not definitely causal. The genetic risks we know of today cannot be used for prediction.[6]

ADHD is not homogeneous, but a continuum. The American Psychiatric Association's *Diagnostic and Statistical Manual of Mental Disorders 5th Edition (DSM-5)* describes three main forms: primarily inattentive, primarily impulsive/hyperactive, and a combination of the two. These forms are not expected to be stable. Children diagnosed with ADHD can change the form of their disorder over time.[7, 8, 9]

ADHD controversies include concerns about the condition's actual existence, its causes, alleged over-diagnosis and methods of treatment, especially the use of stimulant medications in children. These controversies have been under discussion since at least the 1970s,[5, 10] and have sometimes had an almost religious intensity, reflecting some people's fundamental distrust of medical treatment and modern healthcare in general.[4, 5, 10] Those who question the existence of ADHD argue that it is more a matter of temperament and parenting style than of an illness, and that its diagnosis and treatment were invented by doctors, pharmacists or other interested parties with the aim of taming individuals who challenge or disregard societal standards, and/ or to maximise profits from medicines used in its treatment. There are also claims that the condition is over-diagnosed, allegedly for the same reasons it was identified in the first place. At the same time, ADHD has been called the 'scourge of the 21st century'. People who were diagnosed with it in childhood have a higher risk of developing sociopathy, alcoholism and addiction diseases in adulthood.

The diagnosis of ADHD is also becoming more common in forensic psychiatry with the condition being linked to criminal behaviour, including arrests and imprisonment. ADHD also increases the risk of dangerous driving in adults.[1]

Altogether, ADHD is a very complex challenge. Not every young person who is very active should be regarded as *hyper*active. It is normal for children and young people to continually challenge adult supervision and to explore the boundaries of what is allowed or forbidden, and how far they can go. Disruptive behaviour, such as throwing tantrums, is common in young people. Occasional low-intensity naughty, defiant or impulsive behaviour, including anger or even stealing, are regarded as normal in preschool children. However, extremely difficult and challenging behaviours outside the age norm and the level of development are regarded as behaviour disorders.[11]

There will always be a tension between understanding and sympathising with young people who challenge social norms, and not tolerating disruptive behaviour to create clear boundaries. There will never be a definitive solution. There are some individuals who during their youth defy the social norms but later achieve great things. Albert Einstein, who was born in Germany, came into conflict with the school system of the German Empire, which was characterised by discipline and order. Teachers said that his disrespect rubbed off on his classmates. Finally, he decided to leave German education without a degree. Later, he graduated in Switzerland.[12] None of this indicated his future stellar career in physics. On the one hand, individual differences in successful, adaptive psychological styles are essential for human development.[6] On the other hand, those who have a successful career after demonstrating defiance and challenging behaviour in childhood are the exception. Altogether, we must always return to the conclusion that each individual deserves to be looked at with common sense. Some claim that ADHD is over-diagnosed, others that is under-diagnosed, but most agree that it is *mis*diagnosed.[8]

Treatment for ADHD

It is more difficult precisely to describe and define behavioural challenges than measurable physical characteristics such as fever, blood count or signs of inflammation. It was a great merit of clinical research in the last decades that criteria were developed for behavioural disorders that allowed the measurement of the effectiveness of treatments. In the case of ADHD, the main symptoms are recognised as inattentiveness, hyperactivity and impulsiveness.[13, 14]

There is no single, promising ADHD treatment. Parents, doctors, healthcare workers and educational professionals have many different methods for treating and trying to help young people with ADHD until they can find their future place in society. Treatment guidelines recommend a combination of multiple, individually-adapted treatment components ('multimodal treatment'). Treatment options include pharmaceuticals, diet, cognitive behavioural techniques, psychoeducation of both parents and young patients, and more.[6, 15,16]

Stimulants are considered the standard pharmaceutical treatment for ADHD, according to the 2011 practice guidelines of the American Academy of Pediatrics (AAP). They work well and are cost-effective. They usually allow patients to manage their treatment independently, and require minimal physician input in the months and years after successfully arriving at an individual dose.[8, 17]

Methylphenidate (MPH), a stimulant, is sold as Ritalin and many other brand names. This drug was first authorised for use in the US in 1955 and is prescribed relatively frequently. Children with ADHD who use stimulant medications generally have better relationships with peers and family members, perform better in school, are less distractible and impulsive, and have longer attention spans. On the other hand, MPH is not a wonder drug that will resolve all problems.

As MPH was authorised in 1955, it was not affected by US or EU paediatric legislation. However, for another FDA-approved ADHD drug, guanfacine,[18, 19] the FDA offered a financial incentive by extending its patent protection by six months in return for a 'paediatric' randomised, double-blind, placebo-controlled, parallel-group trial in adolescents (aged 13 to 17 years) with ADHD.[20] In the EU, for the same drug, the EMA has demanded one study in adolescents aged 13 to 17 years, one study in 'children' aged 6 to 17 years, and one double-blind, randomised placebo-controlled, efficacy & safety study with a third, active reference arm (atomoxetine) in 'children' from 6 to 17 years of age.[21] A guanfacine ADHD study at the time of writing is recruiting 'children' aged 6 to 17 years in 55 centres in the US, Austria, Belgium, Germany, the Netherlands, Portugal, Spain, Sweden and the UK.[22] As I have explained elsewhere, placebo-controlled randomised, double-blind studies are appropriate in substances whose efficacy we do not yet know, but guanfacine is already FDA-approved in adults. To test it against placebo exposes young patients in the placebo group to no treatment at all. This harms not only the patients by omission, but all patients and their parents by deceit. It is in breach of the Declaration of Helsinki (see page 21).

Parents who are asked for permission to let their child participate in an ADHD study should first of all check if the respective drug is already registered in adults. If this is the case, separate proof of efficacy is pointless and parents should refuse their permission. Parents whose child is already participating in such a study[22] should consider discussing this with their physician, refusing further participation, and insisting on switching to medication that is already available on the basis of their child's individual needs.

Advice for parents

ADHD is very complex, as explained in the introduction to this chapter. There is the temptation just to ask for an effective drug and then forget about it, but unfortunately, this often fails. The prescription of stimulants has increased considerably over the past few years.[7] As in all complex challenges, parents have to consider all treatment options, invest time and energy, use their common sense, and regularly reassess the situation. However, the participation of their child in a questionable study should not be an option. When we know a drug is effective in adults we must remind ourselves that ADHD in an individual patient does not change its characteristics on the night of their 18th birthday[21, 22, 23] and research should focus instead on the correct dose for physically immature individuals where a drug may be helpful.

Chapter 13

Inflammatory skin diseases

Our skin is our first line of defence against pathogens, harmful substances and hazards with the potential to cause damage, such as insects, sharp objects, heat, dehydraton and much more.[1] It continually renews itself, preserving integrity against the many environmental challenges. Stem cells in the basal layer are crucial in keeping the balance between wear and tear and continuous regeneration. They also regenerate hair follicles, and are involved in repairing damage. Injuries to adult skin usually result in scars, while early in pregnancy the skin of the unborn baby regenerates without any scar formation. The development of the baby's skin in the mother includes the formation of hair follicles and sweat glands. Additional cells types migrate into the outer layer of the skin, including cells that produce pigments (absent in albinos), immune cells to coordinate attacks against pathogens, and nerve cells that coordinate skin sensation.

Cells in the lower skin layers continuously divide, differentiate and move upwards towards the surface. Near the surface, they acquire a barrier function, becoming flat, harden, and create a tight seal, continuously replenished by cells from the deeper layers that migrate upwards. The dead cells of the outer, hardened layer are constantly sloughed off and replaced by new cells. This multi-step process involves complex signalling between the deeper layers of the skin and the rest of the body.[2]

In social life, the skin plays a key role in first impressions. It allows a rough estimate of the other person's age. It plays a key role in our attractiveness. We perceive attractiveness through different sensory channels: the eyes see how the skin looks; the nose perceives how it smells; and our hands feel texture, elasticity and the age of the other person's skin.

The barrier function of the skin can be disrupted by an injury or by chronic inflammation, such as atopic dermatitis, psoriasis, ichthyosis or irritant contact dermatitis. When this occurs, the rapid non-specific innate immune response kicks in first (see page 168). If the disruption continues, the slower, pathogen-specific immune response will try to clear and defeat relevant invaders.[1]

Several challenges can affect the skin of young and older people. The details of these are relevant to related drug trials in adults and 'children' so I will describe them next.

Acne vulgaris

Acne, most frequently acne vulgaris, affects the majority of young adults between 12 and 25 years old, but may persist into the 30s and 40s. It occurs regardless of socioeconomic status, race, nationality or sex. Its incidence in late adolescence and early adulthood is rising worldwide; it might have a connection to Western diets, earlier onset of puberty, or some unknown environmental factors. It can just be annoying, but can also lead to scarring, unfavourable pigment changes, depression, anxiety and low self-esteem.

Acne usually begins with the onset of puberty. During puberty, the body increases the production of several hormones, including androgens, testosterone and growth hormone. They cause the skin's follicle glands to grow and produce more oil ('sebum'). At least four interrelated processes are involved: over-production of sebum; abnormal shedding of the hair roots in the outermost skin layer; colonisation of the hair roots by an otherwise harmless bacterium; and inflammation. Sebum over-production results from excessive/unbalanced hormones or an increased sensitivity of the glands to normal hormone levels, or both. There are also genetic components. We know many of the details but do not as yet have a clear picture. Also, today's foods and drinks, particularly sugary drinks, starchy foods, highly processed foods and skimmed milk, appear to affect the severity of acne. Further factors are psychological stress, smoking and other unhealthy habits. The lesions typically occur on the face, chest and/or upper back. They may be non-inflammatory closed papules (lesions) formed by accumulated sebum and/or keratin within the hair follicle; open papules with resulting oxidation of lipids and deposition of dark pigments; or inflammatory lesions resulting from the rupture of follicles plus the activities of bacteria that are normally harmless. Acne is classified as mild, moderate or severe.[3, 4, 5]

Atopic dermatitis

Atopic dermatitis is characterised by itchy, red, swollen and cracked skin. It is the most common inflammatory skin condition in young patients. Its characteristic features are dry skin and severe itching. It is thought to be the result of a complex interaction of genetic and environmental factors that leads to impaired epidermal barrier function and an immune dysregulation.

Atopic dermatitis can also be the initial manifestation of the so-called 'atopic march', leading to further types of allergic disease. Sensitisation through the skin is probably an important initial step.

It mostly begins in early childhood and goes away later in many patients, but not all. It has long been associated with other disorders, such as food allergies, asthma and allergic rhinitis. It has a strong impact on the quality of life. A better understanding of its causes is allowing new therapeutic directions in addition to good skin care and established anti-inflammatory creams and ointments as first-line treatments.[6, 7]

Severe atopic dermatitis significantly interferes with quality of life. Its main features are skin barrier disturbance and immune dysregulation. It is seen in the context of the interplay between genetic predisposition and exposure to harmful environmental factors. Allergen sensitisation is involved when it persists or gets worse.[8, 9, 10]

Psoriasis

Psoriasis is a systemic immune-mediated disease characterised by red, hardened, scaly, itchy and often painful skin plaques. It affects 2-5% of the general population, starting in childhood in about one third of patients. It can manifest as just small, localised patches, but can also affect the entire body. The most frequent form is plaque psoriasis ('psoriasis vulgaris'). It is driven by pro-inflammatory cytokines. It is also associated with other diseases, including psoriatic arthritis, cardiovascular disease and diabetes mellitus.[11, 12]

Ichthyosis

Ichthyoses are a family of genetic skin disorders characterised by dry, thickened, scaly skin. They are a group of skin diseases in which a horny layer of the skin develops, caused by excessive loss of water through the skin. Most ichthyoses are inherited and today can be pin-pointed to specific genetic mutations. The condition typically presents at birth or within the first few years of life. There is no cure, but modern drugs can help to some degree. Despite this, it considerably impairs quality of life. Management depends on disease severity and includes topical agents (creams, gels and ointments) and lifestyle modifications with or without oral retinoid drugs.[13]

Treatments

Today, we no longer see acne, atopic dermatitis, psoriasis, ichthyosis and other challenges just as disorders of the skin. Instead, we have begun to understand the complex interplay between the different organs, cells and functions of the body. We can also increasingly influence underlying imbalances of the immune system and can limit inflammatory processes. Usually, treatment of mild forms of these skin disorders starts with topical therapies, with varying degrees of efficacy and patient satisfaction. Healthcare professionals also advise on lifestyle. Severe cases continue to present therapeutic challenges.[6] These can include secondary infections.

Effective anti-infective treatments emerged during World War II, followed by effective anti-inflammatory treatments. Paediatric warnings on US antibiotic information sheets emerged from 1962 on, reflecting toxicities observed in newborn babies in the 1950s (see page 12).[14, 15, 16, 17] These real dangers were then exaggerated into alleged dangers for all drugs in all 'children' defined by the administrative age limit of 18 years as described in the Introduction to this book.[14, 15, 16, 17, 18, 19, 20]

Today, we have new powerful anti-inflammatory treatments, based on a better understanding of how the body deals with live pathogens and substances the body classifies as harmful. As mentioned in the introduction to this chapter, we have two main immune systems: innate immunity that is general to all invaders, and acquired immunity that is antigen-specific and able to learn and memorise challenges. Key learnings of immunology included the detection of the ABO blood group systems (essential for transplantation, blood transfusion and understanding how the mother's blood group can interfere with the baby in her body); and the detection of antibodies produced by special white blood cells (B cells or plasma cells). We know now how antibodies induce white blood cells to recognise pathogens as potentially harmful, to attack and to destroy them. We are beginning to understand the role of cytokines in cell signalling. They cannot enter cells, but have a key role in the communication between cells and the regulation of the immune systems. They also regulate inflammation. Interleukins are a sub-group of cytokines that regulate inflammatory processes. Increasingly, we understand the role of receptors, receptor antagonists and many more compounds involved in inflammatory processes.

Many diseases discussed in this book are to some degree based on an over-reaction of the immune system; this includes atopic dermatitis and psoriasis. These findings are today also applied in clinical areas beyond dermatology, including allergology, oncology and internal medicine.[21, 22]

This greater understanding of inflammation and the immune system has not changed medical practice by itself, but it has been used by pharmaceutical companies to develop new drugs that increasingly revolutionise bedside care. While the classic drugs with which we are most familiar are mostly created through chemical processes, many modern pharmaceuticals are produced from living organisms or contain components of living organisms – human, animal, plant, fungal, microbial, viral – and are therefore known as 'biologics'. These include monoclonal antibodies – identical, cloned antibodies. They bind to antigens and can be used for diagnostic and therapeutic purposes. Some antibodies block receptors that play a key part in particular disorders. Today, we can produce human antibodies in cells of animal origin. The immune system does not classify them as potentially hostile and tolerates them. Modern drugs and biologics can down-regulate inflammatory processes in a targeted way with many fewer side effects than steroids or chemotherapeutics.

Children's skin

The skin of newborn children is as thick as that of adults, but is younger (of course) and more elastic. All organs mature, including the skin. However, a baby's skin works as a barrier just as well as adult skin. And at birth the baby's skin is not fundamentally different from adult skin.

There are, however, some differences. The baby's immune system has still to mature, and the skin constantly interacts with the immune system. The biggest exception is that the skin of premature newborns is much thinner. When we apply topical medicines to the skin of a preterm newborn, we must be aware that much more of it can be absorbed and enter general circulation.[15, 16, 17, 23]

'Paediatric' studies

Atopic dermatitis, psoriasis, acne and ichthyosis are not specifically 'paediatric' disorders and do not change their mechanism of disease on any given birthday. All the diseases discussed in this chapter occur in both adults and minors, though with different causes. As described, acne is caused by an increase in the body's hormones and a complex interplay with additional factors. Atopic dermatitis is caused by a breakdown of the skin's barrier function and a complex interaction with the immune system. Psoriasis is driven by pro-inflammatory cytokines and an interaction with the immune system. Ichthyosis is predominantly caused by genetic defects. However, all these challenges neither begin nor end on a specific birthday. There is no reason that a drug will work after a given birthday, but not before. As with other conditions described in this book, both the US's

Food and Drug Administration (FDA) and the EU's European Medicines Agency (EMA) demand separate 'paediatric' studies for under 18s, but there is no valid medical rationale for the 18th birthday as an age limit for drug approval. Furthermore, today the process of puberty in our western society begins and ends earlier than formerly.[22]

In some areas of dermatology, the FDA has relented from blindly demanding 'paediatric' studies for new drugs. The topical treatment crisaborole for atopic dermatitis was approved based on studies in patients aged 2 to 79 years.[23] This was a concession to common sense. However, the FDA has not stepped back from its general demand for separate 'paediatric' studies, while the EMA continues with few exceptions to demand separate 'paediatric' studies in dermatology set out in 'paediatric investigation plans' (PIPs) negotiated with the relevant pharmaceutical company.[15, 16, 17]

For the monoclonal antibodies dupilumab (against atopic dermatitis) and brodalumab (against severe plaque psoriasis), the FDA has demanded 'paediatric' studies in patients aged 2 to 17 years. For a large number of monoclonal antibodies that target psoriasis (tildrakizumab, brodalumab, secukinumab, usteki-numab, bimekizumab, ixekizumab, guselkumab, risankizumab and mirikizumab) the EMA has demanded PIPs in patients aged 6 to 17 years old; for adalimumab and briakinumab, in patients aged 4 to 17 years old. EU PIPs for monoclonal antibodies that treat atopic dermatitis demand 'paediatric' studies in patients aged 2 to 17 years of age, some even in younger patients (dupilumab, tralokinumab, nemolizumab). Other EU PIPs demand such studies also for other types of modern biologics that are already known to be effective against atopic dermatitis (baricitinib, updacitinib, abrocitinib). Such studies include open-label studies (where both patients and health providers know what drug is being tested), but also placebo-controlled efficacy studies or a comparison against methotrexate, which definitely has a higher risk of toxicity than adalimumab, the monoclonal antibody for which the PIP has been issued.[24] (This means half the patients in the study will receive a treatment that is known to be more toxic.)

Many industry-sponsored 'paediatric' studies in psoriasis are ongoing in patients aged 6 to 17 years – e.g. ixekizumab,[25] tildrakizumab[26] – or 12 to 16 years (brodalumab).[27] Similarly, many such studies are ongoing in atopic dermatitis, e.g. a placebo-controlled study in tralokinumab in 'children' aged 12 to 17 years.[28]

In the treatment of acne the EMA has relented and asked for clinical studies in 'children' and adults for clindamycin[29] and trifarotene.[30] Here we see another dilemma for the EMA: it may be aware that separate 'paediatric' studies lack medical sense, but there remains a legal obligation to demand 'paediatric' studies. It would have been more reasonable to waive a PIP for these two drugs altogether.

For tazarotene for the treatment of ichthyosis, the EMA PIP demands 'paediatric' studies in patients aged 2 to 17 years.[31] In the meantime, the relevant pharmaceutical company has notified the EMA that the 'paediatric' development of tazarotene for ichthyosis has been discontinued.[32] Tazarotene is an FDA-approved topical for the treatment of psoriasis, acne and sun-damaged skin.[33]

In humans of any age, only those clinical studies that have the potential to improve treatment, diagnostics and understanding of the mechanism of disease are justified, as stated in the Declaration of Helsinki (page 21). Those who profit from the 'paediatric' studies listed above are: paediatric researchers, keeping their jobs and advancing their careers; officers of the FDA and the EMA, again keeping their jobs and advancing their careers; employees in pharmaceutical companies and clinical research organisations who advance their 'paediatric' careers; and pharmaceutical companies that are financially rewarded for 'paediatric' studies by patent extensions.[17]

Conclusion

As we have seen throughout this book, researchers and businesses benefit from unnecessary 'paediatric' studies of efficacy, but patients do not. At best they risk receiving a second-rate treatment when the greater efficacy of another is already known. At worst (in a placebo-controlled study) they may be randomly assigned to no treatment at all.

Parents who are asked to allow their child to participate in such a study should be sceptical. If the drug in question has already been approved for adults, separate studies in 'children' usually make no sense unless they serve to confirm doses that have already been calculated in the treatment of younger patients. If the study in question is only conducted in adolescents, then it is certainly pointless. Parents should then refuse to allow their child to participate. Depending on the age of their child, they can also ask their medical doctor to prescribe the respective medication off-label.

Chapter 14

Juvenile idiopathic arthritis (JIA)

Inflammatory joint diseases

Arthritic disorders (arthritides) affect the joints, tissues around the joints and connective tissues. They mostly cause pain and stiffness of the joint(s), often accompanied by warmth, swelling and a decreased range of motion. Other organs can also be affected. They can begin suddenly or gradually.

The term 'arthritis' stands for more than 100 types of inflammatory disease.[1, 2] Inflammatory joint diseases can be caused by pathogens, such as bacteria, or there are no externally detectable pathogens. In this case, the inflammation is based on the body's immune system attacking the joints and other body tissues. A third option is the wear and tear of the joints with age, which then turns into inflammatory processes.

The most common type of arthritis is osteoarthritis, a degenerative disease. The most common symptoms are joint pain and stiffness. Usually the symptoms progress slowly over years, initially perhaps occurring only after exercise but then becoming constant over time. Osteoarthritis can be caused by injuries, inherited factors and usage. Overweight/obesity is a key risk factor.

In osteoarthritis, the joints alone, and not the other internal organs, are affected.[3] In contrast, rheumatoid arthritis, another relatively common type of arthritis, is a long-term autoimmune disorder that primarily affects the joints but can affect many other organs as well. Its cause is not clear but is believed to involve a combination of genetic and environmental factors. Rheumatoid arthritis begins mostly between the ages of 30 and 50 years, although it can also start earlier or later. Typical signs are warm, swollen and painful joints. Pain and stiffness often worsen after rest. Most commonly, the wrists and hands are involved, often the same joints on both sides of the body. Symptoms also include general fatigue, weight loss and low-grade fever in active disease. Disability is common and significant. Rheumatoid arthritis is a complex disease with strong autoimmune hereditary mechanisms, but non-genetic factors are also involved – smoking, for example, massively increases the risk of developing rheumatoid arthritis.[4, 5] In the following, we will focus on those inflammatory joint diseases that are based on autoimmune processes.

Adult versus 'paediatric' arthritic disorders

At present, medical terminology distinguishes arthritic disorders in adults from those in minors, as if these populations were fundamentally different. However, administrative age limits define societal status but not physical/biological status. Paediatricians can treat patients up to 21 years of age, and older if the patient has special medical needs.[6] This is a reasonable, administrative classification, but the medical mainstream has not managed to distinguish administrative classifications from the division of diseases themselves into 'adult' and allegedly 'paediatric' ones.

Two main schools of thought have emerged in research into the treatment of arthritic conditions in minors over recent decades. To understand how this has come about, we need to look back at past developments.

As infectious diseases ceased to be the childhood killers of the past, due to advances in housing, hygiene, nutrition, clothing, education and anti-infective treatments, a number of rare conditions that had barely been recognised before began to be taken seriously. This was further augmented by advances in diagnostics, medical understanding, surgery and intensive care.[7, 8] Until this time, it had been assumed that most arthritic disorders were a consequence of ageing. Now inflammatory systemic (and other) diseases began to be recognised in young patients also. As inflammatory diseases that affected the joints as well as the rest of body were initially noted only in young patients, researchers and clinicians assumed that these diseases were a specifically paediatric form of rheumatic disease. The US Pediatric Rheumatology Collaborative Study Group (PRCSG) was consequently established in 1973 as a research network linking many academic clinical paediatric rheumatology centres. Its mission was 'to foster, facilitate, and conduct high quality clinical research in the field of paediatric rheumatology'.[9, 10] Eventually, the leadership of the PRCSG was involved in training the leaders of the European Paediatric Rheumatology International Trials Organisation (PRINTO), founded in 1996.[9, 11]

Initially, the terms 'juvenile rheumatoid arthritis' and 'juvenile chronic arthritis' were used. The term 'juvenile idiopathic arthritis' (JIA) was introduced in 1995 by the International League of Associations for Rheumatology (ILAR) in an attempt to provide a globally standardised description of chronic arthritis that begins in childhood.[12] ('Idiopathic' means 'of unknown cause'.)

Early treatment of inflammatory joint diseases

Since its synthesis and first manufacture in 1899, acetylsalicylic acid (aspirin) had been considered by the public and the medical profession as an effective anti-inflammatory and analgesic medication, with few side effects when taken at standard doses.[13]

It was also the most prescribed drug for chronic inflammation in young people.[14] There were no better alternatives. Clinical studies in JIA began when new non-steroidal anti-inflammatory drugs (NSAIDs) had been developed, and when the first group of dedicated investigators started collaborating on a national US basis in the early 1970s.[15, 16] The PRCSG performed the first systematic study to alleviate the symptoms of JIA, comparing tolmetin (an NSAID) with aspirin in young patients.[17] This led to FDA approval of tolmetin for JIA.

Over the next decade the PRCSG published findings from trials of five additional new NSAIDs (fenoprofen, ketoprofen, meclofenamate, pirprofen and proquazone).[16, 17]

Methotrexate was originally developed, and continues to be used, for chemotherapy, either alone or in combination with other agents. It is effective for the treatment of a number of cancers, and is used as a disease-modifying treatment (DMT) for several autoimmune diseases, including rheumatoid arthritis, juvenile dermatomyositis, psoriasis, psoriatic arthritis and lupus erythematosus. It was originally given in high doses, but today is given in low doses and is regarded as a generally safe and well-tolerated drug.

JIA and 'paediatric drug development'

From 1968 on, the mantras discussed in the first part of this book that 'children are therapeutic orphans' and 'children are not little adults' gained influence. The first US Pediatric Law in 1997 offered financial incentives for studies in patients younger than 17 years. Chapter 5 of this book discusses the impact of these on paediatric oncology. Here I want to look at the impact on the diseases that today are summarised under the umbrella term of 'juvenile idiopathic arthritis' (JIA).

This term uses the administrative age limit of 16 years. Whoever develops rheumatic joint inflammation before their

16th birthday is classified as having JIA. The classification further differentiates patients with inflammation in only a few joints ('oligoarticular arthritis'); inflammation in many joints ('polyarticular arthrits'), sub-divided again into those who are rheumatoid-factor negative and rheumatoid-factor positive; arthritis that is systemic from the outset ('systemic-onset arthritis'); inflammation of the sites where tendons or ligaments insert into the bone ('enthesitis-related arthritis'); psoriatic arthritis; and a seventh – 'undifferentiated' JIA – as a catchall for cases that do not fit into any category or that fit into more than one.[4, 12, 16] However, the umbrella term 'JIA' is misleading. These diseases often begin at a young age, but they do not suddenly turn into classic rheumatoid arthritis on the patient's 16th, 17th or 18th birthday.

The two schools of thought

The two schools of thought that have been shaped by the 'children are different' mantra and separate 'paediatric' research are: (1) that arthritic diseases in young people before the age of 16 are completely separate diseases to adult arthritic diseases versus (2) that this distinction is artificial, based on the age at diagnosis.

We have seen in previous chapters in this book how research can be divided into that which genuinely endeavours to break new ground and that which merely aims to fulfil regulatory requirements. The latter has profited significantly from the funds the pharmaceutical industry has had to invest in so-called 'paediatric' studies.[7, 17] JIA is a good example of how financial incentives for 'paediatric' studies have shaped clinical research in an entire sub-discipline into a misleading disease description.

The term 'JIA' gives the impression that we are dealing with 'juvenile' (young) patients, but this is not necessarily the case. The seven diseases that are subsumed under the term 'JIA' usually begin before the age of 16 years, but sufferers do not change when they reach their 16th or a later birthday. Meanwhile, older patients are often misclassified by adult rheumatologists as having adult-type rheumatoid arthritis; this can result in the prescription of the wrong medication.[5, 7]

Equally, patients who have been diagnosed with one of the seven types of 'JIA' before turning 16 are growing older and seeking help after their 18th birthday. This has resulted in the establishment of the second school of thought that has correctly (when one looks at the evidence) concluded that the distinction between adult and children's joint inflammation is artificial and flawed. This second school of thought emphasises that current nomenclature reflects the fact that adult and paediatric rheumatologists historically addressed disease classification separately rather than together: 'We are left therefore not with forms of juvenile arthritis and forms of adult arthritis, but rather with forms of arthritis, period',[5] to quote the director of the Center for Adults with Pediatric Rheumatic Illness (CAPRI) at the Brigham and Women's Hospital in Boston, Massacusetts.[18]

New treatments for auto-inflammatory diseases

While cancer is potentially lethal, arthritic disorders are chronic and affect the sufferer's quality of life over long periods of time. For cancer in young patients, effective drugs – chemotherapeutic agents – were already available for adults, allowing the lives of hundreds of thousands of young cancer patients to be saved from the 1950/60s on (see Chapter 5). Such effective treatments did not exist for arthritic disorders in young patients during the first two thirds of the 20th century. Treatment improved somewhat with NSAIDs and methotrexate, but a true revolution occurred only later, with first the scientific discovery and then the commercial development of modern pharmaceuticals, including substances that are identical to the body's own key signalling proteins.

These include: erythropoetin which stimulates the production of red blood cells; growth hormone that stimulates growth; human insulin and its analogues; monoclonal antibodies; interleukins and interleukin antagonists; interferons; tumour necrosis factor antagonists that interfere with inflammatory and other biological processes; and more.[19] Most of these modern pharmaceuticals are called 'biologics' because they are produced from living organisms or contain components of them (human, animal, plant, fungal, bacterial and viral cells and tissues).[20, 21]

The first monoclonal antibody was approved by the FDA in 1986 to prevent rejection of a transplanted kidney. It was a mouse antibody and had the inherent risk of triggering immune reactions in the human body. Eventually, antibodies were developed with much less potential to trigger allergic reactions, by replacing animal parts of the antibody with human sequences.[22] Clinically, this allowed the treatment of young patients with inflammatory diseases to improve dramatically.[23]

A generation ago, young patients with arthritis faced a lifetime of misery. Their parents were fortunate if they could find a rheumatologist to treat them at all, but even the best available therapies were barely able to effectively treat and prevent a childhood of pain and disability. Furthermore, when the facial joints were involved, this led to external disfigurement. Today, the outlook for young people with JIA has massively improved.[23]

Nevertheless, adult rheumatologists tend to under-dose when they treat young patients, generally out of the concern, often shared by the parents, that these patients might be especially vulnerable to adverse drug effects. (This is because of the ingrained 'children are different' mantra discussed through-out this book.[7, 17, 27]) Correct dosage is of course essential, but disease-modifying anti-rheumatic drugs and even biologics are considered first-line therapeutics in many young patients with JIA today.[23, 24, 25, 26]

In young patients, suppression of inflammation is the only acceptable therapeutic outcome.[23] To achieve this, modern effective drugs are essential. Representatives from the PRCSG and PRINTO (see page 143) claim that treatment has progressed because of the 'paediatric' studies they have performed. Indeed, PRINTO representatives report that the paediatric laws (requiring separate research in minors), the international research networks and the availability of new efficient drugs have improved JIA treatment, *in that order*.[9, 28, 29] In joint publications, representatives of the European Medicines Agency (EMA) and PRINTO have lauded EU paediatric legislation specifically.[30, 31]

However, a 15-year-old patient with an autoimmune-based inflammatory disease is biologically no longer a child, and many of patients in the clinical trials organised by PRCSG/PRINTO have been biologically and physically young but mature humans. As we have seen, several of the diseases classified as 'JIA' are the same in adults and children making a nonsense of testing drug efficacy in different age groups.[5, 32] In these diseases, the demand for separate 'paediatric' studies of drug efficacy is not based on science, but on the dogmatic classification of patients younger than 16 years as 'children', regardless of the biological maturity of their body.

The PRCSG demonstrated its major scientific and therapeutic merits in its early days when its members started out focusing on young patients with inflammatory joint disorders, but the basis of the improved treatment has not been the allegedly 'paediatric' studies, but the industrial production and availability of modern anti-inflammatory drugs. In so far as young patients with an arthritic condition covered by the JIA criteria have the same disease as adults, there is no scientific basis to demand separate 'paediatric' efficacy studies. These studies advance careers, but not the healthcare of young patients. (In very young patients, dose finding is required, not separate proof of efficacy. If we know that a particular drug works in humans, there is no need to separately prove that it works in younger patients. What we need is additional data on the dose. Additional safety information is required for babies.)

How modern pharmaceuticals changed the course of rare joint disease: the example of canakinumab

There are a number of very rare diseases whose root causes have been detected only with the availability of modern interleukin antagonists. One example of these is canakinumab, a monoclonal antibody against interleukin-1-beta (IL-1β). Unlike the two other modern drugs that are effective against IL-1β (anakinra (daily dose) and rilonacept (weekly dose)), canakinumab does not require frequent administration.[33, 34]

Canakinumab was first developed for rheumatoid arthritis, but the clinical response was insufficient. Then the development team looked for diseases characterised by over-production of IL-1β, and found several. They are all rare and have acronyms as names that indicate their complicated causes or disease processes. They include crypoyrin-associated periodic syndrome (CAPS); adult-onset Still's disease; mevalonate kinase deficiency (MKD); TNF-receptor associates periodic syndrome (TRAPS); and familial Mediterranean fever (FMF). They are all connected to over-production of IL-1β, with irregular fever attacks. Canakinumab is highly effective in disorders caused by this over-production,[33] which occurs in both minors and adult patients. In other words, IL-1β is the same before and after the 17th/18th birthday.

Of course, in young patients it is necessary to determine the correct dose of drugs like canakinumab, but there is no valid justification for separate *efficacy* studies before and after the 17th/18th birthday. However, both the FDA and the EMA demand many 'paediatric' studies in patients aged 2 to 17 years to look at the effectiveness of modern effective monoclonal antibodies, small molecules, and other modern anti-inflammatory biologic drugs though these have already been approved in adults.[7, 17]

Conclusion

The diseases that are grouped under the umbrella term 'JIA' can begin at a young age, but they do not stop at the end of adolescence. What is unique about JIA is that the artificial division between 'paediatric' and adult disease definitions has created two completely separate schools, one of which thrives on pointless studies while the other takes care of the real problems of patients who have now grown up. As in many other areas of illness, the recognition that this is a fundamental challenge at the interface of drug development and drug approval and goes beyond just this disease area, is not yet widespread.

Chapter 15

Multiple sclerosis

Multiple sclerosis is a chronic autoimmune, inflammatory disease of the central nervous system (CNS) – that is, the brain and spinal cord. CNS nerve cells consist of the main cell body plus long fibre bundles (axons) that emanate from the main body, branch repeatedly, and innervate (connect) every part of the body. The axons are sheathed in myelin, a fatty coating that protects and insulates them and increases the rate at which electrical impulses can be passed along them. In multiple sclerosis, the body's immune system attacks and destroys the myelin and the axons to varying degrees. This damage disrupts the ability of parts of the nervous system to transmit signals. Symptoms can include double vision, blindness in one eye, muscle weakness, impaired sensation and impaired motor coordination.

The course of multiple sclerosis is unpredictable and different from patient to patient. It begins mostly in adults aged 20 to 45 years but can also start in childhood and in late middle age.[1, 2] It is probably caused by a combination of genetic predisposition and non-genetic triggers that could be viral, metabolic or environmental. Together this results in an autoimmune disorder that leads to recurrent immune attacks on the central nervous system. In most patients, it begins with episodes of reversible neurological deficits, followed by progressive deterioration over the years. So far there is no cure, but today's treatments help to some degree (see below).

Like other paediatric disciplines, paediatric neurology became a clinical specialty in the course of the 20th century. One hundred years ago, paediatrics was in its infancy; neurology and psychiatry were just beginning to separate. Today, neurology, psychiatry and paediatrics are mature disciplines.[3] However, the fact that a young patient is seen by a paediatric neurologist does not make that individual a child; nor does being seen by an adult neurologist make that patient an adult. The age limit of 18 years is used to define 'paediatric' multiple sclerosis, often also called 'paediatric-onset multiple sclerosis' (POMS),[4, 5, 6, 7, 8] but as we have seen elsewhere, the 18th birthday is an administrative and legal marker that does not correspond to any overnight physical change.[9, 10, 11, 12] The human body becomes mature during the process of puberty, which has accelerated during the last 100 years.[13] However, the terms 'paediatric multiple sclerosis' and 'paediatric-onset multiple sclerosis' (POMS) are used broadly in the medical literature as if there were two distinct types of multiple scerosis, one that starts before, and the other after, the 18th birthday.[4, 5, 6, 7, 8] The unthinking use of these terms helps to strengthen the flawed assumption that minors are fundamentally different from adults and have different diseases.

Treatments

No curative therapy for multiple sclerosis exists as yet[1] but there are treatments that can improve the lives of sufferers. These treatments can be divided into disease-modifying therapies that are relatively specific to the envolved structures of the immune system, and symptomatic therapies that can help with pain, depression, spasticity, epileptic seizures and other problems associated with multiple sclerosis.[14] Today, several disease-modifying drugs are available. They shorten the duration of attacks, reduce their frequency and provide symptomatic relief.

Most disease-modifying modern drugs are so-called 'biologics', pharmaceuticals that are produced from living organisms or contain their components, including cells/tissues from humans, animals, plants, fungi, bacteria and viruses. They include substances identical to the body's own signalling messengers, hormones and monoclonal antibodies.[15, 16] Other drugs able to suppress the inflammatory process of multiple sclerosis include glatiramer acetate, a synthesised mixture of peptides, and mitoxantrone, which otherwise is used in the treatment of cancer. Corticosteroids can be given to suppress acute attacks. In the short term, they shut down inflammatory processes, but they have severe systemic side effects if given long-term.

An increasing number of effective drugs against multiple sclerosis are in clinical development. Most are biologics with the potential to deliver a more targeted treatment, with fewer side effects than steroids or chemotherapeutics.

Regulatory control of treatment development

The US's Food and Drug Administration (FDA) and the EU's European Medicines Agency (EMA) approve disease-modifying drugs against multiple sclerosis initially only in adults and require separate 'paediatric' studies of efficacy for approval for use in children, defined as patients younger than 18 years of age. The potentially longest-lasting FDA-required study is a placebo-controlled 'paediatric' study looking at the efficacy of ozanimod designed to run until 2033.[17] The longest EMA-required 'paediatric' studies would be two for ocrelizumab designed to run until 2025; these require 'children' aged 10 to 17 years old; the second one is a comparison of ocrelizumab with interferon β-1a.[18]

Young people of 17 years old are no longer physically children. A drug approved for adults will work for physically mature young people though they are under the age of 18. All FDA/ EMA-required 'paediatric' studies withhold effective treatments completely from those in the placebo group or, in a comparison group, expose those patients to a treatment that is known from adult studies to be sub-standard. Furthermore, they harm all patients and their parents by deceiving them about the need for such studies. These studies are in open breach of the principles of the Declaration of Helsinki (see page 21), which limits clinical studies in humans to those that advance treatment, diagnosis or understanding of the relevant disease. The Declaration does not allow pointless studies to fulfill dogmatic regulatory demands yet these are required by US and EU law.

In the meantime, among clinicians increasing resistance has developed to these FDA and EMA-required separate 'paediatric' studies. Comparably to clinical criticism of separate 'paediatric' studies in epilepsy (see Chapter 8),[9, 10, 11, 12, 19, 20] the International Paediatric Multiple Sclerosis Study Group (IPMSSG) has published a key paper that challenges separate 'paediatric' clinical studies in minors with multiple sclerosis, arguing that the biological processes involved in the condition are the same in older and younger patients. Treatments that have proven efficacious for the care of adults have a biological rationale for use in minors as well. The group has also expressed ethical concerns against clinical trials in young patients that compare effective treatments with placebo.[21] In other words, this group acknowledges that multiple sclerosis is the same disease before and after the 18th birthday.[12] The IPMSSG is a global network of neurologists, scientists, clinicians, multiple sclerosis societies and other organisations that want to optimise healthcare, education and research in paediatric multiple sclerosis and other comparable diseases.[22]

In addition to the three 'paediatric' studies mentioned above, several double-blind placebo-controlled 'paediatric' multiple sclerosis studies are ongoing worldwide for fingolimod, tecfidera, plegridy and other compounds that are already approved in the treatment of patients who are more than 18 years of age. These ongoing 'paediatric' studies recruit patients aged 5 to 17 years,[23] 10 to 17 years,[24, 25, 26, 27] and 10 to 18 years.[28, 29, 30] Most are multi-centre international studies. They require complex logistics, cost a great deal of money, but are medically pointless. They not only waste precious funds and manpower, but they expose young patients to the general risks of study participation and to inferior treatment in a sub-standard comparison group, or no treatment at all in placebo groups.

Today, we already have several drugs that are effective in treating multiple sclerosis. Young patients deserve to be treated as early as possible. Research should be investigating how treatment can be improved over the decades of life that young patients still have ahead of them. In the past, the mainstream doctrine was that treatment should begin with clinical symptoms and visible organ damage. Today, there is a growing belief that treatment should begin with the most effective drugs as early as possible.[6, 7]

Advice for parents

The IPMSSG reports increasing resistance by parents to consent to study participation.[21] Parents' scepticism is based on gut feeling, knowledge, or both, that separate 'paediatric' studies with drugs that we already know to work in humans are questionable. The parents' 'gut feeling' is nearer to the truth than the pseudo-scientific regulatory justification for 'paediatric drug development'.[31] Parents should refuse to consent to let their children participate in such studies. Those who realise that they have already consented to such participation should consider withdrawing and ask the treating physician to change the ongoing treatment to an effective one, be it on-label or off-label. They should also consider sueing the treating study centre, the sponsor of the study, the relevant institutional review board (IRB) and/or the ethics committee (EC) that has approved the specific study, for damages and punitive damages.

Institutional review boards (IRBs) and/or ethics committees (ECs) should urgently review all ongoing 'paediatric' studies in multiple sclerosis. They should suspend any that are ongoing after making sure that all patients who are already enrolled will be switched to effective treatment. They should also from now on refuse authorisation for newly submitted 'paediatric' multiple sclerosis studies.

Chapter 16

COVID-19

The potentially lethal coronavirus infectious disease COVID-19 is, as we cannot but be aware, causing havoc worldwide. Its manifestations range from asymptomatic to fever, cough, fatigue, breathing difficulties, sore throat, loss of smell and taste, pneumonia, multisystem failure and death. Symptoms can begin soon after infection, or with a delay of up to two weeks. In most cases, it causes only mild symptoms. It is mainly transmitted by inhaled droplets and micro-droplets. Immune events, still poorly understood, lead either to the development of a protective immune response or to an exacerbated inflammatory response which can result in acute inflammation, immune dysregulation, a cytokine storm, acute lung injury, acute respiratory distress syndrome (ARDS), multiple-organ system dysfunction, and death. Organs can also be damaged long-term after the initial crisis. A significant sub-group of patients continue to experience effects long after the initial infection, including fatigue, memory loss and muscle weakness. Diabetes, cardiovascular disease and an impaired immune system result in the highest risk of severe disease and death. However, advanced age is the best predictor of a severe course.[1, 2, 3]

Initially, the incidence of COVID-19 in children was underestimated. Today, published research agrees that children become infected as much as adults but have fewer symptoms and develop severe disease forms much more rarely.[4, 5, 6, 7, 8, 9, 10] Nevertheless, the role of children in COVID-19 transmission needs to be considered. It is possible young people might be a reservoir.

Multi-system inflammatory syndrome (MIS)

During the first wave of the pandemic, a 'multi-system inflammatory syndrome' (MIS) in children (MIS-C) was described.[11, 12] MIS has some similarities with Kawasaki disease, an acute febrile (high temperature) illness of unknown cause in children younger than 5 years, with fever, rash and inflammation of multiple tissues.[13] The US Centers for Disease Control and Prevention (CDC) published a warning about 'MIS-C', defining it as occurring in patients younger than 21 years with fever, inflammation, hospital admission, two or more organs involved and COVID-19 infection or exposure.[14] The American Academy of Pediatrics (AAP) issued comparable MIS-C guidance.[15] The CDC warning triggered many medical publications listed on PubMed. PubMed is a free search engine maintained by the US National Library of Medicine at the US National Institutes of Health. PubMed is widely used by the international medical and scientific community and allows a quick and easy first glance at the number of papers a researcher has published and at the number of publications that have been published worldwide on a given topic, such as here, MIS-C.[16, 17]

Unfortunately, the term MIS-C is based on flawed thinking. While Kawasaki disease affects patients younger than 5 years of age,[13] the CDC warning defines MIS-C as occurring in patients up to 20 years old, when they are no longer 'children' either physically or administratively.[14] The first MIS-C publications reported a 'challenge' in children – most authors were paediatricians. Later in 2020, the CDC published a report of MIS also occurring in adults, referring to 'MIS-A'.[18, 19, 20] MIS simply occurs in both children and adults. To distinguish 'MIS-C' and 'MIS-A' is artificial and pointless. Different names for the same disease are often used if that disease occurs both before and after the 18th (or another significant) birthday.

There are several other autoimmune disorders that can be triggered by a viral infection, including macrophage activation syndrome (MAS). The syndrome that has been named MIS might simply be MAS.[19, 21, 22] MIS is definitely not a purely 'paediatric' challenge.

The CDC warning triggered the worldwide use of MIS-C in the title of several hundred PubMed-listed articles, illustrating a fundamental weakness in modern medicine. Physicians are good at caring for patients within the existing framework. If an authority uses a new term, as with MIS-C, it is accepted and uncritically repeated worldwide. Modern medicine has this weakness to multiply and maintain flawed concepts and terms as long as they are used by a respected institution.

Vaccination and treatment of COVID-19

Thus far (at the time of writing) COVID-19 treatment is symptomatic. It tries to prevent a cytokine storm or to interrupt such at an early stage before it triggers overwhelming inflammation and causes severe organ damage or death. For this, steroids, modern anti-inflammatory pharmaceuticals, and antiviral drugs have been used. Furthermore, oxygen is required if the patient's breathing is not sufficient. Invasive mechanical ventilation and intubation are used as a last resort.

In 2020, the FDA approved remdesivir for the treatment of COVID-19 infections in patients down to the age of 12 years with a minimum weight of 40 kg.[23] Also in 2020, the FDA expanded this emergency authorisation for hospitalised children weighing more than 3.5 kg, giving dosing recommendations based on body weight.[24]

However, the key to containing the pandemic is to prevent COVID-19 infection through vaccination. This approach has helped to contain most other viral infectious diseases in the past, although to this day we do not have an effective vaccine against human immunodeficiency virus (HIV). Three COVID-19 vaccines have received FDA approval for emergency use[25] (one of which has been fully approved at the time of writing); four have been approved by the European Medicines Agency (EMA).[26] A broad worldwide vaccination campaign is under way.

The current vaccines against COVID-19 have demonstrated efficacy with a very low risk of adverse events. However, venous thromboses in the brain following vaccination have been reported between days and a few weeks after the vaccination, accompanied by a fall in the number of platelets (thrombocytes). The medical term for a low number of platelets is 'thrombocytopenia'. Some of these thrombotic events have resulted in death. These events occur more in adult women than in men, are very rare, but have unsettled people around the world. Some governments in EU member states temporarily suspended COVID-19 vaccinations, but restarted them again soon afterwards, which of course further increased the general uncertainty. It appears that the thromboses are due to the platelets being attacked by the immune system after the vaccination, which can cause a cascade that leads to a thrombotic event. Although these thrombotic events are very rare, it is essential for emergency clinicians, medical doctors and healthcare professionals in general to be on the alert so that appropriate treatment is initiated fast.[27, 28, 29, 30]

Eventually, children and adolescents will have to be vaccinated as well as adults, not only for their own sake but also to prevent their becoming a reservoir for continuing infections, even if they do not show symptoms. The Pfizer/BioNTech vaccine is now FDA-approved for 12 years and up,[31] the Moderna and the Janssen vaccines from 18 years and up.[32, 33] This does not mean that they are unsafe in patients earlier than their 12th or 18th birthday. The age of the patients who are included in vaccination trials aimed at getting approval is the decision of the companies developing the vaccines. The FDA uses the age of the youngest participant in the particular trial as the lower age limit for a vaccine's approval.

A rational assessment as to how to approach the question of COVID-19 in young people needs to consider two different issues:

(1) is there an age before which 'adult' *treatments* should not be used?

(2) would the *vaccines* be unsafe or ineffective in individuals younger than the current licensing age limits?

Are COVID-19 treatments safe in 'children'?

To tackle the first issue, is there any age limit where symptomatic treatment of young patients with moderate to severe symptoms of a COVID-19 infection would need to be fundamentally different? The answer is no. Antiviral drugs, anti-inflammatory monoclonal antibodies, receptor blockers and other modern pharmaceuticals work the same before and after the 18th birthday. Neither the 18th birthday nor the 12th nor the 10th is an age limit that would influence the body's response to COVID-19 medication. The medical literature uses the term 'child' predominantly in its physiological meaning – that is, relatively young children – or speaks of 'children and adolescents'. For young, pre-adolescent children, we need dosing recommendations but not separate international, randomised studies to prove efficacy that is already known. Meanwhile, dosing recommendations should be based on the principle of 'opportunistic' trials that do not require complex logistics and essentially verify and, if necessary, correct paediatric doses calculated by modelling and simulation.[34, 35]

How to treat newborns and premature newborns with a COVID-19 infection is a special challenge, but thankfully there are few severe COVID-19 infections in this group. In such cases, we have to rely on the training, experience and common sense of the relevant physician.

Will vaccines work in younger age groups?

The second key question is whether there are any logical reasons not to vaccinate young people, or, the other way around, should any age groups be excluded from vaccination? As children are rarely affected by severe symptoms, there is no urgent need to vaccinate them or to change the priority of other established early vaccinations, such as for tetanus, diphtheria and pertussis (whooping cough) (DPT). The question as to the age from which vaccination for COVID-19 should be done is not ultra-urgent compared with the havoc the pandemic is causing in adults and the elderly.

Nevertheless, the FDA and the EMA have produced a joint statement on submitting 'paediatric development plans' for the prevention and treatment of COVID-19.[36] COVID-19 is not a rare or orphan disease, so US paediatric legislation demands a paediatric development plan, as does the EU. The FDA document for 'paediatric drug development' is called an 'initial pediatric study plan' (iPSP); the EMA document meanwhile is the well-known 'paediatric investigation plan' (PIP) encountered many times already in this book. Although the procedures for FDA and EMA approval are different, both agencies insist on separate 'paediatric' studies and separate 'paediatric' approval. As we have seen, this requirement is not based on science, but on regulatory dogmatism. It also reflects the general weakness in modern medicine that has allowed an administrative division of humankind into two populations to develop.

The EMA discusses on its website how it wants to accelerate development, support and evaluation procedures for COVID-19 treatments and vaccines.[37] For PIPs, it offers a reduction in the usually lengthy submission procedures, but the question of whether PIPs make any sense at all in the COVID-19 pandemic is not even addressed. Their need is taken for granted.

In its remdesivir PIP, the EMA demands three 'paediatric' clinical studies in 'children' with confirmed COVID-19 infection: one open-label, single-arm study on pharmacokinetics (how a drug is processed by the body), safety, tolerability and efficacy in hospitalised 'children' from birth to 17 years of age; one study in 'paediatric subjects' from birth to 17 years; and one efficacy and safety extrapolation study from adult subjects to 'paediatric patients' from birth to 17 years.[38] ('Open-label' studies are those where participants – both health professionals and patients – know what drug is being tested; 'single-arm' studies are those where there is no comparison group.)

There are now EMA PIPs for the first two COVID-19 vaccines, EMEA-002861-PIP02-20 for the Pfizer-BioNTech vaccine[39] and EMEA-002893- PIP01-20 for the Moderna vaccine.[40] The former requires three double-blind studies: one in adolescents and adults; one dose-finding safety and immunogenicity study in 5 to 17 year-olds; one dose-finding, safety and immunogenicity in children from birth to 4 years for prevention of COVID-19; and one open-label prevention study in immuno-compromised children (see below) from birth to 17 years.[39] The PIP for the Moderna vaccine demands one double-blind study in adolescents aged 12 to 17 years, one dose-finding and safety study in children from birth to 11 years and one open-label study in immuno-compromised 'children and adolescents' from birth to 17 years.[40] We see in this PIP the same claims and demands as in all others, and the same flaws: adolescents are physically no longer 'paediatric subjects', 'paediatric patients' or 'children'. The EMA feels empowered to demand 'paediatric' studies in young humans who are already physically mature, but are legally still minors. For adolescents, these studies are pointless; for younger patients who have not yet reached the end of puberty, they are over-the-top. Dose finding can be done in an opportunistic framework (see page 93),[34, 35] without exposing young patients to separate study participation. It is worth noting that for remdesivir, adult and 'paediatric' administration is the same: it is given intravenously.[23]

Meanwhile we need to think particularly about immuno-compromised patients. These are those whose immune systems are under-functioning due to chemotherapy for cancer, or immune suppression following organ transplantation to prevent the rejection of the transplanted organ. The best thing that can be done for these patients is to protect them against COVID-19 by vaccinating them as early as possible, instead of exposing them to a pointless additional PIP-required study.

The PIP-dictated 'paediatric' studies for COVID-19 vaccines lack medical logic. Parents should not allow their children to be included in such studies. In those relatively rare cases where a child has an acute COVID-19 infection, parents in Europe should insist that their child is treated with remdesivir or other FDA-approved medications based on the FDA dosing recommendations, instead of allowing them to be abused as guinea pigs in EMA-PIP-dictated questionable studies.

Conclusion

Even in the face of a worldwide pandemic that is known to have killed, at the time of writing, almost 4 million people,[41] the regulatory authorities maintain a dogmatic approach. At least the FDA has approved remdesivir for use in children with a minimum weight of 3.5 kg, the average weight of a healthy newborn. The EMA, however, is even more caught up in its dogmatic requirements, and demands the developing company commit to additional 'paediatric' studies as a condition for approving remdesivir in adults.[38]

The flawed division of humankind into 'adults' and 'children' results in a worldwide waste of energy, mirrored in the many PubMed-listed publications about MIS-C, probably resulting in over-diagnosis of MIS in minors and under-diagnosis in adults. MIS is a medical, not just 'paediatric', challenge. These barriers reflect the damage caused by this flawed concept in today's medicine which results in wrong diagnoses and treatments, flawed disease definitions and pointless or even harmful clinical studies.

Chapter 17

Infectious diseases, antibiotics and other antimicrobials

In an infection the human body is invaded by living organisms. These multiply, and the body reacts to them and the toxins they sometimes produce. Infections can be local or they can affect the entire body, for which we use the label 'systemic'. The main agents with which our bodies and their immune systems have to fight are bacteria, viruses, fungi and parasites. Antimicrobial drugs support the body's own immune system to fight against the infectious agents and tip the balance in our favour.

Antibiotics either prevent bacteria from growing, or kill them directly. There are many different types of antibiotic. They intervene in the functioning and growth processes of bacteria, such as preventing the growth and renewal of bacterial cell walls, cell membranes or internal bacteria-specific metabolic processes. Antifungals kill or prevent the growth of fungi. Antiparasitics destroy parasites or inhibit their growth. Antiviral drugs, however, do not destroy viruses; instead, they inhibit their development.

Antibiotics are relatively new in human history. Their impact on medical care did not begin when their therapeutic potential was detected and scientifically described for the first time, but only when their industrial production made them available worldwide. More than a decade passed between the discovery of penicillin and its finally becoming broadly available. Without World War II, it would probably have taken even longer. Let us hope that wars will not be necessary in the future for further ground-breaking discoveries. Though penicillin was discovered in the UK, its industrial production was made possible only by the support of US governmental structures and the project management capabilities of US pharmaceutical companies at that time.[1]

The development of immunity

All humans are born with an immune system that consists of two parts – the innate and the adaptive. In the womb, the baby's immune system must remain tolerant of the antigens, cells and tissues of the mother. From birth on, the baby is exposed to environmental antigens and agents, and must rapidly adapt. The innate immune system provides an early first-line of defence. Its cells develop and mature during development in the womb. The adaptive immune system matures and acquires memory, but goes into decline in old age.

The function of all components of innate immunity is weak in newborns compared with in later life. The adaptive immune system is also weaker in newborns compared with older children and adults. Before we had good nutrition, hygiene and comprehensive vaccination, there was high mortality in infants and young children due to infection.

The immune system gradually matures during the first months and years. A partial early protection against many infectious diseases through which the mother has gone many years earlier is provided by antibodies transferred from the mother to the child through the placenta before birth, and in the mother's milk after birth. While this initial protection fades away, children begin to be better armed with their maturing innate and adaptive immune systems. Without today's vaccinations, many children would still be victims of many attacking agents.[2]

The use of antibiotics in infants and young children is higher than in any other age group under 65 years. Penicillins are among the most commonly dispensed antibiotics in primary care.[3] The way in which a very young body absorbs, distributes, metabolises and excretes antibiotics is different from adults.[4] There were early tragic experiences with antibiotic use in the very young in the 1950s: as a result, reports of toxicities in preterm newborns were published to warn other medical doctors.[5] However, while children's metabolism is different at birth, it matures fast. Children do not remain newborns until they officially come of age.[6, 7] Antimicrobial drugs have the same mechanism of action in patients of any age.

During the second half of the last century, the special paediatric sub-discipline of neonatology, the care of preterm and low-weight infants, developed successfully, not least because of the availability of antimicrobial medicines.[8] These have been invaluable when used with appropriate caution.

The call for more 'paediatric' drug trials

Several papers have been published complaining about how few studies there have been of antibiotic efficacy in the 'paediatric population', about the relatively low number of clinical studies in 'children', and lauding US and the EU paediatric laws that push for more paediatric studies.[9, 10] There is a catch in this. These complaints would be justified if child mortality had remained high over the last century, but the contrary has occurred worldwide.[5] Without any doubt, further improvements are always possible, but already we can see that there is a flaw in the complaints.[9, 10] They are *artificial*. They use a *regulatory* logic and pretend that a low number of paediatric studies means that children are not treated satisfactorily. As we have seen throughout this book, some researchers use artificial and twisted arguments to blur the interface between medicine and legal age limits to demand more 'paediatric' studies of drug efficacy. These calls appeal to our instincts to protect children. Most importantly, they suggest that more 'paediatric' studies will improve children's healthcare, but the contrary is the case. Young patients do not need 'more' studies per se. They need studies that will really advance healthcare. As we have seen in many clinical areas, many of the allegedly 'paediatric' clinical studies not only lack medical sense but often even cause harm. This is no different with antimicrobial drugs – antibiotics, antifungals and antivirals.

Nevertheless, requirements for separate 'paediatric' studies in antimicrobials follow the same rigid scheme as for all other drugs. They pretend that in 'children' (defined by legal age limits) everything is different, and that for 'paediatric' drug approval separate 'paediatric' efficacy studies are therefore needed. These studies define 'children' not by their degree of physical maturity, but by the administrative age limit of 'younger than 18 years'. In adolescents these studies lack any medical logic; the bodies of these young people are already mature. The following are some stark examples of the consequences of this approach.

The antibiotic moxifloxacin

Moxifloxacin is an antibiotic that is FDA-approved in adults (18 years-of-age or older) for the treatment of intra-abdominal infections.[11] For approval in young patients, the FDA has demanded 'paediatric' data although patients who are 17, 16, 15, or even 12 years old in many cases no longer have the body of a child. Meanwhile, the paediatric investigation plan (PIP) agreed between the pharmaceutical company developing moxifloxacin and the European Medicines Agency (EMA) requires four 'paediatric' studies for complicated intra-abdominal infection – that is, a bacterial infection of the abdominal cavity.[12] Bacteria do not ask for the legal status or age of a patient; they infect, and if they can, they kill. When they take hold, the patient needs the best treatment available, immediately, yet the fourth of the studies required by the PIP involves a prospective, randomised, active-controlled, multinational, multi-centre, clinical trial in 'paediatric patients' with complicated intra-abdominal infection (a relatively rare condition so patients will be slow to recruit), aged from 3 months to 17 years.

Two 'paediatric' studies of moxifloxacin's efficacy have already been completed, one in 'children' aged 3 months to 14 years,[13] the other in 'children' aged 3 months to 17 years.[14] All the studies in the moxifloxacin PIP have lacked medical sense from the outset given we already know this antibiotic works. For the medical care of young patients with a complicated intra-abdominal infection we do not need separate 'paediatric' studies to prove efficacy. We merely need to determine the right dose.

I am pleased to say that, at the time of writing, the study in the moxifloxacin PIP has not yet been listed on www.clinicaltrials. gov – this means it has not yet started. Let us hope that with the publication of this book parents will refuse their children's participation, and that institutional review boards/ethics committees will refuse to allow the start of this study, and many others that are like it.

Antivirals, antifungals and monoclonal antibodies

In the same way, dubious studies are required by the EMA for many other antibiotics, antivirals, antiparasitics and antifungals.[16] Some are completely over-the-top. Baloxavir marboxil is an antiviral agent that is FDA-approved for patients suffering from influenza who are 12 years of age or older.[17] The baloxavir PIP requires 13 (thirteen!) 'paediatric' studies in various 'paediatric' age groups from birth to 17 years, some of which must be placebo-controlled.[18] This means that a proportion of the young people in such a study would be denied active treatment for flu.

Voriconazole is an FDA-approved antifungal drug. The FDA prescribing information lists one study in 22 patients aged 12 to 18 years.[19] The voriconazole EMA PIP requires six 'paediatric' studies. The sixth of these asks for 'extrapolation' of efficacy from adults to patients aged 2 to 17 years.[20] Why should voriconazole not work before the 18th birthday and why would fungi not invade a younger person?

Ibalizumab is an FDA-approved monoclonal antibody used in heavily treatment-experienced adults with multi-drug resistant HIV-1 infection whose current anti-retroviral regimen is failing.[21] The ibalizumab PIP requires two studies in 'children' aged 6 to 17 years with human immunodeficiency virus (HIV) infection to extrapolate efficacy from adults. Why should ibalizumab not work an hour, day, week or month before the 18th birthday? The HIV virus does not ask for a young patient's ID before it infects them.[22]

Conclusion

The artificial division of patients needing treatment for infections into an 'adult' and a 'paediatric' population, based on the 18th birthday, is flawed with potentially harmful consequences for patients and their families. EMA-required 'paediatric' studies involve recruiting patients who may already have an adult body – this will tell us nothing about efficacy in very young children, or about dosage.

In younger patients, additional information on the dosing is necessary, but not in over-the-top international multi-centre studies that serve the careers of researchers rather than the health of young patients. Dose finding can be done in small studies with young patients who need the respective antimicrobial medication anyway.

Parents who are asked for participation in a study should ask why the study is being performed. If it is required only for regulatory purposes, parents should refuse. If the study involves dose finding, parents should first ask if the respective drug is already approved in adults. Furthermore, if it is a large international, multi-centre study, the probability is high that it is unnecessary and parents should ask more searching questions. If they get the impression that there is something fishy, they should refuse participation.

Chapter 18

Inflammatory bowel disease (IBD)

Our current understanding of IBD

Inflammatory bowel disease (IBD) is an umbrella term for several types of serious inflammatory disease in the gastrointestinal tract. The main forms are Crohn's disease, which affects the entire gastrointestinal tract from mouth to anus, and ulcerative colitis, which mainly affects the large intestine (colon) and rectum; there are also forms that are difficult to classify, called 'unclassifiable IBD', 'indeterminate colitis' and 'IBD-U'.[1, 2, 3, 4]

Today, this classification has been relaxed to a certain extent. Earlier classification was focused on what could be observed by the treating physician and on the patient's description of their symptoms; more recently we have become increasingly aware of the role of the immune system in IBD, which is no longer seen as involving only local inflammation,[5] though the main symptoms are diarrhoea, abdominal pain and, in ulcerative colitis, rectal bleeding. Between one in 300 (Crohn's disease) and one in 200 (ulcerative colitis) people in Europe suffer from IBD.[2] Manifestations beyond the gut can affect the joints, eyes, skin and virtually any other organ. These extra-intestinal manifestations can also arise before the bowel disease starts.[2] Extra-intestinal manifestations are so common that some authors make the case for IBD no longer being regarded as a disease of the gastrointestinal tract, but as a systemic (body-wide) disorder.[5]

Most humans live in harmony with the 10 trillion bacteria and fungi in their gut; this is remarkable when we consider that only one layer of intestinal epithelial cells separates these organisms from our own immune cells that circulate in the intestinal 'mucosa' (lining). Somehow, in patients with IBD this co-existence is disturbed. A dysregulated immune response to environmental triggers plays a major part. These environmental triggers are related to modern western food, but we do not yet know in detail exactly which elements are to blame. We know about this connection from observing people who immigrate to our cultures from cultures in which IBD is very rare (see below). These environmental triggers reside inside the body after they have been ingested with food; in addition, smoking can contribute to an increased susceptibility to IBD.

The patient's genes also have an important role, but they are not decisive on their own. If one identical twin has IBD, the probability that the other will also develop the condition is around 50%. The incidence of IBD has increased during the last few decades, faster than could be explained by a change in our genes. IBD also used to be less common in developing countries, but as these have become more developed and their diets more 'westernised', the incidence has risen too. The children of people who have immigrated from developing countries to westernised countries develop IBD with a frequency that is comparable to that of the adopted country. It is clear that environmental factors associated with a western lifestyle contribute to a predisposition to IBD.[6]

Traditionally, IBD has been seen as predominantly an adult disease, but at present not only is its incidence increasing worldwide, but it is increasingly affecting minors, in whom the classic symptoms of bloody diarrhoea and abdominal pain are accompanied by insufficient growth, late pubertal development and psychosocial problems.[7] Proposed mechanisms leading to development of the disease include increased antibiotic use, decreasing exposure to parasites and other infections, and nutrition, including ready-meals, all of which contribute to alterations in the microbial colonisation of the gut.[8]

IBD jeopardises young people's physical, psychosocial and occupational development.[3] In the past, when an immunologist was called to see a young child with IBD, the condition was mostly due to immunodeficiency. Today it is more difficult to distinguish children with an inborn error of immunity from those who are otherwise relatively healthy but are now affected by IBD. Children with early-onset IBD – that is, onset of disease during the first years of life – suffer from a high burden of the condition.[8]

Treatments

Treatment of IBD traditionally included corticosteroids and other anti-inflammatory pharmaceuticals,[9] with surgery often as the treatment of last resort.[10] A big step forward was the introduction of modern anti-inflammatory pharmaceuticals that are no longer produced chemically, but with the help of human, animal, plant and other cells and tissues – so-called 'biologics' – including monoclonal antibodies. Biologics against tumour necrosis factor (TNF), a messenger substance that plays a major part in inflammatory processes, has revolutionised treatment. Anti-TNF biologics are administered by infusion (infliximab) or subcutaneous injection (adalimumab, certolizumab pegol and golimumab).

As long as treatment options were limited, the primary goal was to reduce the symptoms. Now, with biologics targeting TNF, the mucosa can heal, growth improve and IBD's natural history be modified. Treatment aims at eliminating symptoms and restoring quality of life and normal growth.

Early monoclonal antibodies were completely or partially of non-human animal origin and had the risk of triggering immune defence reactions. Modern monoclonal antibodies are 'humanised' – that is, they are made partially or completely identical to the natural antibodies present in the human body and will therefore not trigger any unwanted immune reactions. Vedolizumab is such a humanised monoclonal antibody; it helps IBD symptoms by inhibiting the migration of white blood cells into the intestine. It is the most recently approved treatment for Crohn's disease and ulcerative colitis in adults and is starting to be used in older children whose IBD does not respond to more established anti-TNF agents.[6, 10]

Regulatory challenges

We see the same hurdles for IBD treatment in minors as for all other diseases. The regulatory authorities differentiate between treatment for adults and for 'children', defined as being younger than 18 years, as if the 18th birthday changes the body.

In the case of anti-inflammatory biologics, these are initially approved in adults only. Treatment of minors is either done off-label (without the backing of official approval), or massively delayed by separate 'paediatric' studies. As IBD in minors remains relatively rare, the numbers are not available for quick research even if parents wanted their children to participate.

In 'children' younger than 18 years, infliximab and adalimumab are currently the only biologics with FDA or EMA approval for IBD treatment. Infliximab was FDA-approved for adults in 1998. In 2006 it was FDA-approved for Crohn's disease in children and adolescents. In 2012, adalimumab was approved for 'paediatric' Crohn's disease, but is still being investigated for 'paediatric' ulcerative colitis.

Certolizumab pegol is another monoclonal antibody that is used off-label in 'paediatric' patients in some countries. It is effective in reducing symptoms of moderate to severely active Crohn's disease in adults who do not respond well to conventional therapy. Golimumab, another anti-TNF monoclonal antibody, is comparable with infliximab, but is fully 'humanised' (less risk of an immune reaction) and given subcutaneously instead of by intravenous infusion, which is a much more invasive procedure. (Intravenous administration of a drug has to be done by a doctor or nurse and involves puncturing a vein to establish access. This often goes wrong, hurts, causes bruising and has to be repeated. Subcutaneous administration, though requiring an injection, is less likely to go wrong and usually works the first time.) Despite its advantages, golimumab is approved for moderate to severe ulcerative colitis in over-18 IBD patients only.[6, 7]

Discussion of IBD treatment in 'children' in the clinical world has not so far concluded that the regulatory framework is a problem. Allegedly, off-label use of new treatments in 'children' would prevent the development of an adequate 'paediatric' treatment strategy.[11] However, the regulatory definition of 'children' is, as ever, flawed. To investigate safety issues, regulatory studies are not optimal. Clinicians who demand more studies in 'children' do not distinguish between useful studies with the potential to advance treatment and pointless studies that can harm patients and parents. When clinicians lament that there are not enough 'data' on 'paediatric' treatment,[9] there is too little focus on what is really needed and useful.

For adalimumab, the EMA requires a double-blind, randomised, multi-centre placebo-controlled study of efficacy, safety and pharmacokinetics (drug processing) in 'children' aged 4 to 17 years with moderate to severe ulcerative colitis.[12] As we have seen in earlier chapters, placebo-controlled studies make sense as long as we do not know if a medication works at all, such as in pivotal studies leading to either approval or rejection of a new drug, but the repetition of proof-of-efficacy in minors is both unnecessary and inhumane. To expose minors to placebo is to deliberately withhold treatment that is known to be effective.

For vedolizumab, the EMA requires a double-blind, placebo-controlled multi-centre study in 'paediatric' patients with moderate to severe Crohn's disease.[13] If this study ever begins, it will withhold effective treatment from all those participants who receive placebo. These studies only *pretend* to care for young patients. Parents should not consent.

For tofacitinib, the EMA requires a two-step study of ulcerative colitis in 'children' aged 2 to 17 years. Step one involves determining the pharmacokinetics (how the body processes the drug) in 20 'children' aged 12 to 17 years before enrolment of younger patients.[14] This study too is pointless – the drug's pharmacokinetics are already known and there is nothing to suggest these will differ in adolescents just because they are younger than 18. Parents should not consent. If an adolescent needs tofacitinib, it should be given off-label. Dosage differences are of course important, but an FDA paper has shown that in 95% of the drugs investigated in 'children' the doses recommended for adolescents and adults are identical.[15]

Conclusion

The current situation puts parents whose child suffers from IBD in a difficult position. I have explained which studies are completely pointless and which parents should therefore categorically refuse to give their consent to. Support for this position is, however, not currently widespread. There are now associations of patients who suffer from IBD, but so far these have not grasped the dangerous and harmful artificial differentiation between adults and 'children' that lies behind much 'paediatric' research and the withholding of effective treatments from under 18s.

Individual parents can try to have their child treated 'off-label' with the best drug available for adults. Unfortunately, the reimbursing or funding institution/health insurer may then refuse to pay for this treatment. If parents can afford this treatment nevertheless, this is good for the young patient. If parents are members of a patient association, they can put collective pressure on the reimbursing institutions, politicians and the press to address the challenges I have described. However, it is looking like it will be a while before individual criticism turns into general public demand for change. On the bright side, at least this book is available to highlight the problems and show parents how to understand the blurring between law, medicine and drug approval.

Chapter 19

Rare and ultra-rare diseases

After World War II, the development of effective drugs and medical technologies exploded.[1] Major healthcare challenges, including hypertension, gastric ulcer, diabetes, depression and epilepsy did not go away, but became manageable. Later innovations included keyhole surgery.[2]

In the 1980s, several new movements began. One was the demand for separate drug development in 'children' as described throughout this book. Another called for drug development for rare diseases.

The term 'rare diseases' has various meanings. *Clinically,* it means that a disease affects fewer than a certain number or percentage of the total population. The US National Organization for Rare Disorders (NORD) aims to provide support for individuals with rare diseases by advocating and funding research, education and networking among service providers. It grew out of an informal coalition of support groups and families in the 1970s and 80s. The initial coalition was led by a mother whose son had Tourette syndrome, which begins in childhood or adolescence and is characterised by multiple tics, including blinking, coughing, sniffing and facial movements; these involuntary movements are typically preceded by an unwanted urge in the affected muscles, can sometimes be suppressed temporarily and characteristically change in location, strength and frequency. Such tics often go unnoticed by casual observers but are difficult for sufferers to live with. Tourette syndrome was estimated by the National Institutes of Health (NIH) to affect 100,000 people in the US – that is, roughly only one in 30,000. The development of an experimental drug was halted by the manufacturer on the assumption it would not be profitable due to the low number of patients. The US Orphan Drug Act (ODA) was then passed in 1983, after which the informal coalition founded NORD, which continued to grow with the help of federal grants and donations.[3, 4]

Since the enactment of the US ODA, the term 'orphan disease' has acquired a *formal regulatory* meaning. Drugs, vaccines and diagnostic methods can qualify for orphan status if they target a disease affecting fewer than 200,000 US citizens. Orphan status can result in tax reductions, patent extensions and other incentives; it has facilitated the development of many new drugs. Other countries have also introduced orphan disease laws, including Japan and the EU. Each country defines orphan diseases slightly differently.

In the decades since the ODA was passed, the landscape of drug development has changed dramatically. Today, these 'orphan' diseases have come to command a market worth around 90 billion US dollars annually that serves at least 25 million Americans afflicted with around 7000 recognised rare diseases. Taken together, 'rare diseases' are not that rare,[5] and the interest in developing drugs for them has increased over the last decades because there are already many effective drugs for common diseases that are no longer protected by a patent – so-called 'generics'. Their production is generally inexpensive and they are available at relatively low prices.

The same is now true for 'biologic' drugs (see pages 136 and 147). Generic versions of these are are known as 'biosimilars'.[6] Their working principle is the same as for the original products, but they are offered by the generic competition at a lower price.

Overall, the abundance of generics and biosimilars has resulted in many fewer market opportunities for those common diseases for which many effective drugs have been developed in recent decades. In the case of rare diseases, however, the situation is completely different. Sometimes there are drugs that can alleviate symptoms; sometimes there is little or nothing. The medical need is much greater, and with it comes the chance to achieve a good price for an effective new pharmaceutical.

Orphan status has advanced drug development for many diseases internationally. In the US, the FDA has no authority to demand additional 'paediatric' studies in diseases with orphan status, with the (recent) exception of anticancer drugs; for these the FDA has had the authority to demand 'paediatric' studies in minors aged from birth to 11 years since 2018 (see Chapter 5). However, in the EU things have been different from the very beginning. The European Medicines Agency (EMA) requires a 'paediatric investigation plan' (PIP) for every single new drug, unless it targets a disease explicitly listed as not occurring in 'children' – that is, before the 18th birthday. Most EMA-required 'paediatric' studies lack a sound medical basis, as we have seen, and many cause harm by exposing young patients to ineffective placebo or sub-standard treatments. Unfortunately, 'paediatric' studies in rare diseases are no better.

As ever, the EMA pretends that in 'children' every medical condition is fundamentally different. Today, it classifies the following diseases as 'paediatric': liver cancer, kidney cancer, atherosclerosis of the heart and peripheral arteries, dementia, Parkinson's disease, Huntington's chorea and amyotrophic lateral sclerosis (ALS, Lou Gehrig disease).[7] All these diseases typically occur in older age, but occasionally affect people before their 18th birthday.

Today we also distinguish between rare and 'ultra-rare' diseases. The most common and pragmatic definition of a rare disease is one that affects no more than 50 out of 100,000 people and of an ultra-rare disease as one that affects fewer than one in 100,000 people.[8] Currently there is no separate legislation for ultra-rare diseases.

US 'paediatric' legislation was introduced predominantly as a result of pressure from the worlds of academia and the regulatory authorities. Orphan and 'paediatric' laws sometimes have contradictory consequences: paediatric laws prevent modern, effective drugs being available for minors as soon as possible and the rarer the condition in under 18s, the longer will be the delay.[9, 10, 11]

Examples of rare and ultra-rare diseases

Rare and ultra-rare diseases can have a multitude of different causes. Some we know, others not. Furthermore, knowing the cause(s) does not mean we can predict their course or can treat the root problem.

Sturge-Weber syndrome

Sturge-Weber syndrome (SWS) is a congenital disorder that affects one in 20,000 to 50,000 newborns, characterised by a facial port-wine stain, glaucoma, epileptic seizures, partial paralysis of one side of the body, often mental disability, as well as many other symptoms. Its course is unpredictable, which makes it very difficult to handle.[12] It results from a spontaneous mutation that occurs in the sixth week of pregnancy.[13] If the mutation affects the entire body, it is lethal. However, if it affects only a part of the body, the person lives; as it affects only some cells, it is what is called a 'mosaic' disease.[14] Today, we even know the genetic mutation in the affected cells,[15] but this does not allow us to treat the cause. We can only treat the symptoms, including laser treatment for the port-wine mark; anticonvulsants for the epileptic seizures; medical and/or surgical treatment for the eye(s), and more.[12, 13, 16] SWS is thus an example of an ultra-rare disease for which no effective drugs will be developed in the foreseeable future.

Periodic fever syndromes

Another example of a group of ultra-rare conditions are the periodic fever syndromes, a set of disorders characterised by recurrent episodes of systemic and/or organ-specific inflammation. Unlike autoimmune disorders in which the disease is caused by abnormalities in the *adaptive* immune system (see page 168-9), which attacks the person's own body or specific structures in their body (these include multiple sclerosis and juvenile idiopathic arthritis), patients with periodic fever syndromes do not have antibodies that attack their own tissues, or antigen-specific white blood cells that have turned hostile. Instead, these are 'auto-inflammatory' diseases with underlying errors in the *innate* immune system (see page 168-9). They include cryopyrin-associated periodic syndrome (CAPS); tumour necrosis factor (TNF) receptor-associated periodic syndrome (TRAPS) and familial Mediterranean fever (FMF).[17] Within CAPS, sub-diseases are familial cold auto-inflammatory syndrome (FCAS), Muckle–Wells syndrome (MWS) and 'neonatal-onset multisystem inflammatory disease' (NOMID), also called 'chronic infantile neurologic cutaneous and articular syndrome' (CINCA).[18] Apologies for the many acronyms. Many were first clinically observed by specialists who were helping patients with diseases that were relatively less rare, such as familial Mediterranean fever (FMF).[19] Step by step, underlying mechanisms were discovered, based on genetic mutations, metabolic errors or other pathways. Treatment was initially anti-inflammatory with steroids (with known side effects), or colchicine for treating FMF, but colchicine does not work well in all FMF patients.[19] A next step was the development of the biologic interleukin-1-beta (IL-1β) antagonists, including anakinra, rilonacept and canakinumab: IL-1β has a key role in many different auto-inflammatory processes involving the innate immune system. Canakinumab is a human monoclonal antibody against human IL-1β.[20] It has a long half-life, meaning it stays in the body a long time and does not require frequent administration.[21] It was initially developed for rheumatoid arthritis, failed in clinical development, and was then directed towards diseases characterised by an overproduction of IL-β.[13] Today, it is FDA- and EMA-approved for the treatment of many syndromes and diseases.[20, 21, 22, 23]

Cystic fibrosis

A third example of a rare disorder (30,000 in the US) is the genetic disorder cystic fibrosis (CF). This occurs when both genes for the transport protein 'cystic fibrosis transmembrane conductance regulator' (CFTR) are defective. The body is unable to produce mucus of normal viscosity. Without treatment in the past, this resulted in impaired digestion, growth retardation, chronic bacterial lung infections, inflammation and early death.[24, 25] A hundred years ago, babies born with CF did not reach their first birthday. Among rare diseases, CF is relatively common. Treatment improved gradually. Finally, parents of CF children established the Cystic Fibrosis Foundation, which set up CF treatment centres and invested with 'venture philanthropy' in for-profit pharmaceutical companies.[26, 27, 28] Ivacaftor, FDA-approved in 2012, supports the defective CFTR in mutations that affect roughly 5% of CF patients. Treament options were then expanded with CFTR correctors as the next development. The triple combination of ivacaftor, tezakaftor and lumakaftor (Trikafta®), FDA-approved in 2019, helps about 90% of CF patients. Today, patients born with CF can expect to live as long as healthy people provided they get appropriate treatment. (See

Chapter 20 for more detail on this condition and the barriers to appropriate treatment despite very powerful patient/parent advocacy.)

Regulatory problems with treatment development for 'children'

The development of treatments for rare diseases is a mixture of luck, chance, parents' determination, historical circumstances, and more. Without parents' commitment, advanced treatment for cystic fibrosis would not exist. Without IL-1β antagonists, treatment of familial Mediterranean fever (FMF) and other periodic fever syndromes would be less advanced. Maybe future generations will see advanced treatment for Sturge-Weber syndrome.

The artificial differentiation between 'adult' and 'paediatric' based on the 18th (or 16th or 17th) birthday leads to absurdities here too. A patient who reports having their first attacks of fever before their 16th birthday and is found to have an overproduction of IL-1β will be classified as having the seventh category of juvenile idiopathic arthritis (JIA) – that is, undifferentiated JIA, the catch-all for cases that do not fit into any other JIA category (see Chapter 14). However, first diagnosis *after* their 16th birthday will leave them 'only' with CAPS, TRAPS or FMF as potential diagnoses, though IL-1β over-production is the same before and after the 16th or 18th birthday. There is no valid justification for separate 'paediatric' studies of canakinumab efficacy, yet the EMA requires these.

For the combination of lumacaftor + ivacaftor, the EMA PIP requires 10 'paediatric' studies that would go on until 2024.[29] For the combination of elexacaftor + tezacaftor + ivacaftor it requires 11 'paediatric' studies that would run until 2029.[30,31] These studies have no prospect of contributing to better treatment for cystic fibrosis. They are once again dictated by a regulatory authority that regards young patients more as objects of administration than as human beings.

Safety and dosage in under 18s

There are, of course, safety concerns with young patients. To address these, 'registry studies' (known as 'registries') are sufficient. In clinical studies, drugs are given to study participants as part of a research protocol, and the results are usually used for regulatory purposes. In contrast, registry studies are observational. The respective drug is prescribed with caution to patients by their treating physician on the basis of clinical need and patients are carefully monitored. Also in registry studies the clinical data are collected. The critical difference is that in registries the intervention occurs because the clinical decision was made that the chosen intervention was the appropriate treatment. Therefore, registries are usually performed only with pharmaceuticals that are already approved.

For dose finding in younger patients, small studies in an 'opportunistic framework' are generally sufficient. An opportunistic framework means that patients below a certain age limit are treated with a given new drug that is already approved in adults. The doses for minors are calculated in advance according to certain pharmaceutical models and are confirmed by taking additional blood samples. For confirming the dose of a drug that has already shown efficacy in adult humans, international multi-centre studies are not necessary. Instead, small studies in a few centres are sufficient.[32, 33, 34]

It should also be mentioned that the recruitment of underage patients in rare and ultra-rare diseases is very difficult for the many regulatory studies that are required, primarily by the EMA. There are simply not enough patients to fulfil these demands. Meanwhile, these studies cost a lot of money (see Chapter 3) and time and tie up resources that are then not available for other purposes.

Conclusion

We cannot possibly list all the rare diseases needing treatments in this book – only some key examples. Every day one or several new, rare and ultra-rare diseases are described, recognised or re-named after a new common mechanism of disease has been identified.

In the short term, parents of children with a rare condition should refuse to let their children participate in 'paediatric' studies that will not add anything useful to our ability to treat that disease. When parents and their child are approached for study participation, they should carefully inquire whether the drug is already approved for adults, who is funding the study and why. If the reason is simply that otherwise EU approval of the drug concerned will be refused, parents should decline to consent. Chapter 4 gives a more detailed guide to what to look out for.

Chapter 20

Cystic fibrosis: an example of a rare disease

Cystic fibrosis (CF) is a rare disease (as described in Chapter 19 – more than 30,000 patients in the US) that is due to a defective transport protein ('cystic fibrosis transmembrane conductance regulator' (CFTR)). In a normal body, this transport protein is present in all cells of the body that produce mucus. When the CFTR transport protein does not work properly, the body's internal secretions are too thick and sticky (viscous).

CF is a genetic disorder: the patients' blueprint for the CFTR transport protein is defective. Our genes come 50/50 from our father and mother. Individuals with only one working CFTR gene copy, from either their father or the mother, are clinically healthy, but they are 'carriers' of one defective gene copy. Roughly one in 25 people are carriers of a defective gene copy. If both father and mother are carriers, there is a high chance that the child will have CF.

Not all people with defective CFTR genes have full-scale CF disease. Some develop symptoms late or have 'only' lung problems or liver problems, or are infertile. In such individuals, the diagnosis of CF is often made later in adolescence or adulthood. Today, most developed countries screen all newborns for CF.[1]

Until a century ago, most babies with CF died before their first birthday. Stepwise, symptomatic treatments were developed, including enzyme supplementation to improve digestion, then antibiotics to suppress airway inflammation, then drugs that helped to increase the viscosity of lung secretions.

In 1955, a group of parents whose children had CF established the Cystic Fibrosis Foundation (CFF).[2, 3] In 1962, the predicted survival of CF patients was 10 years. It rose to 16 years in 1970 and to 18 years in 1980.

Until the 1960s, most disease-related non-profit organisations and charities had done their fundraising and investments to support academic medical research. In contrast, the CFF developed the concept of 'venture philanthropy' by investing money in for-profit companies with the aim of developing better and more effective drugs. In 2000, the CFF invested US$40 million in a company that later became Vertex, to find and develop drugs with the potential to help improve CFTR function. As described above, CFTR is produced by the body of CF patients, but is defective. The idea was to develop compounds that would somehow improve its activity. At the time, such compounds did not exist. The investment was a calculated risk.

When the first CFTR corrector, ivacaftor, was FDA-approved in 2012, the CFF sold its royalty rights for several billion US$. With this, it had sufficient funds to become a truly major player in CF research. It funded more research programmes with leading biopharmaceutical companies worldwide. Comparable approaches have in the meantime also been undertaken by other rare-disease non-profit organisations and charities, and the US National Institutes of Health (NIH).[4, 5, 6]

The idea of helping the CFTR transport protein to work properly emerged when the CFTR gene was identified in 1989. We know today there are more than 2000 different mutations that result in a defective CFTR transport protein. Compounds beyond ivacaftor that help to improve CFTR function include tezakaftor, lumacaftor and elexacaftor, and are currently at several stages of development.[7]

The first CFTR modulator, ivacaftor, could improve CFTR activity in patients with a specific mutation (G551D), which affects roughly 5% of all CF patients. It was approved by the FDA and the EMA in 2012 in CF patients from 6 years of age on. It was the first drug able to treat the cause of CF rather than just relieving symptoms. Today, it is approved for several more mutations that lead to CF.[7, 8]

There is no scientifically justifiable reason to approve CF drugs separately in adults and 'children'. There is no 'paediatric' CFTR. As explained, CF used to be mainly a childhood disease because children with CF rarely survived into adulthood. Nevertheless, the FDA has insisted on separate double-blind placebo-controlled studies in young patients. In adults, the EMA followed FDA approvals, 'only' lagging behind. For young patients, it has issued 'paediatric investigation plans' (PIPs) that have added nothing new to the scientific and regulatory work already done by the FDA. However, submitting, negotiating and modifying PIPs is a huge and useless additional burden for new CF treatments, without adding any clinical value.

Until a CF treatment has been licensed in young patients, it can be given off-label but this has to be done privately. The new CF medications are expensive, so few parents can afford to have their child treated this way.

The FDA offered a paediatric written request for ivacaftor – that is, six months' patent extension for funding/performing 'paediatric' studies. From the beginning, it had been approved in patients aged 6 years and above, making it 'on-label' for this group but 'off-label' for younger patients.[9]

The EMA's PIPs for the many compounds meanwhile developed to treat CF have included separate 'paediatric' placebo-controlled efficacy-and-safety studies in adolescents and younger children. These studies will not improve the treatment of young patients with CF. They are completely superfluous in adolescents, and massively exaggerated in younger patients, where dose finding is required, not separate repeated proof of efficacy. Clinical studies should investigate new clinical questions, not formally confirm that the respective new drug also works before the 18th, 12th, or 6th birthday.

Thanks to modern drugs, CF is becoming a chronic disease with which a normal life is possible, provided you take your medication regularly. This is a true medical revolution, comparable to the beginning of the industrial production of antibiotics during World War II,[11] the early successes of paediatric oncology, the development of effective antidepressants, and the development of tisagenlecleucel for relapsed or refractory acute lymphoblastic leukaemia (ALL).[12, 13]

The EMA's requirement for submitting and negotiating at least 17 PIPs with altogether 52 PIP modifications that require 110 'paediatric' clinical studies is an enormous additional burden for the companies developing new CF treatments, yet these studies will not improve the clinical treatment of CF in young patients. Furthermore, these studies will have to run until 2029 to fulfil their brief. This means they will compete with studies for the next generation of CF drugs that will be developed over the coming years.[14] If your child had CF, which type of study would you prefer them to take part in?

The CFF has changed the course of a formerly lethal disease and continues to further improve the prospects for anyone with this condition.[3, 4, 5] Effective treatment is now available for roughly 90% of patients. Research will hopefully find ways to improve the chances of the remaining 10%.[15]

Advances such as in the treatment of CF and the prevention of organ damage from birth onwards, or even before, cannot be facilitated by methods that represent a flawed Stone-Age logic. Surgery and other forms of treatment of the baby in the mother's womb are now routine, including for kidney anomalies and other complex challenges.[16, 17] CF is an excellent paradigm to reflect how drug development for rare diseases and its regulatory handling could and should be improved. Instead of demanding hundreds of pointless studies in young patients that do nothing but repeat what we already know, waste resources and block patients from studies that could make a real difference, the regulatory authorities should ask only for studies with the potential to advance treatment. The true challenge here is that the medical community has not yet fully recognised what is happening nor stood up to it. What will it take to change the situation? Once researchers who have participated in pointless PIP-required 'pediatric' studies are no longer accepted for more senior positions, and as soon as institutional review boards and ethics committees reject such studies and suspend those that are ongoing, then the spectre of this pointless and wasteful research will quickly disappear.

Science and commercial drug development are both necessary to handle complicated genetic disorders such as CF, but the learning is the same as in the fight against the COVID-19 pandemic: both challenges require high-tech solutions, be they in the development of effective vaccinations against COVID-19 or in the development of CFTR modulators to improve the fate of patients with CF. Both require an increasing understanding of the genetic foundations of diseases and of the ways in which cells, bacteria and viruses replicate and can be prevented from infecting the body. The moralistic outrage over the profits that the pharmaceutical industry makes is not a good basis for developing better drugs. On the contrary, this outrage creates false incentives that lead to pseudo-scientifically justified senseless studies that promote 'paediatric' careers in various institutions, but do not help young patients. Where the focus is on forcing pharmaceutical companies to fund research – any research – on an ideological basis rather than on what the research is actually aiming to achieve, there are increased chances of wasting resources. In 'paediatric' research, there are still many people with an anti-profit-making attitude who believe that studies the pharmaceutical industry is forced to commit to will automatically help young patients. Unfortunately the opposite is true. For the moment, there is no movement in the pharmaceutical industry generally to oppose these pointless 'paediatric' studies nor specifically to do so in the companies that develop life-saving drugs for CF. So far, they appear not to be able to see any other way than to commit to the dictates of the FDA and EMA and 'paediatric' legislation.

Conclusion

How to restore public trust in science, medicine, clinical research and the regulatory authorities

Drug development today is a complex process. The many examples set out in this book show that within this complexity there is a simple fundamental flaw in the ongoing medical research in young patients. A gap has opened up between the daily clinical care of young patients and academic paediatric research as a result of this flaw, arising from a dogmatically exaggerated use of 'evidence-based medicine'.[1]

Behind the pointless repetition of proof-of-efficacy studies in young patients of drugs we already know to work, lurk massive conflicts of interest. Contrary to the widespread belief that fraud in research is primarily individual, committed by evil lone perpetrators (such lone perpetrators do exist),[2] the worldwide systematic abuse of young patients is the institutionalised result of the flawed mantras that 'children are therapeutic orphans' and 'children are not small adults'.

All mantras have a core of truth. The younger children are, the less we should treat them as small adults, but children grow and mature. The older they grow, the more mature they become, with their bodies generally maturing faster than their minds. Behind the deliberate blurring of the meanings of the word 'child', as illustrated throughout this book, lie structural conflicts-of-interest that have developed and become entrenched over the past half century.

Economically, pharmaceutical companies have worked very profitably and have acquired great wealth. Relevant parts of the academic world wish to get a share of this wealth. The greed of the academic world for the funds available from pharmaceutical companies as a result of the US 'paediatric' legislation led to a system that has resulted in many pointless and potentially harmful studies involving young patients. This approach was taken up, amplified and expanded by the European Union (EU) through the EU 'Paediatric' Regulation to such a degree that the representatives of the European Medicines Agency (EMA) have admitted there are not enough patients worldwide for all the studies they have demanded.[3, 4] However, the EMA continues to issue PIP (paediatric investigation plan) after PIP. There are at the time of writing more than 2000 PIP decisions listed on the EMA website.[5] The studies demanded in these PIPs are sold to the public and especially to patients and their parents as advancing child healthcare. Which heartless person would dare to stand up against the development of 'better medicines for children'?[6]

The flawed claim that 'children' of any age between birth and 17 years needed separate clinical studies of drug efficacy and the assertion that pharmaceutical companies would not conduct these studies on their own initiative led to the demand for state control of drug development in young people. The flawed concept of 'paediatric drug development' for the administratively defined 'paediatric population' was born. '"Children" should have the same right as adults to modern, well investigated medicines' became the watchwords of those seeking to benefit from 'better medicines for children'.[6, 7, 8, 9, 10, 11]

This is the first instance in modern times of an entire scientific discipline becoming the standard bearer for a flawed concept, but we have only to follow the flow of research funding to get an inkling of what is going on. 'Paediatric' careers have emerged in regulatory authorities,[9, 10] in commercial clinical research organisations (CROs),[11] in the pharmaceutical industry,[12] and in academic research.[13, 14]

All the 'paediatric' studies discussed in this book have been, or are being, performed worldwide in institutions that in theory are committed to the highest standards of medical ethics, as for example defined by the Declaration of Helsinki.[15] They are published in medical and scientific journals that follow the recommendations of the International Committee of Medical Journal Editors (ICMJE),[16] are supported by experts in paediatric clinical pharmacology and by representatives of the US and EU regulatory authorities;[8, 9, 10, 11, 17, 18, 19, 20] they are demanded by US and EU laws,[4] and are accepted by institutional review boards (IRBs) and ethics committees (ECs). All appear to share a blind spot when it comes to providing the best medicines for our children and drop their critical thinking as soon as they see the key vocabulary of evidence-based medicine – 'double-blind', 'randomised', 'placebo-controlled', etc.

What should be done about paediatric research?

To improve things, we must get politicians and institutions out of their comfort zone and confront them with the reality. 'Paediatric' drug development is probably only a tiny part of the many things that go wrong, but at least it is something that has now been identified and therefore can be addressed.

How can we interrupt and stop the conveyor belt of pointless studies in young people that at best lack medical sense, but often cause harm? This is a fundamentally new challenge at the beginning 21st century. Myths, misunderstandings, and flawed concepts have silently invaded science, regulatory authorities and guidelines for drug development. The only people who hesitate and have become increasingly more sceptical are the parents of children who are asked to participate in these studies.[4, 7, 21, 22] Some clinicians too laudably now challenge placebo-controlled studies of drug efficacy in young patients when the efficacy of that drug in humans has already been proved.[23, 24, 25] Often, parents' refusal has been based on their gut feeling that a study is not in their child's best interests. If nothing else, parents can refuse their consent and ask the searching questions that need to be asked (see Chapter 4 and below).

The role of academic publishing

The key to overcoming the flawed concept of 'paediatric drug development' can only be for it to be so utterly condemned by the public worldwide that decent medical and scientific journals will no longer accept articles describing the separate investigation of drugs in physically mature young people administratively defined as 'children'.

The traditional system of peer review has failed in the case of 'paediatric drug development'. A certain section of academia has subscribed to a false concept that has secured research funding from industry in the short and medium term for 'paediatric' studies. This has so far been accepted and condoned by the other parts of the academic sciences involved in healthcare. All control mechanisms that had been in place since the 1960s/1970s have failed. This undermines the foundations of public trust in science and in researchers being honest and not telling lies or half-truths.[9, 11, 17, 18, 19]

The current system of scientific publishing is in a state of profound change. In the traditional system, researchers submitted their manuscript to a journal. After a first check to establish that the manuscript had some merit, it went out for 'peer review'.

Peer review is the critique by scientists of the same rank as the author(s) (their 'peers'). They reviewed the manuscript and recommended acceptance, rejection or acceptance on condition that some corrections be made. The submission of manuscripts was free of charge for most journals. Scientific journals were financed by the subscription fees paid by universities and institutional libraries. The published articles were usually read in the university library, in the hospital library or at home, by those who could afford the journal.

The number of scientific journals has increased steadily over the past few decades, and the number of publications has skyrocketed. Meanwhile, the traditional system is being transformed by several movements, including the 'open access' movement that requires all publicly-funded research to be freely available. The internet makes it possible to read journals outside of the library. Respected and new journals from traditional large publishers can now be read through an academic gateway that allows authorised readers to log in with a password. However, many new journals have developed a different funding system: the author pays a publication fee once the manuscript has been accepted. Then, the article is made available on an 'open access' basis on the internet. Anyone can read it. This has led to many 'predatory' journals that publish almost everything they are offered without critical control. Collecting publication fees has become a global business. The flood of journals is growing and it is difficult to keep up with this growth.[26, 27, 28]

Today, all clinical studies that are to be submitted for publication, or to be used to obtain regulatory approval, must be listed in an internet-based register. To prevent fraud and the misreporting of clinical studies, publicly accessible trial registries have been established worldwide, and the International Committee of Medical Journal Editors (ICMJE) has established guidelines that demand entry of clinical studies into a trial register if they are to be considered for later publication.[16] Such registers had been desired by scientists for a long time. The first one was established under pressure from human immunodeficiency virus (HIV) activists. As is well known now, HIV infection results in acquired immunodeficiency syndrome (AIDS) and leads to death, if left untreated, but this took a long time to be accepted. A US law of 1988 led to the development of a database of AIDS studies.[36] Other interest groups then demanded something comparable for all diseases. The US FDA Modernization Act (FDAMA) of 1997, of which the first US paediatric law (see Part I) was a part, resulted in the establishment of www.clinicaltrials.gov in 2000. Today it is the largest clinical trials database in the world with almost 400,000 registered studies.

The ICMJE is in a position to influence what is published. By looking at this database journal editors can easily see the premise for any study that has resulted in a research paper they are offered. To bring needless 'paediatric' studies to an end the ICMJE should review and revise its recommendations, taking into consideration the validity of studies in young patients.[4, 16]

The time has come for leading medical and scientific journals to stop accepting reports of pointless studies and to start accepting critical articles that question 'paediatric' studies.

Likewise, as soon as researchers and/or clinicians are denied new positions because they listed participation in pointless and harmful clinical trials in underage patients on their résumé, interest in the publication of such questionable studies will decline. Even predatory journals will no longer receive payments for the publication of such studies.

The role of regulatory authorities

The days when regulatory authorities did not have conflicts of interest have gone. Furthermore, many publications by FDA and EMA employees reflect the desire of these institutions to document their scientific competence.

Conclusion

Western societies are dynamic and we are experienced in dealing with contradictions and conflicts of interest, provided, of course, that we are aware of these. 'Paediatric drug development' is not the first case of abuse of patients in questionable or pointless research studies in modern history, and it will not be the last, but it has new characteristics that should put us on the alert. The regulatory authorities have become part of the political theatre in our increasingly controlled world. They have a high reputation. The higher the reputation of an institution, the more public funding they receive.

This is particularly problematic where medicine and its professional representative bodies have committed to a flawed concept. (These representative bodies include the American Academy of Pediatrics (AAP), the American Medical Association (AMA), the European Society of Developmental Perinatal and Paediatric Pharmacology (ESDPPP), the European national professional representative bodies of the paediatric profession, and many disease-specific representative bodies, including the PRCSG[29] and PRINTO.[30]) The flawed concept has ensured a steady flow of funds to their members but is based on a questionable foundation. Paediatrics is a discipline that people trust. Trust takes a long time to build but can be destroyed quickly. As soon as the public takes note of the problems presented in this book, trust in the research projects described and in the regulatory authorities that demand these questionable studies will be fundamentally jeopardised. A revision of 'paediatric' legislation will be needed to restore trust but this could take many years.

In the meantime, institutional review boards and ethics committees should undergo urgent training in drug development and regulatory drug approval to distinguish between reasonable and unnecessary or harmful 'paediatric' studies. They should suspend ongoing questionable 'paediatric' studies and reject newly submitted ones.

The World Medical Association (WMA) needs to adapt the Declaration of Helsinki to the challenges of clinical research in young patients.[15]

The role of charities

Charitable giving is the act of giving money, goods or time as a humanitarian act to those in need.[31] Today, charities are organisations whose primary objective is activities serving the public interest, common good or philanthropy.[32] 'Charity' aims to relieve specific social problems, whereas 'philanthropy' attempts to address the roots of such problems. Thus, philanthropy and charity are different, but there is also some overlap.[33]

Altogether, it is not easy to get an overview of the world of charities. The US-based Charity Navigator (www. charitynavigator.org) claims to be the world's largest and most trusted non-profit evaluator.[34] It classifies charities into the following categories (with the numbers of charities within each category given in brackets): animals (531); arts, culture, humanities (1343); community development (926); education (714); environment (457); health (927); human services (2614); human and civil rights (398); international (642); religion (476); and research & public policy (225). In total, in the US giving to charitable organisations amounted to US$410.02 billion in 2017.[35] Furthermore, giving has increased continuously since 1977 with the exception of three years. Health charities received US$38.27 billion – that is, 9% of all donations.[36] As there is an overlap with other charity categories that are also related to health issues, the total amount of health-related donations is certainly even higher. There are charities for specific diseases such as cystic fibrosis, multiple sclerosis, cancer and leukaemia to name but a very few. There are many more charities worldwide beyond those in the US, all of which are trying to improve the lot of humanity (and animals, and the environment).

The flawed concept of 'paediatric drug development' and its pseudoscientific justifications are of extreme interest to all health-related charities. They will have to learn that when distinguishing between adults and children it is necessary to differentiate between the administrative and the bodily characteristics of human beings. Research projects that address issues such as 'paediatric' cancer research, 'paediatric' multiple sclerosis, and the myriad other alleged childhood diseases require critical review in the light of the issues described in this book. Where the objectives of research projects turn out to be pseudoscientific and misleading, financial support should be discontinued as should encouragment of patients and parents to participate.

The role of parents

Parents today are the last line of defence against questionable studies involving their loved ones. Hopefully, this book will motivate even more parents to question their child's participation in regulatory studies and to refuse where the study is unnecessary and/or potentially harmful. Paediatric researchers have been reporting for many years an increasing resistance from parents to 'paediatric' studies.[3] This resistance is mostly based on parents' gut feeling as well as an awareness that many effective drugs are already available. However, gut feeling is not enough to differentiate senseless/harmful studies from studies with the potential to save lives.

So far, parents have been active in patient advocacy groups, but are mostly unaware of the true dangers of 'paediatric' clinical studies. It is hoped this book will provide a useful guide to determining the value of any study that might be relevant to their child.

The role of individual clinicians

Most clinicians want to help patients and to improve treatment. Some want to contribute to the growing body of medical knowledge that is codified in medical publications, textbooks, and more. Most clinicians are part of an institution and participate in the maintenance of that institution.

Individual clinician can prescribe medication for adolescents that is approved only for 'adults' and not for 'children' – what is known as 'off-label' prescribing. Depending on the institution, this can generate trouble with the administration, with clinician's superiors, and/or with both. If the clinician participates in an institutional review board (IRB) or ethics committee (EC), they can share their concerns regarding flawed 'paediatric' studies with their IRB/EC colleagues, propose to reject submitted questionable new studies and to suspend ongoing questionable studies.

If the clinician sits on the organising committee of a scientific conference and is asked for input as to which issues should be discussed at the next upcoming conference, they can propose to address 'paediatric drug development' within the specific clinical discipline, or as a general issue.

If the clinician is interested in publishing, they can approach the author of this book.

As with anyone working in an institution, the individual clinician should be aware that discussing the challenges outlined may violate taboos, especially if the chief physician is heavily involved in 'paediatric drug development'. Even in our free western society, opening your mouth too much can be a risk, but any individual clinician can refer to this book and make colleagues aware of it. In the end, 'paediatric drug development' will fall with the fact that more and more professional medical representatives will distance themselves from this concept, but it may take a while until then.

The role of lawyers

The problems highlighted in this book are also of interest to lawyers. The first US 'paediatric' legislation was triggered by warnings from US drug manufacturers that wanted to avoid damage lawsuits in the litigious US legal landscape. If anything, litigiousness has increased since then. It is only a question of time before the first damage lawsuits will be brought against companies that have organised clinical studies that have harmed young patients, such as the two terminated trials in 'paediatric' melanoma (see Chapter 5). These young patients received treatment below the current standard-of-care. Parents cannot sue the regulatory authorities, but they can sue everybody else, including paediatric research centres, institutional review boards, ethics committees, clinical investigators and clinical research organisations. There will never be criminal proceedings against those who are responsible for harmful studies. The FDA and EMA follow the letter of the law. The law, however, also forbids harming patients and parents. With open contradictions in the legal framework, judges will eventually have to decide who pays for damages. The first US verdict awarding a few billion US$ in punitive damages will suffice to wake up the pharmaceutical industry. Then, things will move fast.

Change will take time

As this challenge is new, the traditional structures that usually allow for public discussion are not available. The ending of the thalidomide disaster in 1961, the publication by Beecher in 1966 that unveiled many unethical studies in the US,[37] and the termination of the Tuskegee study in 1972[38, 39, 40, 41] occurred once major newspapers reported them. Thalidomide was on the market for three years. In the Tuskegee study, organised by the US Public Health Service, illiterate African American men with syphilis were observed, but not given antibiotics when these had become broadly available after World War II. The social worker Peter Buxtun tried for seven years internally to have the Tuskegee study terminated, before he understood that internal channels would never work and went public.[37] Complex societies have a certain inertia. Questions and critical observations that jeopardise our accepted ideas are not necessarily popular immediately. It is usually just a few who resist the general pressure to conform. It takes time for accepted dogma to change, I hope for the better in the case of developing treatments for children.

The role of the individual reader

This book describes a complex challenge at the interface of medicine and law, of drug development and drug approval. But it also describes a challenge to which thousands of mothers and fathers have reacted with correct gut feelings by rejecting the participation of their child in a questionable or even harmful 'paediatric' study. Most abuses in medical research have in the end not been terminated because of critical scientific publications, but as a result of public outrage when the abuse was exposed. Anyone who works in healthcare can talk to colleagues about this.

This book describes the involvement of a relevant portion of medical research and science in what is, collectively, the most extensive abuse of humans in medical research. The best that any individual can do is talk about it with their partner, parents, friends, co-workers and others, and bring up this book on social media. Anyone who knows a journalist who might be interested in reporting on this should contact them. The author's contact details are open to everyone on the internet.

End note

This book discusses a challenge that has not yet reached mainstream scientific discussion or patient and parent advocacy groups. Advocacy groups have achieved remarkable successes, such as the development of effective drugs for cystic fibrosis (see Chapter 20), but the abuses highlighted in this book are currently so far from what we would imagine the regulatory authorities and researchers in children's medicine would allow and even encourage that there has been no systematic discussion as yet – that the regulatory agencies and paediatric researchers would ask for pointless and harmful studies to be funded on which to base their careers is beyond current comprehension.

For this reason, there are no groups or networks to which I can currently direct my readers. Patient advocacy groups still trust the regulatory authorities. There is academic criticism of 'paediatric' studies, including in epilepsy, pain treatment, multiple sclerosis and juvenile idiopathic arthritis (JIA), but these critical voices have so far remained within the bounds of their respective clinical sub-specialty and have not yet reached the world of critical parents. There might be critical parents in many advocacy groups, but until now their voice has not found any systematic representation. *Blind Trust* aims to join the dots, so to speak, between these individual voices.

Defending ourselves against the abuse of our children in 'paediatric' pseudo-research will be one of the great challenges of the 21st century. Interested parents are welcome to contact me, the author (https://klausrose.net/contact). As soon as international travel is possible again after COVID-19, I will again welcome invitations to lectures and discussions.

References

Chapter 1: Introduction

1. Food and Drug Administration (FDA) 2018. Pediatric Product Development. www.fda.gov/drugs/development-resources/pediatric-product-development
2. European Medicines Agency (EMA). Paediatric Medicines: Overview. www.ema.europa.eu/en/human-regulatory/overview/paediatric-medicines-overview
3. Rose K, Neubauer D, Grant-Kels JM. Rational Use of Medicine in Children – The Conflict of Interests Story. A Review. *Rambam Maimonides Med J* 2019; 10(3): e0018. doi:10.5041/RMMJ.10371. www.rmmj.org.il/userimages/928/2/PublishFiles/953Article.pdf
4. Rose K. *Considering the Patient in Pediatric Drug Development. How good intentions turned into harm.* Elsevier, London, 2021. www.elsevier.com/books/considering-the-patient-in-pediatric-drug-development/rose/978-0-12-823888-2 and www.sciencedirect.com/book/9780128238882/considering-the-patient-in-pediatric-drug-development
5. Medicines and Healthcare products Regulatory Agency (MHRA) December 31, 2020. Legal requirements for children's medicines. An overview of the legal requirements for children's medicines that Marketing Authorisation Holders (MAHs) need to abide by. www.gov.uk/government/publications/legal-requirements-for-childrens-medicines

6. Kearns GL, Abdel-Rahman SM, Alander SW, Blowey DL, Leeder JS, Kauffman RE. Developmental pharmacology – drug disposition, action, and therapy in infants and children. *N Engl J Med* 2003; 349(12): 1157-1167 https://pdfs.semanticscholar.org/55f8/1745303e9aaec7f4cb85f0b5921eec14a9c0.pdf
7. Wikipedia: Iron lung. https://en.wikipedia.org/wiki/Iron_lung
8. Rodriguez McRobbie L. The man in the iron lung. *The Guardian* 26 May 2020. www.theguardian.com/society/2020/may/26/last-iron-lung-paul-alexander-polio-coronavirus
9. Adamson PC. Improving the outcome for children with cancer: Development of targeted new agents. *CA Cancer J Cli* 2015; 65(3): 212-220. www.ncbi.nlm.nih.gov/pmc/articles/PMC4629487/
10. CDC. Leading causes of death www.cdc.gov/injury/images/lc-charts/leading_causes_of_death_by_age_group_2017_1100w850h.jpg

Chapter 2: The business of paediatric research

1. Ballentine C. Sulfanilamide Disaster. *FDA Consumer Magazine* June 1981. www.fda.gov/files/about%20fda/published/The-Sulfanilamide-Disaster.pdf
2. Rägo L, Santo B: Drug Regulation: History, Present and Future (chapter 6). In: van Boxtel CJ, Santo B, Edwards IR (editors). *Drug Benefits and Risks: International Textbook of Clinical Pharmacology*, revised 2nd edition. IOS Press & Uppsala Monitoring Centre, Uppsala, Sweden 2008: pp. 65-77. www.who.int/medicines/technical_briefing/tbs/Drug_Regulation_History_Present_Future.pdf
3. Vargesson N. Thalidomide-induced teratogenesis: History and mechanisms. *Birth Defects Res C Embryo Today* 2015; 105(2): 140–156. www.ncbi.nlm.nih.gov/pmc/articles/PMC4737249/
4. Wikipedia. Thalidomide. https://en.wikipedia.org/wiki/Thalidomide
5. Lachmann PJ. The penumbra of thalidomide, the litigation culture and the licensing of pharmaceuticals. *QJM* 2012; 105(12): 1179-1189. www.ncbi.nlm.nih.gov/pmc/articles/PMC3516063/pdf/hcs148.pdf

References

6. Wikipedia: US Food and Drug Administration (FDA) https://en.wikipedia.org/wiki/Food_and_Drug_Administration

7. Wikipedia: European Medicines Agency (EMA) https://en.wikipedia.org/wiki/European_Medicines_Agency

8. Wikipedia: Medicines and Healthcare products Regulatory Agency. https://en.wikipedia.org/wiki/Medicines_and_Healthcare_products_Regulatory_Agency

9. Rose K, Neubauer D, Grant-Kels JM. Rational Use of Medicine in Children – The Conflict of Interests Story. A Review. *Rambam Maimonides Med J* 2019; 10(3): e0018. Review. doi:10.5041/RMMJ.10371. www.rmmj.org.il/userimages/928/2/PublishFiles/953Article.pdf

10. Rose K. The Challenges of Pediatric Drug Development. *Curr Ther Res Clin Exp* 2019; 90: 128-134. doi.org/10.1016/j.curtheres.2019.01.007

11. Rose K. *Considering the Patient in Pediatric Drug Development. How good intentions turned into harm.* Elsevier, London: 2020. www.elsevier.com/books/considering-the-patient-in-pediatric-drug-development/rose/978-0-12-823888-2 and www.sciencedirect.com/book/9780128238882/considering-the-patient-in-pediatric-drug-development

12. Shirkey H. Therapeutic Orphans. *J Pediatr* 1968; 72 (1): 119-120. https://pdfs.semanticscholar.org/f1cb/acdbac19fa56236b919fb7799eaacaa10c77.pdf

13. Plate V. The Impact of Off-Label, Compassionate and Unlicensed Use on Health Care Laws in preselected Countries. https://bonndoc.ulb.uni-bonn.de/xmlui/bitstream/handle/20.500.11811/4152/1936.pdf?sequence=1&isAllowed=y

14. Dunne J, Murphy MD, Rodriguez WJ. The globalization of pediatric clinical trials. *Pediatrics* 2012; 130(6): e1583-91.

15. Rose K. Pediatric pharmaceutical legislation in the USA and EU and their impact on adult and pediatric drug development. In: Bar-Shalom D, Rose K, editors. *Pediatric Formulations: A Roadmap.* Springer Publishers, New York, NY, USA: 2014.

16. Sinha MS, Najafzadeh M, Rajasingh EK, Love J, Kesselheim AS. Labeling Changes and Costs for Clinical Trials Performed Under the US Food and Drug Administration Pediatric Exclusivity

Extension, 2007 to 2012. *JAMA Intern Med* 20181; 178(11): 1458-1466. www.ncbi.nlm.nih.gov/pmc/articles/PMC6248195

17. Kim J, Ross JS, Kapczynski A. Pediatric Exclusivity and Regulatory Authority: Implications of Amgen v HHS. *JAMA* 2018; 319(1): 21-22.

18. FDA. The Pediatric Exclusivity Provision. Executive Summary. 2018. www.fda.gov/science-research/pediatrics/pediatric-exclusivity-provision

19. FDA. The Pediatric Exclusivity Provision. Status Report to Congress. 2021. www.fda.gov/downloads/Drugs/DevelopmentApprovalProcess/DevelopmentResources/UCM049915.pdf

20. Sinha MS, Najafzadeh M, Rajasingh EK, Love J, Kesselheim AS. Labeling Changes and Costs for Clinical Trials Performed Under the US Food and Drug Administration Pediatric Exclusivity Extension, 2007 to 2012. *JAMA Intern Med* 2018; 178(11): 1458-1466. www.ncbi.nlm.nih.gov/pmc/articles/PMC6248195/

21. Hathaway C, Manthei J, Scherer C. Exclusivity Strategies in the United States and European Union. *Food and Drug Law Institute (FDLI) Update* May/June 2009. www.lw.com/upload/pubcontent/_pdf/pub2655_1.pdf

22. FDA. Best Pharmaceuticals for Children Act and Pediatric Research Equity Act. Status Report to Congress. July 2016. www.fda.gov/media/99184/download

23. Regulation (EC) No 1901/2006 of the European Parliament and of the Council of 12 December 2006 on Medicinal Products for Paediatric Use and Amending Regulation (EEC) No 1768/92, Directive 2001/20/EC, Directive 2001/83/EC and Regulation (EC) No 726/2004. http://ec.europa.eu/health/files/eudralex/vol-1/reg_2006_1901/reg_2006_1901_en.pdf

24. EMA. Opinions and decisions on paediatric investigation plans (PIPs). 2020. www.ema.europa.eu/en/medicines/ema_group_types/ema_pip

25. EMA. 10-year Report to the European Commission. General report on the experience acquired as a result of the application of the Paediatric Regulation. 2016. https://ec.europa.eu/health/sites/health/files/files/paediatrics/2016_pc_report_2017/ema_10_year_report_for_consultation.pdf

26. EU Commission. Report from The Commission To The European Parliament And The Council. State of Paediatric Medicines in the EU – 10 years of the EU Paediatric Regulation. 2017. https://ec.europa.eu/transparency/regdoc/rep/1/2017/EN/COM-2017-626-F1-EN-MAIN-PART-1.PDF

27. EU Commission. State of Paediatric Medicines in the EU. 10 years of the EU Paediatric Regulation. Report from the Commission to the European Parliament and the Council. COM (2017) 626. 2017. https://ec.europa.eu/health/sites/health/files/files/paediatrics/docs/2017_childrensmedicines_report_en.pdf

28. EMA. Paediatric Medicines. Overview. 2018. www.ema.europa.eu/en/human-regulatory/overview/paediatric-medicines-overview

29. Tamborlane WV, Barrientos-Pérez M, Fainberg U, et al. Liraglutide in Children and Adolescents with Type 2 Diabetes. *N Engl J Med* 2019; 381(7): 637-646. www.nejm.org/doi/pdf/10.1056/NEJMoa1903822?articleTools=true

30. Danne T, Biester T, Kapitzke K, et al. Liraglutide in an Adolescent Population with Obesity: A Randomized, Double-Blind, Placebo-Controlled 5-Week Trial to Assess Safety, Tolerability, and Pharmacokinetics of Liraglutide in Adolescents Aged 12-17 Years. *J Pediatr* 2017; 181: 146-153. e3. www.jpeds.com/article/S0022-3476(16)31210-0/pdf

31. Wirth S, Emil SGS, Engelis A, et al. Moxifloxacin in Pediatric Patients With Complicated Intra-abdominal Infections: Results of the MOXIPEDIA Randomized Controlled Study. *Pediatr Infect Dis* 2018; 37(8): e207-e213.

32. FDA. Liraglutide label. 2019. www.accessdata.fda.gov/drugsatfda_docs/label/2019/022341s031lbl.pdf

33. FDA. Liraglutide pediatric written request. 2015. www.fda.gov/media/125521/download

34. EMA liraglutide PIP EMEA-000128-PIP01-07-M08 for diabetes mellitus. www.ema.europa.eu/en/documents/pip-decision/p/0218/2017-ema-decision-9-august-2017-acceptance-modification-agreed-paediatric-investigation-plan_en.pdf

35. EMA liraglutide PIP EMEA-000128-PIP02-09-M03 for obesity. www.ema.europa.eu/en/documents/pip-decision/

p/0383/2019-ema-decision-4-december-2019-acceptance-modification-agreed-paediatric-investigation-plan_en.pdf

36. Wikipedia: Declaration of Helsinki. https://en.wikipedia.org/wiki/Declaration_of_Helsinki

37. FDA. FDA approves new treatment for pediatric patients with type 2 diabetes. 2019. www.fda.gov/news-events/press-announcements/fda-approves-new-treatment-pediatric-patients-type-2-diabetes

38. Micale SJ, Kane MP, Hogan E. Off-label use of liraglutide in the management of a pediatric patient with type 2 diabetes mellitus. *Case Rep Pediatr* 2013; 2013: 703925. http://downloads.hindawi.com/journals/cripe/2013/703925.pdf

39. European Network of Pediatric Research at the EMA (Enpr-EMA). www.ema.europa.eu/en/partners-networks/networks/european-network-paediatric-research-european-medicines-agency-enpr-ema

40. Enpr-EMA. 2018 Annual workshop of the European Network of Paediatric Research at the European Medicines Agency (Enpr-EMA). www.ema.europa.eu/en/events/2018-annual-workshop-european-network-paediatric-research-european-medicines-agency-enpr-ema

41. Ruperto N, Eichler I, Herold R, et al. A European Network of Paediatric Research at the European Medicines Agency (Enpr-EMA). *Arch Dis Child* 2012; 97(3): 185-188. doi: 10.1136/archdischild-2011-300286

42. EMA 2007: The European paediatric initiative: History of the Paediatric Regulation. www.ema.europa.eu/en/documents/other/european-paediatric-initiative-history-paediatric-regulation_en.pdf

43. Moghadami M. Narrative Review of Influenza: A Seasonal and Pandemic Disease. *Iran J Med Sci* 2017; 42(1): 2-13. www.ncbi.nlm.nih.gov/pmc/articles/PMC5337761/pdf/IJMS-42-2.pdf

44. EMA 2018: PIP EMEA-001782-PIP01-15-M03. www.ema.europa.eu/en/documents/pip-decision/p/0211/2018-ema-decision-17-july-2018-acceptance-modification-agreed-paediatric-investigation-plan/h1n1/h3n2-b/yamagata-linea_en.pdf

45. Kearns GL, Abdel-Rahman SM, Alander SW, Blowey DL, Leeder JS, Kauffman RE. Developmental pharmacology – drug disposition,

action, and therapy in infants and children. *N Engl J Med* 2003; 349(12): 1157-1167. www.semanticscholar.org/paper/Drug-Disposition-%2C-Action-%2C-and-Therapy-in-Infants-Kearns-Abdel-Rahman/55f81745303e9aaec7f4cb85f0b5921eec14a9c0

46. Beunen GP, Rogol AD, Malina RM. Indicators of biological maturation and secular changes in biological maturation. *Food Nutr Bull* 2006; 27(4 Suppl Growth Standard): S244-S256. doi: 10.1177/15648265060274S508

47. Van Norman GA. Limitations of Animal Studies for Predicting Toxicity in Clinical Trials. Is it Time to Rethink Our Current Approach? *JACC Basic Transl Sci* 2019; 4(7): 845-854. https://reader.elsevier.com/reader/sd/pii/

48. Hajar R. Animal Testing and Medicine. *Heart Views* 2011; 12(1): 42. www.ncbi.nlm.nih.gov/pmc/articles/PMC3123518/

49. Jacobs AC, Hatfield KP. History of Chronic Toxicity and Animal Carcinogenicity Studies for Pharmaceuticals. *Vet Pathol* 2013; 50(2): 324-333. doi: 10.1177/0300985812450727

50. ICH 2009. ICH Harmonised Tripartite Guideline M3(R2), nonclinical safety studies for the conduct of human clinical trials and marketing authorization or pharmaceuticals, M3(R2), 2009. https://database.ich.org/sites/default/files/M3_R2__Guideline.pdf

51. Ganesh Suntharalingam, Perry MR, Ward S, et al. Cytokine Storm in a Phase 1 Trial of the anti-CD28 Monoclonal Antibody TGN1412. *N Engl J Med* 2006; 355(10): 1018-1028. www.nejm.org/doi/pdf/10.1056/NEJMoa063842?articleTools=true

52. Van Norman GA. Limitations of Animal Studies for Predicting Toxicity in Clinical Trials. Part 2: Potential Alternatives to the Use of Animals in Preclinical Trials. *JACC Basic Transl Sci* 2020; 5(4): 387-397.

53. National Institute of Environmental Health Sciences 2019: Toxicology. www.niehs.nih.gov/health/topics/science/toxicology/index.cfm

54. FDA 2018. Step 2: Preclinical Research. www.fda.gov/patients/drug-development-process/step-2-preclinical-research

55. ICH preclinical safety guidelines ICH S 1 through ICH S 12. www.ich.org/page/safety-guidelines

56. FDA 2006. Guidance for Industry. Nonclinical safety evaluation of pediatric drug products, CDER, 2006. www.fda.gov/media/119658/download

57. EMA 2008. Guideline on the need for non-clinical testing in juvenile animals of pharmaceuticals for paediatric indications. Ref. EMEA/CHMP/ www.ema.europa.eu/en/documents/scientific-guideline/guideline-need-non-clinical-testing-juvenile-animals-pharmaceuticals-paediatric-indications_en.pdf

58. International Council For Harmonisation Of Technical Requirements For Pharmaceuticals For Human Use (ICH) 2020. ICH Harmonized Guideline. Nonclinical Safety Testing In Support Of Development Of Paediatric Pharmaceuticals S11. https://database.ich.org/sites/default/files/S11_Step4_FinalGuideline_2020_0310.pdf

59. Supp DM. Animal Models for Studies of Keloid Scarring. *Adv Wound Care* 2019; 8(2): 77-89. www.ncbi.nlm.nih.gov/pmc/articles/PMC6906757/pdf/wound.2018.0828.pdf

60. de la Torre Hernández JM, Edelman ER. From Nonclinical Research to Clinical Trials and Patient-registries: Challenges and Opportunities in Biomedical Research. *Rev Esp Cardiol* (Engl Ed) 2017; 70(12): 1121-1133. www.ncbi.nlm.nih.gov/pmc/articles/PMC5975372/pdf/nihms969120.pdf

61. Francione GL. Some brief comments on animal rights. *Anim Front* 2020; 10(1): 29-33. www.ncbi.nlm.nih.gov/pmc/articles/PMC6952855/pdf/vfz050.pdf

62. Rollin BE. Animal Rights as a Mainstream Phenomenon. *Animals* 2011; 1(1): 102-115. www.ncbi.nlm.nih.gov/pmc/articles/PMC4552208/pdf/animals-01-00102.pdf

63. Beversdorf DQ, Roos RP, Hauser WA, et al. Animal extremists' threats to neurologic research continue: Neuroreality II. *Neurology*

2015; 85(8): 730-734. www.ncbi.nlm.nih.gov/pmc/articles/PMC4553027/pdf/NEUROLOGY2015640318.pdf

64. Djulbegovic B, Guyatt GH. Progress in evidence-based medicine: a quarter century on. *Lancet* 2017; 390(10092): 415-423.

65. Wikipedia: Evidence-Based Medicine https://en.wikipedia.org/wiki/Evidence-based_medicine

66. Wikipedia: Garbage in, garbage out. https://en.wikipedia.org/wiki/Garbage_in,_garbage_out

67. Sackett DL, Rosenberg WM, Gray JA, et al. Evidence based medicine: what it is and what it isn't. *BMJ* 1996; 312(7023): 71-72. www.ncbi.nlm.nih.gov/pmc/articles/PMC2349778/pdf/bmj00524-0009.pdf

68. Tebala GD. The Emperor's New Clothes: a Critical Appraisal of Evidence-based Medicine. *Int J Med Sci* 2018, 15: xx. www.medsci.org/v15p1397.pdf

69. Wikipedia: Cochrane https://en.wikipedia.org/wiki/Cochrane_(organisation)

70. Emily Whitehead: A Young Girl Beats Cancer with Immunotherapy. www.cancerresearch.org/immunotherapy/stories/patients/emily-whitehead

71. FDA 2017. Tisagenlecleucel label. www.fda.gov/files/vaccines%2C%20blood%20%26%20biologics/published/Package-Insert---KYMRIAH.pdf

72. Frey NV. Chimeric antigen receptor T cells for acute lymphoblastic leukemia. *Am J Hematol* 2019; 94(S1): S24-S27. https://onlinelibrary.wiley.com/doi/epdf/10.1002/ajh.25442

73. Emily Whitehead Foundation – 2020 Stem Cell & Regenerative Medicine Action Award honoree. www.youtube.com/watch?v=GW42FUhflkY

74. Rose K, Walson PD. Are Regulatory Age Limits in Pediatric Melanoma Justified? *Curr Ther Res Clin Exp* 2019; xx: xx-xx. doi.org/10.1016/j.curtheres.2019.01.003

75. Rose K, Grant-Kels JM. Pediatric Melanoma – The Whole (Conflicts Of Interest) Story. *Int J Womens Dermatol* 2018; 5(2): 110-115. doi: 10.1016/j.ijwd.2018.10.020 www.ncbi.nlm.nih.gov/pmc/articles/PMC6451736/pdf/main.pdf

76. Medicines and Healthcare Regulatory Agency (MHRA) guidance. *Procedures for UK Paediatric Investigation Plan (PIPs)*, 31 December

2020. www.gov.uk/guidance/procedures-for-uk-paediatric-investigation-plan-pips

77. Medicines and Healthcare Regulatory Agency (MHRA) guidance. *Format and content of applications for agreement or modification of a Paediatric Investigation Plan. Also covering requests for waivers or deferrals and concerning the operation of the compliance check.* www.gov.uk/government/publications/format-and-content-of-applications-for-agreement-or-modification-of-a-paediatric-investigation-plan

78. Medicines and Healthcare Regulatory Agency (MHRA). *Guideline on the format and content of applications for agreement or modification of a Paediatric Investigation Plan and requests for waivers or deferrals and concerning the operation of the compliance check.* https://assets.publishing.service.gov.uk/government/uploads/system/uploads/attachment_data/file/948571/Guideline_on_the_format_and_content_of_applications_for_PIP.pdf

Chapter 3: Can 'children' receive 'adult' medicines?

1. Hardin AP, Hackell JM. Committee on Practice and Ambulatory Medicine. Age limit of pediatrics. *Pediatrics* 2017;140(3):e20172151. https://pediatrics.aappublications.org/content/pediatrics/140/3/e20172151.full.pdf

2. Beunen GP, Rogol AD, Malina RM. Indicators of biological maturation and secular changes in biological maturation. *Food Nutr Bull* 2006; 27(4 Suppl Growth Standard): S244-56. https://journals.sagepub.com/doi/pdf/10.1177/15648265060274S508

3. Colón AR. *Nurturing Childen. A History of Pediatrics.* Greenwood Press, Westport, CT; 1999.

4. Wikipedia: American Academy of Pediatrics. https://en.wikipedia.org/wiki/American_Academy_of_Pediatrics

5. Momper JD, Mulugeta Y, Green DJ, et al. Adolescent dosing and labeling since the Food and Drug Administration Amendments Act of 2007. *JAMA Pediatr* 2013; 167(10): 926-932. https://jamanetwork.com/journals/jamapediatrics/fullarticle/1723817

6. Plate V. The Impact of Off-Label, Compassionate and Unlicensed Use on Health Care Laws in preselected Countries. https://bonndoc.ulb.uni-bonn.de/xmlui/bitstream/handle/20.500.11811/4152/1936.pdf?sequence=1&isAllowed=y

7. Rose K. *Considering the Patient in Pediatric Drug Development. How good intentions turned into harm.* Elsevier, London, 2020. www.elsevier.com/books/considering-the-patient-in-pediatric-drug-development/rose/978-0-12-823888-2 and www.sciencedirect.com/book/9780128238882/considering-the-patient-in-pediatric-drug-development

8. Declaration Of The Rights Of The Child. Adopted by UN General Assembly Resolution 1386 (XIV) of 10 December 1959. https://web.archive.org/web/20130926070812/www.un.org/cyberschoolbus/humanrights/resources/child.asp

9. Philip AG. The evolution of neonatology. *Pediatr Res* 2005; 58(4): 799-815. www.nature.com/articles/pr2005743.pdf?origin=ppub

10. Wikipedia: Human embryonic development. https://en.wikipedia.org/wiki/Human_embryonic_development

11. Kearns GL, Abdel-Rahman SM, Alander SW, Blowey DL, Leeder JS, Kauffman RE. evelopmental pharmacology – drug disposition, action, and therapy in infants and children. *N Engl J Med* 2003; 349(12): 1157-1167 https://pdfs.semanticscholar.org/55f8/1745303e9aaec7f4cb85f0b5921eec14a9c0.pdf

12. Beunen GP, Rogol AD, Malina RM. Indicators of biological maturation and secular changes in biological maturation. *Food Nutr Bull* 2006; 27(4 Suppl Growth Standard): S244-S256. https://journals.sagepub.com/doi/pdf/10.1177/15648265060274S508

13. Wikipedia: Neonatology. https://en.wikipedia.org/wiki/Neonatology

14. Jorgensen AM. Born in the USA – The History of Neonatology in the United States: A Century of Caring. http://images.abbottnutrition.com/ANHI/MEDIA/Nurse%20Currents%20NICU%20History%20June%202010.pdf

15. McGuire W, Halliday HL. The Research Cycle: Improving Care and Outcomes for Newborn Infants. *Neonatology* 2018; 114(1): 2-6. www.karger.com/Article/Pdf/487990

16. Patz A. The Role Of Oxygen In Retrolental Fibroplasia. *Trans Am Ophthalmol Soc* 1968; 66: 940-985. www.ncbi.nlm.nih.gov/pmc/articles/PMC1310320/pdf/taos00033-0953.pdf

17. Sardesai S, Biniwale M, Wertheimer F, et al. Evolution of surfactant therapy for respiratory distress syndrome: past, present, and future. *Pediatr Res* 2017; 81(1-2): 240-248. www.nature.com/articles/pr2016203

18. Halliday HL. Surfactants: past, present and future. *J Perinatol* 2008; 28 Suppl 1(Suppl 1): S47-S56. www.ncbi.nlm.nih.gov/pmc/articles/PMC7104445/pdf/41372_2008_Article_BFjp200850.pdf

19. Penkov D, Tomasi P, Eichler I, et al. Pediatric Medicine Development: An Overview and Comparison of Regulatory Processes in the European Union and United States. *Therapeutic Innovation & Regulatory Science* 2017; 51(3): 360-371. https://europepmc.org/backend/ptpmcrender.fcgi?accid=PMC5493316&blobtype=pdf

20. Bucci-Rechtsweg C. Enhancing the Pediatric Drug Development Framework to Deliver Better Pediatric Therapies Tomorrow. *Clin Ther* 2017; 39(10): 1920-1932. www.clinicaltherapeutics.com/action/showPdf?pii=S0149-2918%2817%2930832-9

21. Thomsen MDT. Global Pediatric Drug Development. *Curr Ther Res Clin Exp* 2019; 90: 135-142. www.ncbi.nlm.nih.gov/pmc/articles/PMC6677570/pdf/main.pdf

22. Severin T, Corriol-Rohou S, Bucci-Rechtweg C, et al. How is the Pharmaceutical Industry Structured to Optimize Pediatric Drug Development? Existing Pediatric Structure Models and Proposed Recommendations for Structural Enhancement. *Ther Innov Regul Sci* 6 Feb 2020. https://link.springer.com/article/10.1007/s43441-020-00116-4

23. Willhelm C, Girisch W, Gottschling S, et al. Systematic Cochrane reviews in neonatology: a critical appraisal. *Pediatr Neonatol* 2013; 54(4): 261-266. www.pediatr-neonatol.com/action/showPdf?pii=S1875-9572%2813%2900037-5

24. Thompson G, Barker CI, Folgori L, et al. Global shortage of neonatal and paediatric antibiotic trials: rapid review. *BMJ Open* 2017; 7(10): e016293. www.ncbi.nlm.nih.gov/pmc/articles/PMC5652566/pdf/bmjopen-2017-016293.pdf

25. Iosifidis E, Papachristou S, Roilides E. Advances in the Treatment of Mycoses in Pediatric Patients. *J Fungi* 2018; 4(4). www.mdpi.com/2309-608X/4/4/115

26. Chen SC, Sorell TC. Antifungal Agents. *Med J Aust* 2007; 187(7): 404-409. www.mja.com.au/system/files/issues/187_07_011007/che10188_fm.pdf

27. International Council for Harmonisation of Technical Requirements for Pharmaceuticals for Human Use (ICH). www.ich.org

28. Addendum to ICH E11: Clinical Investigation of Medicinal Products in the Pediatric Population. E11 (R1). https://database.ich.org/sites/default/files/E11_R1_Addendum.pdf

29. Lutsar I, Chazallon C, Trafojer U, et al. Meropenem vs standard of care for treatment of neonatal late onset sepsis (NeoMero1): A randomised controlled trial. *PLoS One* 2020; 15(3): e0229380. www.ncbi.nlm.nih.gov/pmc/articles/PMC7055900/pdf/pone.0229380.pdf

30. Garazzino S. Lutsar I, Bertaina C, et al. New antibiotics for paediatric use: A review of a decade of regulatory trials submitted to the European Medicines Agency from 2000—Why aren't we doing better? *Int J Antimicrob Agents* 2013; 42(2): 99-118. https://iris.unito.it/retrieve/handle/2318/140674/263834/New%20antibiotics%20for%20paediatric%20use_4aperto.pdf

31. Folgori L, Lutsar I, Standing JF, et al. Standardising neonatal and paediatric antibiotic clinical trial design and conduct: the PENTA-ID network view. *BMJ Open* 2019; 9(12): e032592. www.ncbi.nlm.nih.gov/pmc/articles/PMC6955510/pdf/bmjopen-2019-032592.pdf

32. Hanning SM, Lopez FL, Wong IC, et al. Patient centric formulations for paediatrics and geriatrics: Similarities and differences. *Int J Pharm* 2016; 512(2): 355-359. doi: 10.1016/j.ijpharm.2016.03.017.

33. Bar-Shalom D, Rose K (Editors). *Pediatric Formulations – A Roadmap*. AAPS Press & Springer, New York, USA; 2014.

34. Bar-Shalom D, Rose K (Editors). *Pediatric Formulations – A Roadmap*. AAPS Press & Springer, New York, USA; 2014. www.springer.com/gp/book/9781489980106

35. Zajicek A, Fossler MJ, Barrett JS, et al. A Report from the Pediatric Formulations Task Force: Perspectives on the State of Child-Friendly Oral Dosage Forms. *AAPSJ* 2013; 15(4):

1072–1081. www.ncbi.nlm.nih.gov/pmc/articles/PMC3787237/pdf/12248_2013_Article_9511.pdf

36. Salunke S, Tuleu C. Formulating better medicines for children- Still too far to walk. *Int J Pharm* 2016; 511(2): 1124-1126. https://discovery.ucl.ac.uk/id/eprint/1504593/1/Tuleu_Formulating%20better%20medicines%20for%20children%20%20still%20too%20far%20to%20walk%20Final1.pdf

37. European Paediatric Formulation Initiative (*EuPFI*) www.eupfi.org

38. EMA 2006. Reflection paper on the formulations of choice of children. www.ema.europa.eu/en/documents/scientific-guideline/reflection-paper-formulations-choice-paediatric-population_en.pdf

39. EMA 2013. Guideline on pharmaceutical development of medicines for paediatric use. www.ema.europa.eu/en/documents/scientific-guideline/guideline-pharmaceutical-development-medicines-paediatric-use_en.pdf

40. EMA 2020. Paediatric Formulations. www.ema.europa.eu/en/human-regulatory/research-development/paediatric-medicines/paediatric-investigation-plans/paediatric-formulations

41. Trofimiuk M, Wasilewska K, Winnicka K. How to Modify Drug Release in Paediatric Dosage Forms? Novel Technologies and Modern Approaches with Regard to Children's Population. *Int J Mol Sci* 2019; 20(13): 3200. www.mdpi.com/1422-0067/20/13/3200

42. FDA 2015: Spritam (levetiracetam) medical review 207958Orig1s000. www.accessdata.fda.gov/drugsatfda_docs/nda/2015/207958Orig1s000MedR.pdf

Chapter 4: Finding good and identifying bad studies

1. Medicines and Healthcare products Regulatory Agency (MHRA) December 31, 2020. Legal requirements for children's medicines. An overview of the legal requirements for children's medicines that Marketing Authorisation Holders (MAHs) need to abide by. www.gov.uk/government/publications/legal-requirements-for-childrens-medicines

References

2. Penkov D, Tomasi P, Eichler I, et al. Pediatric Medicine Development: An Overview and Comparison of Regulatory Processes in the European Union and United States. *Therapeutic Innovation & Regulatory Science* 2017; 51(3): 360-371. https://europepmc.org/backend/ptpmcrender. fcgi?accid=PMC5493316&blobtype=pdf

3. Bucci-Rechtsweg C. Enhancing the Pediatric Drug Development Framework to Deliver Better Pediatric Therapies Tomorrow. *Clin Ther* 2017; 39(10): 1920-1932. www.clinicaltherapeutics.com/ action/showPdf?pii=S0149-2918%2817%2930832-9

4. Thomsen MDT. Global Pediatric Drug Development. *Curr Ther Res Clin Exp* 2019; 90: 135-142. www.ncbi.nlm.nih.gov/pmc/articles/ PMC6677570/pdf/main.pdf

5. Severin T, Corriol-Rohou S, Bucci-Rechtweg C, et al. How is the Pharmaceutical Industry Structured to Optimize Pediatric Drug Development? Existing Pediatric Structure Models and Proposed Recommendations for Structural Enhancement. *Ther Innov Regul Sci* 2020 Feb 6. https://link.springer.com/article/10.1007/s43441-020-00116-4

6. FDA 2017. Tisagenlecleucel label www.fda.gov/files/ vaccines%2C%20blood%20%26%20biologics/published/ Package-Insert---KYMRIAH.pdf

7. Frey NV. Chimeric antigen receptor T cells for acute lymphoblastic leukemia. *Am J Hematol* 2019; 94(S1): S24-S27. https://onlinelibrary.wiley.com/doi/epdf/10.1002/ajh.25442

8. Emily Whitehead: A Young Girl Beats Cancer with Immunotherapy. www.cancerresearch.org/immunotherapy/stories/patients/ emily-whitehead

9. Emily Whitehead Foundation – 2020 Stem Cell & Regenerative Medicine Action Award honoree. www.youtube.com/watch?v=GW42FUhflkY

10. FDA crisaborole prescribing information. www.accessdata.fda. gov/drugsatfda_docs/label/2016/207695s000lbl.pdf

11. US National Library of Medicine PubMed. https://pubmed.ncbi.nlm.nih.gov/

12. Wikipedia: PubMed. https://en.wikipedia.org/wiki/PubMed

13. Hilts PJ. *Protecting America's Health: The FDA, Business, and One Hundred Years of Regulation.* New York, USA, Alfred A Knopf Publishers 2003 .

14. George SL, Buyse M. Data fraud in clinical trials. *Clin Investig* 2015; 5(2): 161-173. www.ncbi.nlm.nih.gov/pmc/articles/PMC4340084/pdf/nihms662892.pdf

15. Hwang TJ, Tomasi PA, Bourgeois FT. Delays in completion and results reporting of clinical trials under the Paediatric Regulation in the European Union: A cohort study. *PLoS Med* 2018; 15(3): e1002520. https://journals.plos.org/plosmedicine/article/file?id=10.1371/journal.pmed.1002520&type=printable

16. Rose K. *Considering the Patient in Pediatric Drug Development. How good intentions turned into harm.* Elsevier, London, 2021. www.elsevier.com/books/considering-the-patient-in-pediatric-drug-development/rose/978-0-12-823888-2 and www.sciencedirect.com/book/9780128238882/considering-the-patient-in-pediatric-drug-development

17. Goldacre B. *Bad Pharma: How drug companies mislead doctors and harm patients.* Harper Collins Publishers, London, UK; 2012.

18. Angell M. *The Truth about the Drug Companies: How They Deceive Us and What to Do about It.* Random House Publishers, New York, USA; 2004.

19. Gøtzsche P. *Deadly Medicines and Organised Crime: How Big Pharma Has Corrupted Healthcare.* Routledge, London, UK; 2013.

20. Rose K, Grant-Kels JM. Pediatric Melanoma – The Whole (Conflicts Of Interest) Story. *Int J Womens Dermatol* 2018; 5(2): 110-115. doi: 10.1016/j.ijwd.2018.10.020 www.ncbi.nlm.nih.gov/pmc/articles/PMC6451736/pdf/main.pdf

21. Clinicaltrials.gov NCT03665038. A Study to Assess the Safety of Brexanolone in the Treatment of Adolescent Female Participants With Postpartum Depression (PPD). www.clinicaltrials.gov/ct2/show/NCT03665038?recrs=a&cond=Postpartum+Depression&age=0&fund=2&draw=2&rank=1

22. Study of the Pharmacokinetics, Pharmacodynamics, Safety and Tolerability of Fosaprepitant for the Prevention of Chemotherapy-Induced Nausea and Vomiting (CINV) in

Children (MK-0517-029). NCT # NCT01697579
https://clinicaltrials.gov/ct2/show/NCT01697579

23. A Study of MACI in Patients Aged 10 to 17 Years With Symptomatic Chondral or Osteochondral Defects of the Knee. www.clinicaltrials.gov/ct2/show/NCT03588975?term=microfracture&age=0&fund=2&draw=2&rank=1

24. Rose K, Neubauer D, Fumi L, Grant-Kels JM. Comment on: Mumme M et al. Tissue engineering for paediatric patients. *Swiss Medical Weekly* 2020.
https://smw.ch/article/doi/smw.2020.20239

25. Rose K, Kopp MV. Pediatric investigation plans for specific immunotherapy: Questionable contributions to childhood health. *Pediatr Allergy Immunol* 2015; 26(8): 695-701.

26. EMA 2014. Cannabidiol PIP EMEA-000181-PIP02-13 www.ema.europa.eu/en/documents/pip-decision/p/0298/2014-ema-decision-24-november-2014-agreement-paediatric-investigation-plan-granting-deferral/delta-9-tetrahydrocannabinol-sativex-emea-000181-pip02-13_en.pdf

27. Hwang TJ, Tomasi PA, Bourgeois FT. Delays in completion and results reporting of clinical trials under the Paediatric Regulation in the European Union: A cohort study. *PLoS Med* 2018; 15(3): e1002520. www.ncbi.nlm.nih.gov/pmc/articles/PMC5832187/pdf/pmed.1002520.pdf

28. Rose K, Neubauer D, Grant-Kels JM. Rational Use of Medicine in Children – The Conflict of Interests Story. A Review. *Rambam Maimonides Med J* 2019; 10(3): e0018. doi:10.5041/RMMJ.10371. www.rmmj.org.il/userimages/928/2/PublishFiles/953Article.pdf

29. Emily Whitehead: A Young Girl Beats Cancer with Immunotherapy. www.cancerresearch.org/immunotherapy/stories/patients/emily-whitehead

30. Rose K. Pediatric Oncology At The Crossroads: A Call for Change. Editorial. *Pharmaceut Med* 2020 Oct 7. https://rdcu.be/b8drm

Chapter 5: Cancer, leukaemia and other malignancies

1. Nambayan AG. Historical Overview of Pediatric Oncology and Pediatric Oncology Nursing. St. Jude's Children's Research Hospital/ Cure4kids 2005. www.cure4kids.org/private/ courses_documents/m_1/NEM01D02V07.pdf

2. Wikipedia: Cancer https://en.wikipedia.org/wiki/Cancer

3. Saletta F, Seng MS, Lau LM. Advances in paediatric cancer treatment. *Transl Pediatr* 2014; 3(2): 156-182. www.ncbi.nlm.nih. gov/pmc/articles/PMC4729100/pdf/tp-03-02-156.pdf

4. US National Cancer Institute: Childhood Cancers. www.cancer.gov/types/childhood-cancers

5. Krueger G. *Hope and Suffering: Children, Cancer, and the Paradox of Experimental Medicine*. John Hopkins University Press, Baltimore, MD, USA; 2008.

6. Adamson PC. Improving the outcome for children with cancer: Development of targeted new agents. *CA Cancer J Cli* 2015; 65(3): 212-220.

7. DeVita VT Jr, Chu E. A history of cancer chemotherapy. *Cancer Res* 2008; 68(21): 8643-8653. http://cancerres.aacrjournals.org/ content/68/21/8643.full-text.pdf

8. Rose K, Neubauer D, Grant-Kels JM. Rational Use of Medicine in Children – The Conflict of Interests Story. A Review. *Rambam Maimonides Med J* 2019; 10(3): e0018. doi:10.5041/RMMJ.10371. www.rmmj.org.il/userimages/928/2/ PublishFiles/953Article.pdf

9. Rose K. The Challenges of Pediatric Drug Development. *Curr Ther Res Clin Exp* 2019; 90: 128-134. https://doi.org/10.1016/j.curtheres.2019.01.007

10. Rose K. *Considering the Patient in Pediatric Drug Development. How good intentions turned into harm*. Elsevier, London, 2020. www.elsevier.com/books/considering-the-patient-in-pediatric-drug-development/rose/978-0-12-823888-2 and www. sciencedirect.com/book/9780128238882/considering-the-patient-in-pediatric-drug-development

11. Rose K, Grant-Kels JM, Ettienne E, Tanjinatus E, Striano P, Neubauer D. Comment on: A review of the experience with

pediatric written requests issued for oncology drug products. Young patients with malignancies need reasonable studies with therapeutic intention. *Pediatric Blood & Cancer* 2021. Online ahead of print. doi.org/10.22541/au.161280832.22407928/v1

12. FDA Pemetrexed pediatric written request 2001. www.fda.gov/media/80043/download

13. Rose K. Pediatric Oncology At The Crossroads: A Call for Change. Editorial. *Pharmaceut Med* 2020 Oct 7. https://rdcu.be/b8drm

14. Rägo L, Santo B. Drug Regulation: History, Present and Future. In: van Boxtel CJ, Santo B & Edwards IR (editors). *Drug Benefits and Risks: International Textbook of Clinical Pharmacology* revised 2nd edition. IOS Press & Uppsala Monitoring Centre, Uppsala, Sweder, 2008, chapter 6, pp. 65-77. www.who.int/medicines/technical_briefing/tbs/Drug_Regulation_History_Present_Future.pdf

15. Plate V. The Impact of Off-Label, Compassionate and Unlicensed Use on Health Care Laws in preselected Countries. https://bonndoc.ulb.uni-bonn.de/xmlui/bitstream/handle/20.500.11811/4152/1936.pdf?sequence=1&isAllowed=y

16. Janssen WM. A Historical Perspective on Off-Label Medicine: From Regulation, Promotion, and the First Amendment to the Next Frontiers. Food and Drug Law Institute, Levy MC (Editor). First Washington, DC, USA *Off-Label Communications*; 2008.

17. Kearns GL, Abdel-Rahman SM, Alander SW, Blowey DL, Leeder JS, Kauffman RE. Developmental pharmacology – drug disposition, action, and therapy in infants and children. *N Engl J Med* 2003; 349(12): 1157-1167. https://pdfs.semanticscholar.org/55f8/1745303e9aaec7f4cb85f0b5921eec14a9c0.pdf

18. The RACE for Children Act Coalition. www.kidsvcancer.org/race-for-children-act/endorsements-for-race-act/

19. Emily Whitehead: A Young Girl Beats Cancer with Immunotherapy. www.cancerresearch.org/immunotherapy/stories/patients/emily-whitehead

20. Emily Whitehead Foundation – 2020 Stem Cell & Regenerative Medicine Action Award honoree. www.youtube.com/watch?v=GW42FUhflkY

21. EMA 2015. EMA/PDCO Summary Report on the review of the list of granted Class Waivers.

www.ema.europa.eu/en/documents/other/ema/pdco-summary-report-review-list-granted-class-waivers_en.pdf

22. Wikipedia: Melanoma https://en.wikipedia.org/wiki/Melanoma

23. Pappo AS. Pediatric melanoma: the whole (genome) story. *Am Soc Clin Oncol Educ Book* 2014; e432-5. https://ascopubs.org/doi/pdfdirect/10.14694/EdBook_AM.2014.34.e432

24. Bahrami A, Barnhill RL. Pathology and genomics of pediatric melanoma: A critical reexamination and new insights. *Pediatr Blood Cancer* 2018; 65(2): 10.1002/pbc.26792. www.ncbi.nlm.nih.gov/pmc/articles/PMC6500729/pdf/nihms-1009468.pdf

25. Rose K, Grant-Kels JM. Pediatric Melanoma – The Whole (Conflicts Of Interest) Story. *Int J Womens Dermatol* 2018; 5(2): 110-115. doi: 10.1016/j.ijwd.2018.10.020 www.ncbi.nlm.nih.gov/pmc/articles/PMC6451736/pdf/main.pdf

26. Rose K, Senn S: Drug development: EU paediatric legislation, the European Medicines Agency and its Paediatric Committee—adolescents' melanoma as a paradigm. *Pharmaceutical Statistics* 2014; 13(4): 211-213.

27. Geoerger B, Bergeron C, Gore L, et al. Phase II study of ipilimumab in adolescents with unresectable stage III or IV malignant melanoma. *Eur J Cancer* 2017; 86: 358–363.

28. Chisholm JC, Suvada J, Dunkel IJ, et al. BRIM-P: A phase I, open-label, multicenter, dose-escalation study of vemurafenib in pediatric patients with surgically incurable, BRAF mutation-positive melanoma. *Pediatr Blood Cancer* 2018; 65(5) :e26947. www.ncbi.nlm.nih.gov/pmc/articles/PMC5867229/pdf/nihms928012.pdf

29. EMA 2019. Bempegaldesleukin PIP EMEA-002492-PIP01-18. www.ema.europa.eu/en/documents/pip-decision/p/0298/2019-ema-decision-14-august-2019-agreement-paediatric-investigation-plan-granting-deferral_en.pdf

30. Rose K, Grant-Kels JM, Etienne E, Tanjinatus E, Striano P, Neubauer D. Comment on: A review of the experience with pediatric written requests issued for oncology drug products. Young patients with malignancies need reasonable studies with therapeutic intention. *Pediatric Blood & Cancer* 2021. Online ahead of print. doi.org/10.22541/au.161280832.22407928/v1

31. Casanova M, Enis Özyar E, Patte C, et al. International randomized phase 2 study on the addition of docetaxel to the combination of cisplatin and 5- fluorouracil in the induction treatment for nasopharyngeal carcinoma in children and adolescents. *Cancer Chemother Pharmacol* 2016; 77(2): 289-298.

32. Wikipedia: Nasopharyngeal carcinoma. https://en.wikipedia.org/wiki/Nasopharyngeal_carcinoma

33. Wikipedia: Chimeric antigen receptor T cell. https://en.wikipedia.org/wiki/Chimeric_antigen_receptor_T_cell

34. FDA 2018. Kymriah (tisagenlecleucel) prescribing information. www.fda.gov/files/vaccines%2C%20blood%20%26%20biologics/published/Package-Insert---KYMRIAH.pdf

35. FDA 2019. Considerations for the Inclusion of Adolescent Patients in Adult Oncology Clinical Trials. Guidance for Industry. www.fda.gov/media/113499/download

36. Gröbner SN, Worst BC, Weischenfeldt J, et al. The landscape of genomic alterations across childhood cancers. *Nature* 2018; 555(7696): 321-327.

37. Ma X, Liu Y, Liu Y, Alexandrov LB, Edmonson MN, et al. Pan-cancer genome and transcriptome analyses of 1,699 paediatric leukaemias and solid tumours. *Nature* 2018; 555(7696): 371-376.

Chapter 6: Suicide and depression in young people

1. Leading causes of death www.cdc.gov/injury/images/lc-charts/leading_causes_of_death_by_age_group_2017_1100w850h.jpg

2. Ogundele MO. Behavioural and emotional disorders in childhood: A brief overview for paediatricians. *World J Clin Pediatr* 2018; 7(1): 9-26. www.ncbi.nlm.nih.gov/pmc/articles/PMC5803568/pdf/WJCP-7-9.pdf

3. Varley CK. Treating depression in children and adolescents: what options now? *CNS Drugs* 2006; 20(1): 1-13.

4. Brent DA. Master Clinician Review: Saving Holden Caulfield: Suicide Prevention in Children and Adolescents. *J Am Acad Child Adolesc Psychiatry* 2019; 58(1): 25-35.

5. Fornaro M et al. The FDA "Black Box" Warning on Antidepressant Suicide Risk in Young Adults: More Harm Than Benefits? *Frontiers in Psychiatry* 2019; 10: 294. www.ncbi.nlm.nih.gov/pmc/articles/PMC6510161/pdf/fpsyt-10-00294.pdf

6. Wikipedia: Psychoanalytic theory. https://en.wikipedia.org/wiki/Psychoanalytic_theory

7. López-Muñoz F, Alamo C. Monoaminergic Neurotransmission: The History of the Discovery of Antidepressants from 1950s Until Today. *Curr Pharm Des* 2009; 15(14): 1563-1586.

8. Hillhouse TM, Porter JH. A brief history of the development of antidepressant drugs: From monoamines to glutamate. *Exp Clin Psychopharmacol* 2015; 23(1): 1-21. www.ncbi.nlm.nih.gov/pmc/articles/PMC4428540/pdf/nihms667554.pdf

9. Peter C. Gøtzsche. *Deadly Psychiatry and Organised Denial.* Table of contents and introduction. www.deadlymedicines.dk/wp-content/uploads/2014/10/G%C3%B8tzsche-Deadly-Psychiatry-chapter-1.pdf

10. Wharton GT, Murphy MD, Avant D, et al. Impact of pediatric exclusivity on drug labeling and demonstrations of efficacy. *Pediatrics* 2014; 134(2): e512-e518.

11. Rose K, Neubauer D, Grant-Kels JM. Ethical Issues in Pediatric Regulatory Studies Involving Placebo Treatment. *J Pediatr Epilepsy* 2020. www.researchgate.net/publication/342200539_Ethical_Issues_in_Pediatric_Regulatory_Studies_Involving_Placebo_Treatment

12. Rose K, Neubauer D, Grant-Kels JM. Rational Use of Medicine in Children – The Conflict of Interests Story. A Review. *Rambam Maimonides Med J* 2019; 10(3): e0018. www.ncbi.nlm.nih.gov/pmc/articles/PMC6649781/pdf/rmmj-10-3-e0018.pdf

13. Rose K. The Challenges of Pediatric Drug Development. *Curr Ther Res Clin Exp* 2019; 90: 128-134. doi.org/10.1016/j.curtheres.2019.01.007

14. AAP 1995: Guidelines for the Ethical Conduct of Studies to Evaluate Drugs in Pediatric Populations, Committee on Drugs. American Academy of Pediatrics. *Pediatrics* 1995; 95(2): 286-294. https://pediatrics.aappublications.org/content/pediatrics/95/2/286.full.pdf

15. Shaddy RE, Denne SC; Committee on Drugs and Committee on Pediatric Research. Clinical report--guidelines for the ethical conduct of studies to evaluate drugs in pediatric populations. *Pediatrics* 2010; 125(4): 850-860. https://pediatrics. aappublications.org/content/pediatrics/125/4/850.full.pdf

16. FDA 2018. Suicidality in Children and Adolescents Being Treated With Antidepressant Medications. www.fda.gov/ drugs/postmarket-drug-safety-information-patients-and-providers/suicidality-children-and-adolescents-being-treated-antidepressant-medications

17. Gören JL. Antidepressants use in pediatric populations. *Expert Opin Drug Saf* 2008; 7(3): 223-225.

18. Noel C. Antidepressants and suicidality: History, the black-box warning, consequences, and current evidence. *Mental Health Clinician* 2015; 5: 202-211. doi.org/10.9740/mhc.2015.09.202

19. Martinez-Aguayo JC, Arancibia M, Concha S, et al. Ten years after the FDA black box warning for antidepressant drugs: a critical narrative review. Arch. *Clin. Psychiatry* 2016; 43(3). www.scielo.br/pdf/rpc/v43n3/0101-6083-rpc-43-3-0060.pdf

20. Bushnell GA, Stürmer T, Swanson SA, et al. Dosing of Selective Serotonin Reuptake Inhibitors Among Children and Adults Before and After the FDA Black-Box Warning. *Psychiatr Serv* 2016; 67(3): 302-309. www.ncbi.nlm.nih.gov/pmc/articles/ PMC5033112/pdf/nihms811212.pdf

21. Wikipedia 2020: Garbage in, garbage out. https://en.wikipedia. org/wiki/Garbage_in,_garbage_out

22. Rose K, Neubauer D, Grant-Kels JM. Too many avoidable suicides occur worldwide in young patients. *Rambam Maimonides Med J* 2019; 10(4). www.ncbi.nlm.nih.gov/pmc/articles/PMC6824826/ pdf/rmmj-10-4-e0026.pdf

23. Lu CY, Zhang F, Lakoma MD, et al. Changes in antidepressant use by young people and suicidal behavior after FDA warnings and mediacoverage: quasi-experimental study. *BMJ* 2014; 348: g3596. www.bmj.com/content/bmj/348/bmj.g3596.full.pdf

---

Chapter 7: Diabetes

1. Harvard Health Publishing 2019: Diabetes Mellitus Overview. What is it? www.health.harvard.edu/a_to_z/diabetes-mellitus-overview-a-to-z

2. Yeung WC, Rawlinson WD, Craig ME. Enterovirus infection and type 1 diabetes mellitus: systematic review and meta-analysis of observational molecular studies. *BMJ* 2011; 342: d35. www.bmj.com/content/bmj/342/bmj.d35.full.pdf

3. Quianzon CC, Cheikh I. History of insulin. *J Community Hosp Intern Med Perspect* 2012; 2(2). www.ncbi.nlm.nih.gov/pmc/articles/PMC3714061/pdf/JCHIMP-2-18701.pdf

4. Ziegler R, Neu A. Diabetes in Childhood and Adolescence. *Dtsch Arztebl Int* 2018; 115(9): 146-156. www.ncbi.nlm.nih.gov/pmc/articles/PMC5876549/pdf/Dtsch_Arztebl_Int-115_0146.pdf

5. FDA. Insulin. www.fda.gov/media/119149/download

6. Quianzon CC, Cheikh I. History of current non-insulin medications for diabetes mellitus. *J Community Hosp Intern Med Perspect* 2012; 2(3). www.ncbi.nlm.nih.gov/pmc/articles/PMC3714066/pdf/JCHIMP-2-19081.pdf

7. Vieira R, Souto SB, Sánchez-López E, et al. Sugar-Lowering Drugs for Type 2 Diabetes Mellitus and Metabolic Syndrome-Review of Classical and New Compounds: Part-I. *Pharmaceuticals* 2019; 12(4). www.ncbi.nlm.nih.gov/pmc/articles/PMC6958392/pdf/pharmaceuticals-12-00152.pdf

8. FDA 2020. List of issued pediatric written requests. www.fda.gov/drugs/development-resources/written-requests-issued

9. FDA 2018. Insulin glargine label. www.accessdata.fda.gov/drugsatfda_docs/label/2019/021081s072lbl.pdf

10. FDA 2000. Insulin aspart label. www.accessdata.fda.gov/drugsatfda_docs/label/2012/020986s057lbl.pdf

11. FDA 2019. Liraglutide label. www.accessdata.fda.gov/drugsatfda_docs/label/2019/022341s031lbl.pdf

12. Christensen ML, Franklin BE, Momper JD, Reed MD. Pediatric drug development programs for type 2 diabetes: A review. *J Clin Pharmacol* 2015; 55(7): 731-738.

13. Rose K, Neubauer D, Grant-Kels JM. Too Many Avoidable Suicides Occur Worldwide In Young Patients. A Review.

Rambam Maimonides Med J 2019, Sep 18. www.rmmj.org.il/ userimages/965/1/PublishFiles/977OnlineFirst.pdf

14. Ruiz LD, Zuelch ML, Dimitratos SM, et al. Adolescent Obesity: Diet Quality, Psychosocial Health, and Cardiometabolic Risk Factors. *Nutrients* 2019; 12(1): 43. www.ncbi.nlm.nih.gov/pmc/articles/ PMC7020092/pdf/nutrients-12-00043.pdf

15. FDA 2015. Liraglutide pediatric written request. www.fda.gov/media/125521/download

16. Micale SJ, Kane MP, Hogan E. Off-label use of liraglutide in the management of a pediatric patient with type 2 diabetes mellitus. *Case Rep Pediatr* 2013; 2013: 703925. http://downloads.hindawi. com/journals/cripe/2013/703925.pdf

17. Chao AM, Wadden TA, Berkowitz RI. The safety of pharmacologic treatment for pediatric obesity. *Expert Opin Drug Saf* 2018; 17(4): 379-385.

18. Tamborlane WV, Barrientos-Pérez M, Fainberg U, et al. Liraglutide in Children and Adolescents with Type 2 Diabetes. *N Engl J Med* 2019; 381(7): 637-646. www.nejm.org/doi/pdf/10.1056/ NEJMoa1903822?articleTools=true

19. Ladenheim EE. Liraglutide and obesity: a review of the data so far. *Drug Des Devel Ther* 2015; 9: 1867–1875. www.ncbi.nlm.nih.gov/ pmc/articles/PMC4386791/pdf/dddt-9-1867.pdf

20. Danne T, Biester T, Kapitzke K, et al. Liraglutide in an Adolescent Population with Obesity: A Randomized, Double-Blind, Placebo-Controlled 5-Week Trial to Assess Safety, Tolerability, and Pharmacokinetics of Liraglutide in Adolescents Aged 12-17 Years. *J Pediatr* 2017; 181: 146-153.e3. www.jpeds.com/article/S0022-3476(16)31210-0/pdf

21. Rose K. *Considering the Patient in Pediatric Drug Development. How good intentions turned into harm.* Elsevier, London, 2020. www. elsevier.com/books/considering-the-patient-in-pediatric-drug-development/rose/978-0-12-823888-2 and www.sciencedirect. com/book/9780128238882/considering-the-patient-in-pediatric-drug-development

22. Regulation (EC) No 1901/2006 of the European Parliament and of the Council of 12 December 2006 on Medicinal Products for Paediatric Use and Amending Regulation (EEC) No 1768/92, Directive 2001/20/EC, Directive 2001/83/EC and Regulation

(EC) No 726/2004. http://ec.europa.eu/health/files/eudralex/vol-1/reg_2006_1901/reg_2006_1901_en.pdf

23. World Medical Association (WMA) Declaration of Helsinki – Ethical Principles for Medical Research Involving Human Subjects. Adopted by the 18th WMA General Assembly, Helsinki, Finland, June 1964, and amended by the 64th WMA General Assembly, Fortaleza, Brazil, October 2013. www.wma.net/policies-post/wma-declaration-of-helsinki-ethical-principles-for-medical-research-involving-human-subjects/

24. Adashi EY, Walters LB, Menikoff JA. The Belmont Report at 40: Reckoning with Time. *Am J Public Health* 2018; 108(10): 1345-1348. www.ncbi.nlm.nih.gov/pmc/articles/PMC6137767

25. Burckart GJ, Kim C. The Revolution in Pediatric Drug Development and Drug Use: Therapeutic Orphans No More. *J Pediatr Pharmacol Ther* 2020; 25(7): 565-573. www.ncbi.nlm.nih.gov/pmc/articles/PMC7541025/pdf/i1551-6776-25-7-565.pdf

26. Howard M, Barber J, Alizei N, et al. Dose adjustment in orphan disease populations: the quest to fulfill the requirements of physiologically based pharmacokinetics. *Expert Opin Drug Metab Toxicol* 2018; 14(12): 1315-1330.

27. Tamborlane WV, Haymond MW, Dunger D, et al. Expanding Treatment Options for Youth With Type 2 Diabetes: Current Problems and Proposed Solutions. A White Paper From the NICHD Diabetes Working Group. *Diabetes Care* 2016; 39: 323–329. www.ncbi.nlm.nih.gov/pmc/articles/PMC4764039/pdf/dc151649.pdf

28. Karres J, Tomasi P. New medicines for Type 2 diabetes in adolescents: many products, few patients. *Expert Rev Clin Pharmacol* 2013; 6(3): 227-229.

29. Karres J, Pratt V, Guettier JM, et al. Joining forces: a call for greater collaboration to study new medicines in children and adolescents with type 2 diabetes. *Diabetes Care* 2014; 37(10): 2665-2667. https://care.diabetesjournals.org/content/diacare/37/10/2665.full.pdf and www.fda.gov/science-research/pediatrics/joining-forces-call-greater-collaboration-study-new-medicines-children-and-adolescents-type-2

30. EMA 2019. Tirzepatide PIP EMEA-002360-PIP01-18. www.ema.europa.eu/en/documents/pip-decision/p/0311/2019-ema-

decision-10-september-2019-agreement-paediatric-investigation-plan-granting-deferral_en.pdf

31. EMA 2013. Evacetrapib PIP EMEA-001180-PIP01-11. www.ema.europa.eu/en/documents/pip-decision/p/0155/2013-ema-decision-5-july-2013-agreement-paediatric-investigation-plan-granting-deferral-granting_en.pdf

32. Barrett T, Jalaludin MY, Turan S, et al. Rapid progression of type 2 diabetes and related complications in children and young people-A literature review. *Pediatr Diabetes* 2020; 21(2): 158-172. https://onlinelibrary.wiley.com/doi/epdf/10.1111/pedi.12953

Chapter 8: Epilepsy

1. Wikipedia: Encephalography. https://en.wikipedia.org/wiki/Electroencephalography

2. Fisher RS, Acevedo C, Arzimanoglou A, et al. ILAE official report: a practical clinical definition of epilepsy. *Epilepsia* 2014; 55(4): 475-482. https://onlinelibrary.wiley.com/doi/epdf/10.1111/epi.12550

3. Wikipedia: Epilepsy. https://en.wikipedia.org/wiki/Epilepsy

4. Liu G, Slater N, Perkins A. Epilepsy: Treatment Options. *Am Fam Physician* 2017; 96(2): 87-96. www.aafp.org/afp/2017/0715/afp20170715p87.pdf

5. Perucca E. Antiepileptic drugs: evolution of our knowledge and changes in drug trials. *Epileptic Disord* 2019; 21(4): 319-329.

6. Rose K, Neubauer D, Grant-Kels JM. Ethical Issues in Pediatric Regulatory Studies Involving Placebo Treatment. *J Pediatr Epilepsy* 2020; 9(3). DOI:10.1055/s-0040-1712147 www.researchgate.net/publication/342200539_Ethical_Issues_in_Pediatric_Regulatory_Studies_Involving_Placebo_Treatment

7. Burrell L, Noble A, Ridsdale L. Decision-making by ambulance clinicians in London when managing patients with epilepsy: A qualitative study. *Emerg Med J* 2013; 30(3): 236-240. www.ncbi.nlm.nih.gov/pubmed/22433590

8. Berry M, Sander L. Not Always A&E. www.epilepsysociety.org.uk/sites/default/files/Ambulance%20service%20ER%20Issue%2010%20Summer%202014%20spreads-3_0.pdf

9. Wikipedia: Status epilepticus. https://en.wikipedia.org/wiki/Status_epilepticus

10. Trinka E, Cock H, Hesdorffer D, et al. A definition and classification of status epilepticus – Report of the ILAE Task Force on Classification of Status Epilepticus. *Epilepsia* 2015; 56(10): 1515-1523
   https://onlinelibrary.wiley.com/doi/epdf/10.1111/epi.13121

11. Rose K. The Challenges of Pediatric Drug Development. *Curr Ther Res Clin Exp* 2019; 90:128-134. https://doi.org/10.1016/j.curtheres.2019.01.007

12. Rose K. *Considering the Patient in Pediatric Drug Development. How good intentions turned into harm.* Elsevier, London, 2021. www.elsevier.com/books/considering-the-patient-in-pediatric-drug-development/rose/978-0-12-823888-2

13. Rose K, Neubauer D, Grant-Kels JM. Rational Use of Medicine in Children – The Conflict of Interests Story. A Review. *Rambam Maimonides Med J* 2019; 10(3): e0018. Review. doi:10.5041/RMMJ.10371. www.rmmj.org.il/userimages/928/2/PublishFiles/953Article.pdf

14. Rägo L, Santo B. Drug Regulation: History, Present and Future. In: van Boxtel CJ, Santo B & Edwards IR (editors). *Drug Benefits and Risks: International Textbook of Clinical Pharmacology* revised 2nd edition. IOS Press & Uppsala Monitoring Centre, Uppsala, Sweden; 2008, pp 65-77.

15. Sheridan PH, Jacobs MP. The development of antiepileptic drugs for children. Report from the NIH workshop, Bethesda, Maryland, February 17-18, 1994. *Epilepsy Res* 1996; 23(1): 87-92.

16. Shirkey H. Therapeutic Orphans. *J Pediatr* 1968; 72 (1), 119-120. https://pdfs.semanticscholar.org/f1cb/acdbac19fa56236b919fb7799eaacaa10c77.pdf

17. FDA. Drugs for Treatment of Partial Onset Seizures: Full Extrapolation of Efficacy from Adults to Pediatric Patients 2 Years of Age and Older Guidance for Industry. 2019. www.fda.gov/media/130449/download

18. Sun H, Temeck JW, Chambers W, et al. Extrapolation of Efficacy in Pediatric Drug Development and Evidence-based Medicine: Progress and Lessons Learned. *Ther Innov Regul Sci* 2017; 2017: 1-7.

19. Extrapolation Reference #45 EMA 2013. Concept Paper on extrapolation of efficacy and safety in medicine development. www.ema.europa.eu/en/documents/scientific-guideline/concept-paper-extrapolation-efficacy-safety-medicine-development_en.pdf

20. Burckart GJ, Kim C. The Revolution in Pediatric Drug Development and Drug Use: Therapeutic Orphans No More. *J Pediatr Pharmacol Ther* 2020; 25(7): 565-573. www.ncbi.nlm.nih.gov/pmc/articles/PMC7541025/pdf/i1551-6776-25-7-565.pdf

21. Howard M, Barber J, Alizei N, et al. Dose adjustment in orphan disease populations: the quest to fulfill the requirements of physiologically based pharmacokinetics. *Expert Opin Drug Metab Toxicol* 2018; 14(12): 1315-1330.

22. Auvin S, French J, Dlugos D, et al. Novel study design to assess the efficacy and tolerability of antiseizure medications for focal-onset seizures in infants and young children: A consensus document from the regulatory task force and the pediatric commission of the International League against Epilepsy (ILAE), in collaboration with the Pediatric Epilepsy Research Consortium (PERC). *Epilepsia Open* 2019; 4(4): 537-543. https://onlinelibrary.wiley.com/doi/epdf/10.1002/epi4.12356

23. Pellock JM, Carman WJ, Thyagarajan V, Daniels T, Morris DL, D'Cruz O. Efficacy of antiepileptic drugs in adults predicts efficacy in children: a systematic review. *Neurology* 2012; 79(14): 1482-1489. www.ncbi.nlm.nih.gov/pmc/articles/PMC4098824/pdf/znl1482.pdf

24. Pellock JM, Arzimanoglu A, D'Cruz O, et al. Extrapolating evidence of antiepileptic drug efficacy in adults to children ≥2 years of age with focal seizures: The case for disease similarity. *Epilepsia* 2017; 58(10): 1686-1696. https://onlinelibrary.wiley.com/doi/epdf/10.1111/epi.13859

25. Wadsworth I, Jaki T, Sills GJ, et al. Clinical Drug Development in Epilepsy Revisited: A Proposal for a New Paradigm Streamlined Using Extrapolation. *CNS Drugs* 2016; 30(11): 1011–1017 www.ncbi.nlm.nih.gov/pmc/articles/PMC5078157/pdf/40263_2016_Article_383.pdf

26. Garofalo E. Clinical Development of Antiepileptic Drugs for Children. *Neurotherapeutics* 2007; 4(1): 70-74.

www.ncbi.nlm.nih.gov/pmc/articles/PMC7479697/
pdf/13311_2011_Article_40100070.pdf

27. EMA. Guideline on clinical investigation of medicinal products in the treatment of epileptic disorders. 2018
www.ema.europa.eu/en/documents/scientific-guideline/draft-guideline-clinical-investigation-medicinal-products-treatment-epileptic-disorders-revision-3_en.pdf

28. Berde CB, Walco GA, Krane EJ, et al. Pediatric analgesic clinical trial designs, measures, and extrapolation: report of an FDA scientific workshop. *Pediatrics* 2012; 129(2): 354-364.

29. Rose K, Tanjinatus O, Grant-Kels JM, et al. Minors and a dawning paradigm shift in "pediatric" drug development. *J Clin Pharmacol* 2020, Dec 23. Online ahead of print.

30. Thomas S Kuhn. *The Structure of Scientific Revolutions*. Second Edition, Enlarged. International Encyclopedia of Unified Science, The University of Chicago Press, Chicago, IL, USA, 1970. www.lri.fr/~mbl/Stanford/CS477/papers/Kuhn-SSR-2ndEd.pdf

Chapter 9: Knee surgery

1. Wikipedia: Epiphyseal plate. https://en.wikipedia.org/wiki/Epiphyseal_plate

2. Salzmann, GM, Niemeyer P, Hochrein A, et al. Articular Cartilage Repair of the Knee in Children and Adolescents. *Orthop J Sports Med* 2018; 6(3): 2325967118760190. www.ncbi.nlm.nih.gov/pmc/articles/PMC5858627/pdf/10.1177_2325967118760190.pdf

3. Stephen M Schroeder. Locked Knees. Sports Medicine Oregon 2021. www.sportsmedicineoregon.com/sports-medicine-recovery-journal/what-is-a-locked-knee.php

4. Hunziker EB, Lippuner K, Keel MJ, et al. An educational review of cartilage repair: precepts and practice – myths and misconceptions – progress and prospects. *Osteoarthritis Cartilage* 2015; 23(3): 334-350. www.oarsijournal.com/article/S1063-4584(14)01383-1/pdf

5. Sophia Fox AJ, Bedi A, Rodeo SA. The basic science of articular cartilage: structure, composition, and function. *Sports Health*

2009; 1(6): 461-468. www.ncbi.nlm.nih.gov/pmc/articles/ PMC3445147/pdf/10.1177_1941738109350438.pdf

6. Kwon H, Brown WE, Lee CA, et al. Surgical and tissue engineering strategies for articular cartilage and meniscus repair. *Nat Rev Rheumatol* 2019; 15(9): 550-570. www.ncbi.nlm.nih.gov/pmc/ articles/PMC7192556/pdf/nihms-1579623.pdf

7. Accadbled F, Vial J, Sales de Gauzy J. Osteochondritis dissecans of the knee. *Orthop Traumatol Surg Res* 2018; 104(1S): S97-S105. https://reader.elsevier.com/reader/sd/pii/ S1877056817303341?token=2542B06156589093E3099910FC9 CF632D37DFBAE784586DBEA0C6B69EFEDF59025C729AB91 CC701B6361B97EF18B00F1

8. Wikipedia: Endoscopy. https://en.wikipedia.org/wiki/Endoscopy

9. Erggelet C, Vavken P. Microfracture for the treatment of cartilage defects in the knee joint – A golden standard? *J Clin Orthop Trauma* 2016; 7(3): 145-152. www.ncbi.nlm.nih.gov/pmc/articles/PMC4949407/pdf/main.pdf

10. Wikipedia: Microfracture surgery. https://en.wikipedia.org/wiki/Microfracture_surgery

11. Coughlin RP, Gupta A, Sogbein OA, et al. Cartilage Restoration in the Adolescent Knee: a Systematic Review. *Curr Rev Musculoskelet Med* 2019; 12(4): 486-496. www.ncbi.nlm.nih.gov/pmc/articles/ PMC6942099/pdf/12178_2019_Article_9595.pdf

12. Hanna E, Rémuzat C, Auquier P, et al. Advanced therapy medicinal products: current and future perspectives. *J Mark Access Health Policy* 2016; 4. www.ncbi.nlm.nih.gov/pmc/articles/ PMC4846788/pdf/JMAHP-4-31036.pdf

13. Regulation (EC) No 1901/2006 of the European Parliament and of the Council of 12 December 2006 on Medicinal Products for Paediatric Use and Amending Regulation (EEC) No 1768/92, Directive 2001/20/EC, Directive 2001/83/EC and Regulation (EC) No 726/2004. http://ec.europa.eu/health/files/eudralex/ vol-1/reg_2006_1901/reg_2006_1901_en.pdf

14. Hirschfeld S, Saint-Raymond A. Pediatric Regulatory Initiatives. *Handb Exp Pharmacol* 2011; 205: 245-268

15. Rose K. The Challenges of Pediatric Drug Development. *Curr Ther Res Clin Exp* 2019; xx: xx-xx. https://doi.org/10.1016/j.curtheres.2019.01.007

16. Rose K, Grant-Kels JM. The Meanings of "Pediatric Drug Development". A Review. *Ther Innov Regul Sci* 2018: 2168479018812060. https://journals.sagepub.com/doi/pdf/10.1177/2168479018812060

17. Rose K, Neubauer D, Grant-Kels JM. Rational Use of Medicine in Children – The Conflict of Interests Story. A Review. *Rambam Maimonides Med J* 2019; 10(3): e0018. doi:10.5041/RMMJ.10371. www.rmmj.org.il/userimages/928/2/PublishFiles/953Article.pdf

18. Eder C, Wild C. Technology forecast: advanced therapies in late clinical research, EMA approval or clinical application via hospital exemption. *J Mark Access Health Policy* 2019; 7(1): 1600939. www.ncbi.nlm.nih.gov/pmc/articles/PMC6493298/pdf/zjma-7-1600939.pdf

19. Mumme M, Wixmerten A, Miot S, et al. Tissue engineering for paediatric patients. *Swiss Med Wkly* 2019; 149: w20032. https://smw.ch/article/doi/smw.2019.20032

20. Rose K, Neubauer D, et al. Comment on: Mumme M et al. Tissue engineering for paediatric patients. *Swiss Med Wkly* 2020 May 26. https://smw.ch/article/doi/smw.2020.20239

21. A Study of MACI in Patients Aged 10 to 17 Years With Symptomatic Chondral or Osteochondral Defects of the Knee (PEAK). https://clinicaltrials.gov/ct2/show/NCT03588975

22. MACI (Autologous Cultured Chondrocytes on a Porcine Collagen Membrane). www.fda.gov/vaccines-blood-biologics/cellular-gene-therapy-products/maci-autologous-cultured-chondrocytes-porcine-collagen-membrane

23. EMA 2012: PIP EMEA-000736-PIP01-09 www.ema.europa.eu/en/documents/pip-decision/p/0022/2012-ema-decision-27-january-2012-agreement-paediatric-investigation-plan-granting-deferral-granting_en.pdf

24. EMA 2018: PIP EMEA-000979-PIP01-10-M02. www.ema.europa.eu/en/documents/pip-decision/p/0012/2018-ema-decision-30-january-2018-acceptance-modification-agreed-paediatric-investigation-plan_en.pdf

25. EMA 2018: PIP EMEA-001264-PIP01-12-M02. www.ema.europa.eu/en/documents/pip-decision/

p/0161/2018-ema-decision-15-june-2018-acceptance-modification-agreed-paediatric-investigation-plan_en.pdf

26. EMA 2019: PIP EMEA-001823-PIP01-15-M01.
www.ema.europa.eu/en/documents/pip-decision/
p/0074/2019-ema-decision-22-march-2019-acceptance-modification-agreed-paediatric-investigation-plan_en.pdf

27. EMA 2018: PIP EMEA-002217-PIP01-17.
www.ema.europa.eu/en/documents/pip-decision/
p/0282/2018-ema-decision-12-september-2018-agreement-paediatric-investigation-plan-granting-waiver_en.pdf

28. Harris JD, Siston RA, Pan X, et al. Autologous Chondrocyte Implantation: a systematic review. *J Bone Joint Surg Am* 2010; 92(12): 2220-2233. http://citeseerx.ist.psu.edu/viewdoc/download?doi=10.1.1.1004.3559&rep=rep1&type=pdf

29. Ruano-Ravina A, Jato Diaz M. Autologous chondrocyte implantation: a systematic review. *Osteoarthritis Cartilage* 2006; 14(1): 47-51.
www.oarsijournal.com/article/S1063-4584(05)00201-3/pdf

30. Kearns GL, Abdel-Rahman SM, Alander SW, Blowey DL, Leeder JS, Kauffman RE. Developmental pharmacology – drug disposition, action, and therapy in infants and children. *N Engl J Med* 2003; 349(12): 1157-1167 https://pdfs.semanticscholar.org/55f8/1745303e9aaec7f4cb85f0b5921eec14a9c0.pdf

31. Beunen GP, Rogol AD, Malina RM. Indicators of biological maturation and secular changes in biological maturation. *Food Nutr Bull* 2006; 27(4 Suppl Growth Standard): S244-S256. https://journals.sagepub.com/doi/pdf/10.1177/15648265060274S508

32. Non-interventional Study With NOVOCART® 3D for the Treatment of Cartilage Defects of the Knee in Pediatric Patients (JUNOVO). https://clinicaltrials.gov/ct2/show/NCT04186208

33. Facing the challenge. The Lisbon strategy for growth and employment. Report from the High Level Group chaired by Wim Kok November 2004. http://ec.europa.eu/research/evaluations/pdf/archive/fp6-evidence-base/evaluation_studies_and_reports/evaluation_studies_and_reports_2004/the_lisbon_strategy_for_growth_and_employment_report_from_the_high_level_group.pdf

Chapter 10: Perinatal depression

1. Guille C, Newman R, Fryml LD, et al. Management of postpartum depression. *J Midwifery Womens Health* 2013; 58(6): 643-653. www.ncbi.nlm.nih.gov/pmc/articles/PMC4101986/pdf/nihms511665.pdf

2. Rafferty J, Mattson G, Earls MF, et al. Incorporating Recognition and Management of Perinatal Depression Into Pediatric Practice. *Pediatrics* 2019; 143(1): e20183260.
https://pediatrics.aappublications.org/content/pediatrics/143/1/e20183260.full.pdf

3. Galea LAM, Frokjaer VG. Perinatal Depression: Embracing Variability toward Better Treatment and Outcomes. *Neuron* 2019; 102(1): 13-16. www.cell.com/action/showPdf?pii=S0896-6273%2819%2930158-8

4. Pearlstein T, Howard M, Salisbury A, et al. Postpartum depression. *Am J Obstet Gynecol* 2009; 200(4): 357-364. www.ncbi.nlm.nih.gov/pmc/articles/PMC3918890/pdf/nihms310333.pdf

5. Wikipedia: Postpartum Depression.
https://en.wikipedia.org/wiki/Postpartum_depression

6. Beunen GP, Rogol AD, Malina RM. Indicators of biological maturation and secular changes in biological maturation. *Food Nutr Bull* 2006; 27(4 Suppl Growth Standard): S244-S256. https://journals.sagepub.com/doi/pdf/10.1177/15648265060274S508

7. Fortenberry JD. Puberty and adolescent sexuality. *Horm Behav* 2013; 64(2): 280-287. www.ncbi.nlm.nih.gov/pmc/articles/PMC3761219/pdf/nihms460231.pdf

8. Ademiluka 2018 Patriarchy & Women Abuse. www.researchgate.net/publication/329381622_Patriarchy_and_Women_Abuse_Perspectives_from_Ancient_Israel_and_Africa

9. Rawat PS. Patriarchal Beliefs, Women's Empowerment, and General Well-Being. *VIKALPA* 2014; 39(2). https://journals.sagepub.com/doi/pdf/10.1177/0256090920140206

10. Ruggles S. Patriarchy, Power, and Pay: The Transformation of American Families, 1800–2015. *Demography* 2015; 52(6): 1797–1823. www.ncbi.nlm.nih.gov/pmc/articles/PMC5068828/pdf/nihms734181.pdf

11. Clinicaltrials.gov NCT03665038. A Study to Assess the Safety of Brexanolone in the Treatment of Adolescent Female Participants With Postpartum Depression (PPD). www.clinicaltrials.gov/ct2/show/NCT03665038?recrs=a&cond=Postpartum+Depression&age=0&fund=2&draw=2&rank=1

12. Wikipedia: Allopregnanolone. https://en.wikipedia.org/wiki/Allopregnanolone

13. FDA Briefing Document. Psychopharmacologic Drugs Advisory Committee (PDAC) and Drug Safety and Risk Management (DSaRM) Advisory Committee Meeting. November 2, 2018. Topic: New Drug Application 211371/New Drug Application, brexanolone for the Treatment of Postpartum Depression. www.fda.gov/media/121345/download

14. FDA 2010: Brexanolone prescribing information. www.accessdata.fda.gov/drugsatfda_docs/label/2019/211371lbl.pdf

15. Kanes SJ, Colquhoun H, Doherty J, et al. Open-label, proof-of-concept study of brexanolone in the treatment of severe postpartum depression. *Hum Psychopharmacol* 2017; 32(2): e2576. www.ncbi.nlm.nih.gov/pmc/articles/PMC5396368/pdf/HUP-32-na.pdf

16. Brexanolone/ allopregnanolone PIP EMEA-002051-PIP02-16. www.ema.europa.eu/en/documents/pip-decision/p/0357/2017-ema-decision-1-december-2017-agreement-paediatric-investigation-plan-granting-deferral-granting_en.pdf

17. Rose K, Neubauer D, Grant-Kels JM. Rational Use of Medicine in Children – The Conflict of Interests Story. A Review. *Rambam Maimonides Med J* 2019; 10(3): e0018. doi:10.5041/RMMJ.10371. www.rmmj.org.il/userimages/928/2/PublishFiles/953Article.pdf

18. Rose K, Grant-Kels JM. The Meanings of "Pediatric Drug Development". A Review. *Ther Innov Regul Sci* 2019; 53(6): 767-774.

19. Rose K, Neubauer D, Grant-Kels JM. Too many avoidable suicides occur worldwide in young patients. *Rambam Maimonides Med J* 2019; 10(4). www.ncbi.nlm.nih.gov/pmc/articles/PMC6824826/pdf/rmmj-10-4-e0026.pdf

20. Rose K. The Challenges of Pediatric Drug Development. *Curr Ther Res Clin Exp* 2019; xx: xxx-xxx. https://doi.org/10.1016/j. curtheres.2019.01.007

21. Ward RM, Benjamin DK Jr, Davis JM, Gorman RL, Kauffman R, Kearns GL, et al.The Need for Pediatric Drug Development. *J Pediatr* 2018; 192: 13-21.

Chapter 11: Pain relief

1. Woolf CJ. What is this thing called pain? *J Clin Invest* 2010; 120(11): 3742-3744. www.ncbi.nlm.nih.gov/pmc/articles/PMC2965006/ pdf/JCI45178.pdf

2. Wikipedia: Pain. https://en.wikipedia.org/wiki/Pain

3. O'Donnell FT, Rosen KR. Pediatric pain management: a review. *Mo Med* 2014; 111(3): 231-237. www.ncbi.nlm.nih.gov/pmc/articles/ PMC6179554/pdf/ms111_p0231.pdf

4. Wikipedia: Pain management in children. https://en.wikipedia.org/wiki/Pain_management_in_children

5. Unruh AM, McGrath PJ. History of pain in children. In: McGrath P, Stevens B, Walker S, Zempsky W (Editors). *Oxford Textbook of Paediatric Pain*. Oxford, UK: Oxford University Press; 2014: chapter 1, pp 3-11.

6. Sunny Wei 2016. Neonatal Anesthesia – The Origins Of Controversy. www.mcgill.ca/library/files/library/wei_sunny_2016.pdf

7. Wikipedia: History of General Anesthesia. https://en.wikipedia.org/wiki/History_of_general_anesthesia

8. AAP 1987. American Academy of Pediatrics: Neonatal Anesthesia. *Pediatrics* 1987; 80(3): 446. https://pediatrics.aappublications.org/ content/pediatrics/80/3/446.full.pdf

9. AAP 2000. Prevention and management of pain and stress in the neonate. American Academy of Pediatrics. Committee on Fetus and Newborn. Committee on Drugs. Section on Anesthesiology. Section on Surgery. Canadian Paediatric Society. Fetus and Newborn Committee. *Pediatrics* 2000; 105(2): 454-461. https://pediatrics.aappublications.org/content/ pediatrics/105/2/454.full.pdf

10. Wikipedia: Laudanum https://en.wikipedia.org/wiki/Laudanum

References

11. Levy S. Youth and the Opioid Epidemic. *Pediatrics* 2019; 143(2): e20182752. https://pediatrics.aappublications.org/content/pediatrics/143/2/e20182752.full.pdf

12. Opioids for cancer-related pain in children and adolescents. Wiffen PJ, Cooper TE, Anderson AK, et al. *Cochrane Database Syst Rev* 2017; 7(7): CD012564. www.ncbi.nlm.nih.gov/pmc/articles/PMC6484393/pdf/CD012564.pdf

13. Cooper TE, Fisher E, Gray AL, et al. Opioids for chronic non-cancer pain in children and adolescents. *Cochrane Database Syst Rev* 2017; 7(7): CD012538. www.ncbi.nlm.nih.gov/pmc/articles/PMC6477875/pdf/CD012538.pdf

14. Vashishtha D, Mittal ML, Werb D. The North American opioid epidemic: current challenges and a call for treatment as prevention. *Harm Reduct J* 2017; 14(1): 7.

15. Manchikanti L, Helm S 2nd, Fellows B, et al. Opioid epidemic in the United States. *Pain Physician* 2012; 15(3 Suppl): ES9-ES38. www.painphysicianjournal.com/current/pdf?article=MTcwNA%3D%3D&journal=68

16. Jones MR, Viswanath O, Peck J, A Brief History of the Opioid Epidemic and Strategies for Pain Medicine. *Pain Ther* 2018; 7(1): 13-21. www.ncbi.nlm.nih.gov/pmc/articles/PMC5993682/pdf/40122_2018_Article_97.pdf

17. Rose K. *Considering the Patient in Pediatric Drug Development. How good intentions turned into harm.* Elsevier, London, 2020. www.elsevier.com/books/considering-the-patient-in-pediatric-drug-development/rose/978-0-12-823888-2

18. Rose K, Neubauer D, Grant-Kels JM. Rational Use of Medicine in Children – The Conflict of Interests Story. A Review. *Rambam Maimonides Med J* 2019; 10(3): e0018. www.ncbi.nlm.nih.gov/ pmc/articles/PMC6649781/pdf/rmmj-10-3-e0018.pdf

19. Rose K. The Challenges of Pediatric Drug Development. *Curr Ther Res Clin Exp* 2019; 90: 128-134. https://doi.org/10.1016/j.curtheres.2019.01.007

20. Sun H, Temeck JW, Chambers W, et al. Extrapolation of Efficacy in Pediatric Drug Development and Evidence-based Medicine: Progress and Lessons Learned. *Ther Innov Regul Sci* 2017; 2017:

1-7. www.ncbi.nlm.nih.gov/pmc/articles/PMC5587157/pdf/nihms901908.pdf

21. Berde CB, Walco GA, Krane EJ, et al. Pediatric analgesic clinical trial designs, measures, and extrapolation: report of an FDA scientific workshop. *Pediatrics* 2012; 129(2): 354-364.

22. Hertz S 2016. Analgesic Developments for Pediatric Patients. www.fda.gov/downloads/AdvisoryCommittees/CommitteesMeetingMaterials/PediatricAdvisoryCommittee/UCM495096.pdf

23. FDA 2008. Tapentadol prescribing information. www.accessdata.fda.gov/drugsatfda_docs/label/2010/022304s003lbl.pdf

24. FDA 2011. Diclofenac prescribing information. www.accessdata.fda.gov/drugsatfda_docs/label/2011/019201s039s040lbl.pdf

25. EMA 2013. PIP Cebranopadol EMEA-001305-PIP01-12. www.ema.europa.eu/en/documents/pip-decision/p/0145/2013-ema-decision-3-july-2013on-agreement-paediatric-investigation-plan-granting-deferral-granting_en.pdf

26. EMA 2011. Rizatriptan EMEA-000084-PIP02-10. www.ema.europa.eu/en/documents/pip-decision/p/27/2011-ema-decision-28-january-2011on-agreement-paediatric-investigation-plan-granting-deferral_en.pdf

27. EMA 2011. Telcagepant EMEA-000274-PIP01-08-M01. www.ema.europa.eu/en/documents/pip-decision/p/44/2011-ema-decision-3-march-2011-acceptance-modification-agreed-paediatric-investigation-plan/2006-eur_en.pdf

28. EMA 2015. Naloxone EMEA-001567-PIP01-13-M01. www.ema.europa.eu/en/documents/pip-decision/p/0219/2015-ema-decision-2-october-2015-acceptance-modification-agreed-paediatric-investigation-plan_en.pdf

29. EMA 2017. PIP Tapentadol EMEA-000018-PIP01-07-M14. www.ema.europa.eu/en/documents/pip-decision/p/0355/2017-ema-decision-1-december-2017-acceptance-modification-agreed-paediatric-investigation-plan_en.pdf

30. EMA 2019. Fentanyl PIP EMEA-001509-PIP01-13-M02 www.ema.europa.eu/en/documents/pip-decision/p/0237/2019-ema-decision-16-july-2019-acceptance-modification-agreed-paediatric-investigation-plan-fentanyl_en.pdf

Chapter 12: Attention-deficit hyperactivity disorder (ADHD)

1. Gaidamowicz R, Deksnytė A, Palinauskaitė K, et al. ADHD – the scourge of the 21st century? *Psychiatr Pol* 2018; 52(2): 287-307. http://psychiatriapolska.pl/uploads/images/PP_2_2018/ENGver287Gaidamowicz_PsychiatrPol2018v52i2.pdf

2. Mahone EM, Denckla MB. Attention-Deficit/Hyperactivity Disorder: A Historical Neuropsychological Perspective. *J Int Neuropsychol Soc* 2017; 23(9-10): 916-929. www.ncbi.nlm.nih.gov/pmc/articles/PMC5724393/pdf/nihms924361.pdf

3. Franke B, Michelini G, Asherson P, et al. Live fast, die young? A review on the developmental trajectories of ADHD across the lifespan. *Eur Neuropsychopharmacol* 2018; 28(10): 1059-1088. www.ncbi.nlm.nih.gov/pmc/articles/PMC6379245/?report=printable

4. Wikipedia: Attention deficit hyperactivity disorder. https://en.wikipedia.org/wiki/Attention_deficit_hyperactivity_disorder

5. Wikipedia: Attention deficit hyperactivity disorder controversies. https://en.wikipedia.org/wiki/Attention_deficit_hyperactivity_disorder_controversies#Concerns_about_medication

6. Thapar A, Cooper M, Eyre O, et al. What have we learnt about the causes of ADHD? *J Child Psychol Psychiatry* 2013; 54(1): 3-16. www.ncbi.nlm.nih.gov/pmc/articles/PMC3572580/pdf/jcpp0054-0003.pdf

7. Matthews M, Nigg JT, Fair DA. Attention deficit hyperactivity disorder. *Curr Top Behav Neurosci* 2014; 16: 235-266. www.ncbi.nlm.nih.gov/pmc/articles/PMC4079001/pdf/nihms588714.pdf

8. Manos MJ, Giuliano K, Geyer E. ADHD: Overdiagnosed and overtreated, or misdiagnosed and mistreated? *Cleve Clin J Med* 2017; 84(11): 873-880. www.ccjm.org/content/84/11/873.long

9. Manos MJ. Pharmacologic treatment of ADHD: road conditions in driving patients to successful outcomes. *Medscape J Med* 2008; 10(1): 5. www.ncbi.nlm.nih.gov/pmc/articles/PMC2258464/

10. Cohen EF, Morley CP. Children, ADHD, and Citizenship. *J Med Philos* 2009; 34(2): 155-180. www.ncbi.nlm.nih.gov/pmc/articles/PMC3916736/pdf/jhp013.pdf

11. Ogundele MO. Behavioural and emotional disorders in childhood: A brief overview for paediatricians. *World J Clin Pediatr* 2018; 7(1):

9-26. www.ncbi.nlm.nih.gov/pmc/articles/PMC5803568/pdf/ WJCP-7-9.pdf

12. Wikipedia Albert Einstein https://en.wikipedia.org/wiki/ Albert_Einstein

13. NHS Symptoms Attention Deficit Hyperactivity Disorder. www. nhs.uk/conditions/attention-deficit-hyperactivity-disorder-adhd/symptoms/

14. Centers for Disease Control and Prevention (CDC). Attention Deficit Hyperactivity Disorder (ADHD). Symptoms and Diagnosis of ADHD. www.cdc.gov/ncbddd/adhd/diagnosis. html

15. Banaschweski T, Becker K, Döpfner M, et al. Attention-Deficit/ Hyperactivity Disorder. *Dtsch Arztebl Int* 2017; 114(9): 149-159. www.ncbi.nlm.nih.gov/pmc/articles/PMC5378980/pdf/ Dtsch_Arztebl_Int-114-0149.pdf

16. Keen D, Hadijikoumi I. ADHD in children and adolescents. *BMJ Clin Evid* 2011; 2011: 0312. www.ncbi.nlm.nih.gov/pmc/articles/ PMC3217800/pdf/2011-0312.pdf

17. American Academy of Pediatrics (AAP) 2011: ADHD: clinical practice guideline for the diagnosis, evaluation, and treatment of attention-deficit/hyperactivity disorder in children and adolescents. *Pediatrics* 2011; 128(5): 1007-1022. www.ncbi.nlm.nih. gov/pmc/articles/PMC4500647/pdf/nihms701937.pdf

18. FDA 1986 Guanfacine (INTUNIV®) Prescribing Information. www.accessdata.fda.gov/drugsatfda_docs/ label/2013/022037s009lbl.pdf

19. FDA 2013: Guanfacine (Tenex®) Prescribing Information www.accessdata.fda.gov/drugsatfda_docs/ label/2013/019032s021lbl.pdf

20. FDA Guanfacine Original Written Request www.fda.gov/files/ drugs/published/N022037-Guanfacine-Original_WR.pdf

21. EMA PIP EMEA-000745-PIP01-09-M03 Guanfacine for ADHD. www.ema.europa.eu/en/documents/pip-decision/ p/0265/2013-ema-decision-30-october-2013-acceptance-modification-agreed-paediatric-investigation-plan_en.pdf

22. NCT04085172: A Study to Assess the Safety and Efficacy of Guanfacine Hydrochloride Prolonged Release (SPD503)

in Children and Adolescents Aged 6 to 17 Years With Attentiondeficit/Hyperactivity Disorder (ADHD). https://clinicaltrials.gov/ct2/show/NCT04085172

23. Rose K. *Considering the Patient in Pediatric Drug Development. How good intentions turned into harm.* Elsevier, London, 2020 www.elsevier.com/books/considering-the-patient-in-pediatric-drug-development/rose/978-0-12-823888-2

24. Rose K, Neubauer D, Grant-Kels JM. Rational Use of Medicine in Children – The Conflict of Interests Story. A Review. *Rambam Maimonides Med J* 2019; 10(3): e0018. www.ncbi.nlm.nih.gov/pmc/articles/PMC6649781/pdf/rmmj-10-3-e0018.pdf

25. Rose K. The Challenges of Pediatric Drug Development. *Curr Ther Res Clin Exp* 2019; 90: 128-134. https://doi.org/10.1016/j.curtheres.2019.01.007

Chapter 13: Inflammatory skin diseases

1. Richmond JM, Harris JE. Immunology and skin in health and disease. *Cold Spring Harb Perspect Med* 2014; 4(12): a015339. www.ncbi.nlm.nih.gov/pmc/articles/PMC4292093/pdf/cshperspectmed-SKN-a015339.pdf

2. Hu MS, Borelli MR, Hong WX. Embryonic skin development and repair. *Organogenesis* 2018; 14(1): 46-63. www.ncbi.nlm.nih.gov/pmc/articles/PMC6150059/pdf/kogg-14-01-1421882.pdf

3. Lynn DD, Umari T, Dunnick CA, et al. The epidemiology of acne vulgaris in late adolescence. *Adolesc Health Med Ther* 2016; 7: 13-25. www.ncbi.nlm.nih.gov/pmc/articles/PMC4769025/pdf/ahmt-7-013.pdf

4. Purdy S, de Berker D. Acne vulgaris. *BMJ Clin Evid* 2011; 2011: 1714. www.ncbi.nlm.nih.gov/pmc/articles/PMC3275168/pdf/2011-1714.pdf

5. Ogé LK, Broussard A, Marshall MD. Acne Vulgaris: Diagnosis and Treatment. *Am Fam Physician* 2019; 100(8): 475-484. www.aafp.org/afp/2019/1015/afp20191015p475.pdf

6. Psomadakis CE, Han G. New and Emerging Topical Therapies for Psoriasis and Atopic Dermatitis. *J Clin Aesthet Dermatol*

2019; 12(12): 28-34. www.ncbi.nlm.nih.gov/pmc/articles/ PMC7002051/pdf/jcad_12_12_28.pdf

7. Schneider L, Hanifin J, Boguniewicz M, et al. Study of the atopic march: development of atopic comorbidities. *Pediatr Dermatol* 2016; 33: 388-398. www.ncbi.nlm.nih.gov/pmc/articles/ PMC5649252/pdf/nihms912001.pdf

8. Deleanu D, Nedelea I. Biological therapies for atopic dermatitis: An update. *Exp Ther Med* 2019; 17(2): 1061–1067. www.ncbi.nlm.nih. gov/pmc/articles/PMC6327672/pdf/etm-17-02-1061.pdf

9. Kraft MT, Prince BT. Atopic Dermatitis Is a Barrier Issue, Not an Allergy Issue. *Immunol Allergy Clin North Am* 2019; 39(4): 507-519.

10. de la O-Escamilla NO, Sidbury R. Atopic Dermatitis: Update on Pathogenesis and Therapy. *Pediatr Ann* 2020; 49(3): e140-e146.

11. Korman NJ. Management of psoriasis as a systemic disease: what is the evidence? *Br J Dermatol* 2020; 182(4): 840-848. www.ncbi.nlm. nih.gov/pmc/articles/PMC7187293/pdf/BJD-182-840.pdf

12. Kamata M, Tada Y. Efficacy and Safety of Biologics for Psoriasis and Psoriatic Arthritis and Their Impact on Comorbidities: A Literature Review. *Int J Mol Sci* 2020; 21(5): 1690. www.ncbi.nlm. nih.gov/pmc/articles/PMC7084606/pdf/ijms-21-01690.pdf

13. Limmer AL, Nwannunu CE, Patel RR, et al. Management of Ichthyosis: A Brief Review. *Skin Therapy Lett* 2020; 25(1): 5-7. www.skintherapyletter.com/ichthyoses/management-ichthyosis-review/

14. AAP 1995: Guidelines for the Ethical Conduct of Studies to Evaluate Drugs in Pediatric Populations, Committee on Drugs. *Pediatrics* 1995; 95(2): 286-294.

15. Rose K. The Challenges of Pediatric Drug Development. *Curr Ther Res Clin Exp* 2019; 90: 128-134. https://doi.org/10.1016/j.curtheres.2019.01.007

16. Rose K, Neubauer D, Grant-Kels JM. Rational Use of Medicine in Children – The Conflict of Interests Story. A Review. *Rambam Maimonides Med J* 2019; 10(3): e0018. doi:10.5041/RMMJ.10371. www.rmmj.org.il/userimages/928/2/PublishFiles/953Article. pdf

17. Rose K. *Considering the Patient in Pediatric Drug Development. How good intentions turned into harm.* Elsevier, London, 2021

www.elsevier.com/books/considering-the-patient-in-pediatric-drug-development/rose/978-0-12-823888-2

18. Shirkey H. Therapeutic Orphans. *J Pediatr* 1968; 72 (1), 119-120. https://pdfs.semanticscholar.org/f1cb/acdbac19fa56236b919fb7799eaacaa10c77.pdf

19. Thomsen MDT. Global Pediatric Drug Development. *Curr Ther Res Clin Exp* 2019; 90: 135-142. www.ncbi.nlm.nih.gov/pmc/articles/PMC6677570/pdf/main.pdf

20. Mulugeta YL, Zajicek A, Barrett J, et al. Development of Drug Therapies for Newborns and Children: The Scientific and Regulatory Imperatives. *Pediatr Clin North Am* 2017 ; 64(6): 1185-1196. www.ncbi.nlm.nih.gov/pmc/articles/PMC5765998/pdf/nihms931910.pdf

21. Kearns GL, Abdel-Rahman SM, Alander SW, Blowey DL, Leeder JS, Kauffman RE. Developmental pharmacology – drug disposition, action, and therapy in infants and children. *N Engl J Med* 2003; 349(12): 1157-1167. https://pdfs.semanticscholar.org/55f8/1745303e9aaec7f4cb85f0b5921eec14a9c0.pdf

22. Beunen GP, Rogol AD, Malina RM. Indicators of biological maturation and secular changes in biological maturation. *Food Nutr Bull* 2006; 27(4 Suppl Growth Standard): S244-S256. https://journals.sagepub.com/doi/pdf/10.1177/15648265060274S508

23. FDA 2016. Crisaborole label. www.accessdata.fda.gov/drugsatfda_docs/label/2016/207695s000lbl.pdf

24. EMA 2019. Adalimumab PIP EMEA-000366-PIP02-09-M06. www.ema.europa.eu/en/documents/pip-decision/p/0174/2019-ema-decision-15-may-2019-acceptance-modification-agreed-paediatric-investigation-plan_en.pdf

25. Study of Ixekizumab (LY2439821) in Children 6 to Less Than 18 Years With Moderate-to-Severe Plaque Psoriasis (Ixora-peds). https://clinicaltrials.gov/ct2/show/NCT03073200

26. A Study of Tildrakizumab in Pediatric Subjects with Chronic Plaque Psoriasis. https://clinicaltrials.gov/ct2/show/NCT03997786

27. An Open-label, Single-dose Study to Evaluate Safety, Tolerability, and Pharmacokinetics of Brodalumab in Pediatric Subjects. https://clinicaltrials.gov/ct2/show/NCT03240809

28. Tralokinumab Monotherapy for Adolescent Subjects with Moderate to Severe Atopic Dermatitis – ECZTRA 6 (ECZema TRAlokinumab Trial no. 6). https://clinicaltrials.gov/ct2/show/NCT03526861

29. EMA 2010. Clindamycin PIP EMEA-000532-PIP01-0 www.ema.europa.eu/en/documents/pip-decision/p/87/2010-european-medicines-agency-decision-1-june-2010-agreement-paediatric-investigation-plan-granting/bituminosulphonate-sodium-emea-000532-pip0_en.pdf

30. EMA 2017.Trifarotene PIP EMEA-001492-PIP01-13-M01 www.ema.europa.eu/en/documents/pip-decision/p/0099/2017-ema-decision-11-april-2017-acceptance-modification-agreed-paediatric-investigation-plan_en.pdf

31. EMA 2012. Tazarotene PIP EMEA-000510-PIP02-10-M02. www.ema.europa.eu/en/documents/pip-decision/p/0250/2012-ema-decision-24-october-2012-acceptance-modification-agreed-paediatric-investigation-plan_en.pdf

32. EMA 2015. Tazarotene – Notification of discontinuation of a paediatric development which is covered by an agreed PIP Decision. www.ema.europa.eu/en/documents/other/tazarotene-notification-discontinuation-paediatric-development-which-covered-agreed-paediatric_en.pdf

33. FDA 2011. Tazarotene prescription information. www.accessdata.fda.gov/drugsatfda_docs/label/2011/020600s008lbl.pdf

Chapter 14: Juvenile idiopathic arthritis (JIA)

1. Centers for Disease Control and Prevention (CDC) 2016. Arthritis in General. https://web.archive.org/web/20160909205959/http://www.cdc.gov/arthritis/basics/general.htm

2. Wikipedia: Arthritis https://en.wikipedia.org/wiki/Arthritis

3. Wikipedia: Osteoarthritis https://en.wikipedia.org/wiki/Osteoarthritis

4. Wikipedia: Rheumatoid arthritis. https://en.wikipedia.org/wiki/Rheumatoid_arthritis

5. Nigrovic PA, Raychaudhuri S, Thompson SD. Review: Genetics and the Classification of Arthritis in Adults and Children. *Arthritis*

Rheumatol 2018; 70(1): 7-17.
https://onlinelibrary.wiley.com/doi/epdf/10.1002/art.40350

6. Hardin AP, Hackell JM. Committee on Practice and Ambulatory Medicine. Age limit of pediatrics. *Pediatrics* 2017; 140(3): e20172151. https://pediatrics.aappublications.org/content/pediatrics/140/3/e20172151.full.pdf

7. Rose K. *Considering the patient in pediatric drug development. How good intentions turned into harm.* Elsevier, London, 2020. www.elsevier.com/books/considering-the-patient-in-pediatric-drug-development/rose/978-0-12-823888-2 and https://www.sciencedirect.com/book/9780128238882/considering-the-patient-in-pediatric-drug-development

8. Colón AR. *Nurturing Children. A History of Pediatrics.* Westport, CT, USA: Greenwood Press; 1999.

9. Brunner HI, Rider LG, Kingsbury DJ, et al. Pediatric Rheumatology Collaborative Study Group – over four decades of pivotal clinical drug research in pediatric rheumatology. *Pediatr Rheumatol Online J* 2018; 16(1): 45. www.ncbi.nlm.nih.gov/pmc/articles/PMC6042275/pdf/12969_2018_Article_261.pdf

10. Pediatric Rheumatology Collaborative Study Group (PRCSG). www.prcsg.org

11. Paediatric Rheumatology International Trials Organization (PRINTO). www.printo.it

12. *International League of Associations for Rheumatology (ILAR).* www.ilar.org

13. Desborough MJR, Keeling DM. The aspirin story – from willow to wonder drug. *Br J Haematol* 2017; 177(5): 674-683. https://onlinelibrary.wiley.com/doi/epdf/10.1111/bjh.14520

14. Levinson JE, Baum J, Brewer E Jr, et al. Comparison of tolmetin sodium and aspirin in the treatment of juvenile rheumatoid arthritis. *J Pediatr* 1977; 91(5): 799-804.

15. Feger DM, Longson N, Dodanwala H, et al. Comparison of Adults with Polyarticular Juvenile Idiopathic Arthritis to Adults With Rheumatoid Arthritis: A Cross-sectional Analysis of Clinical Features and Medication Use. *J Clin Rheumatol* 2019; 25(4): 163-170. www.ncbi.nlm.nih.gov/pmc/articles/PMC6240403/pdf/rhu-25-163.pdf

16. Lovell DJ, Ruperto N, Giannini EH, Martini A. Advances from clinical trials in juvenile idiopathic arthritis. *Nat Rev Rheumatol* 2013; 9(9): 557-563.

17. Rose K, Tanjinatus O, Ettienne E. The term "Juvenile Idiopathic Arthritis (JIA)" is misleading. It will not be sufficient to just replace this term. Editorial. *Pharmaceut Med* 16 January 2021. https://doi.org/10.1007/s40290-021-00379-8 https://rdcu.be/cdH1x

18. The Brigham and Women's Hospital: Center for Adults with Pediatric Rheumatic Illness (CAPRI). www.brighamandwomens.org/medicine/rheumatology-immunology-allergy/services/pediatric-rheumatology-for-adults

19. Giannini EH, Cawkwell GD. Drug treatment in children with juvenile rheumatoid arthritis. Past, present, and future. *Pediatr Clin North Am* 1995; 42(5): 1099-1125.

20. Wikipedia: Biopharmaceutical. https://en.wikipedia.org/wiki/Biopharmaceutical

21. Wikipedia: Biologics for immunosuppression. https://en.wikipedia.org/wiki/Biologics_for_immunosuppression

22. Liu JK. The history of monoclonal antibody development – Progress, remaining challenges and future innovations. *Ann Med Surg* 2014; 3(4): 113-116. https://reader.elsevier.com/reader/sd/pii/S2049080114000624?token=90A6E71442BE2C923B5B72DD2D6C5FF458BD2DDBAEA958D167B7A07674B3CDF904A53C7895A7100D38756D870310E93A

23. Stoll ML, Cron RQ. Treatment of juvenile idiopathic arthritis: a revolution in care. *Pediatr Rheumatol Online J* 2014; 12: 13. www.ncbi.nlm.nih.gov/pmc/articles/PMC4003520/pdf/1546-0096-12-13.pdf

24. Nigrovic PA 2013 What Adult Rheumatologists Need to Know about Juvenile Arthritis. www.the-rheumatologist.org/article/what-adult-rheumatologists-need-to-know-about-juvenile-arthritis/?singlepage=1&theme=print-friendly

25. Nigrovic PA, White PH. Care of the adult with juvenile rheumatoid arthritis. *Arthritis Rheum* 2006; 55(2): 208-216. https://onlinelibrary.wiley.com/doi/pdf/10.1002/art.21857

26. Healio Rheumatology 2018. Bridging the treatment gap between pediatric, adult rheumatology care. www.healio.com/news/rheumatology/20180821/bridging-the-treatment-gap-between-pediatric-adult-rheumatology-care

27. Shirkey H. Therapeutic orphans. *J Pediatr* 1968; 72(1): 119-120. https://pdfs.semanticscholar.org/f1cb/acdbac19fa56236b919fb7799eaacaa10c77.pdf

28. Ruperto N, Vesely R, Saint-Raymond A, Martini A, for the Paediatric Rheumatology International Trials Organisation (PRINTO). Impact of the European paediatric legislation in paediatric rheumatology: past, present and future. *Ann Rheum Dis* 2013; 72: 1893–1896.

29. Ruperto N, Martini A. Current and future perspectives in the management of juvenile idiopathic arthritis. *Lancet Child Adolesc Health* 2018; 2(5): 360-370.

30. Ruperto N, Eichler I, Herold R, et al. A European Network of Paediatric Research at the European Medicines Agency (Enpr-EMA). *Arch Dis Child* 2012; 97(3): 185-188.

31. Ruperto N, Vesely R, Saint-Raymond A, Martini A, for the Paediatric Rheumatology International Trials Organisation (PRINTO). Impact of the European paediatric legislation in paediatric rheumatology: past, present and future. *Ann Rheum Dis* 2013; 72: 1893–1896.

32. Martini A, Ravelli A, Avcin T, et al. Toward New Classification Criteria for Juvenile Idiopathic Arthritis: First Steps, Pediatric Rheumatology International Trials Organization International Consensus. *J Rheumatol* 2019; 46(2): 190-197. www.jrheum.org/content/jrheum/46/2/190.full.pdf

33. Gram H. The long and winding road in pharmaceutical development of canakinumab from rare genetic autoinflammatory syndromes to myocardial infarction and cancer. *Pharmacol Res* 2019: S1043-6618(18)31983-2. https://reader.elsevier.com/reader/sd/pii/S1043661818319832?token=A6994A4A9579EFFE8C5E11B4E735A08C61A1D579DEBDF679404CD19064C00F22E6A3213D99C400A4D3F1E106DF65EED2

34. Gurung P, Kanneganti TD. Autoinflammatory Skin Disorders: The Inflammasome in Focus. *Trends Mol Med* 2016; 22(7): 545-564.

doi:10.1016/j.molmed.2016.05.003 www.ncbi.nlm.nih.gov/pmc/articles/PMC4925313/pdf/nihms793570.pdf

Chapter 15: Multiple sclerosis

1. Goldenberg MM. Multiple Sclerosis Review. *P&T* 2012; 37(3): 175-184. www.ncbi.nlm.nih.gov/pmc/articles/PMC3351877/pdf/ptj3703175.pdf

2. Wikipedia: Multiple sclerosis. https://en.wikipedia.org/wiki/Multiple_sclerosis

3. Ashwal S, Rust R. Child Neurology in the 20th Century. *Pediatr Res* 2003; 53(2): 345-361.
    www.nature.com/articles/pr2003231.pdf?origin=ppub

4. Pétrin J, Fiander M, Doss PMIA, et al. A Scoping Review of Modifiable Risk Factors in Pediatric Onset Multiple Sclerosis: Building for the Future. *Children* 2018; 5(11): 146. www.ncbi.nlm.nih.gov/pmc/articles/PMC6262383/pdf/children-05-00146.pdf

5. Fisher KS, Cuascut FX, Rivera VM, et al. Current Advances in Pediatric Onset Multiple Sclerosis. *Biomedicines* 2020; 8(4): 71. www.ncbi.nlm.nih.gov/pmc/articles/PMC7235875/pdf/biomedicines-08-00071.pdf

6. McGinley M, Rossman IT. Bringing the HEET: The Argument for High-Efficacy Early Treatment for Pediatric-Onset Multiple Sclerosis. Neurotherapeutics. 2017; 14(4): 985-998. www.ncbi.nlm.nih.gov/pmc/articles/PMC5722772/pdf/13311_2017_Article_568.pdf

7. Sikes EM, Motl RW, Ness JM. Pediatric multiple sclerosis: current perspectives on health behaviors. *Pediatric Health Med Ther* 2018; 9: 17-25. www.ncbi.nlm.nih.gov/pmc/articles/PMC5863894/pdf/phmt-9-017.pdf

8. Alroughani R, Boyko A. Pediatric multiple sclerosis: a review. *BMC Neurol* 2018; 18(1): 27. www.ncbi.nlm.nih.gov/pmc/articles/PMC5845207/pdf/12883_2018_Article_1026.pdf

9. Rose K, Neubauer D, Grant-Kels JM. Rational Use of Medicine in Children – The Conflict of Interests Story. A Review. *Rambam Maimonides Med J* 2019; 10(3): e0018. Review. doi:10.5041/

RMMJ.10371. www.rmmj.org.il/userimages/928/2/PublishFiles/953Article.pdf

10. Rose K, Mueller T. Children with Multiple Sclerosis Should Not Become Therapeutic Hostages. *Ther Adv Neurol Disord* 2016; 9(5): 389–395. www.ncbi.nlm.nih.gov/pmc/articles/PMC4994785/pdf/10.1177_1756285616656592.pdf

11. Rose K. The Challenges of Pediatric Drug Development. *Curr Ther Res Clin Exp* 2019; 90: 128-134. https://doi.org/10.1016/j.curtheres.2019.01.007

12. Rose K. *Considering the Patient in Pediatric Drug Development. How good intentions turned into harm.* Elsevier, London, 2021 www.elsevier.com/books/considering-the-patient-in-pediatric-drug-development/rose/978-0-12-823888-2

13. Beunen GP, Rogol AD, Malina RM. Indicators of biological maturation and secular changes in biological maturation. *Food Nutr Bull* 2006; 27(4 Suppl Growth Standard): S244-S456. https://journals.sagepub.com/doi/pdf/10.1177/15648265060274S508

14. Henze T, Rieckmann P, Toyka KV. Symptomatic Treatment of Multiple Sclerosis Multiple Sclerosis Therapy Consensus Group (MSTCG) of the German Multiple Sclerosis Society. *Eur Neurol* 2006; 56: 78–105. www.karger.com/Article/PDF/95699

15. Wikipedia: Biopharmaceutical: https://en.wikipedia.org/wiki/Biopharmaceutical

16. Wikipedia: Biologics for immunosuppression https://en.wikipedia.org/wiki/Biologics_for_immunosuppression

17. FDA 2020. Ozanimod (zeposia) approval package including approval letter. www.accessdata.fda.gov/drugsatfda_docs/nda/2020/209899Orig1s000Approv.pdf

18. EMA 2019. Ocrelizumab PIP EMEA-000310-PIP03-10-M03. www.ema.europa.eu/en/documents/pip-decision/p/0028/2019-ema-decision-29-january-2019-acceptance-modification-agreed-paediatric-investigation-plan_en.pdf

19. Pellock JM, Arzimanoglou A, D'Cruz O, et al. Extrapolating evidence of antiepileptic drug efficacy in adults to children ≥2 years of age with focal seizures: The case for disease similarity. *Epilepsia* 2017; 58(10): 1686-1696. https://onlinelibrary.wiley.com/doi/epdf/10.1111/epi.13859

20. Wadsworth I, Jaki T, Sills GJ, et al. Clinical Drug Development in Epilepsy Revisited: A Proposal for a New Paradigm Streamlined Using Extrapolation. *CNS Drugs* 2016; 30(11): 1011–1017. www.ncbi.nlm.nih.gov/pmc/articles/PMC5078157/pdf/40263_2016_Article_383.pdf

21. Waubant E, Banwell B, Wassmer E, et al. Clinical trials of disease-modifying agents in pediatric MS. *Neurology* 2019; 92(22): e2538-e2549. https://n.neurology.org/content/neurology/92/22/e2538.full.pdf

22. IPMSSG http://ipmssg.org/professionals/

23. A Study of NeuroVax™, a Novel Therapeutic TCR Peptide Vaccine for Pediatric Multiple Sclerosis. https://clinicaltrials.gov/ct2/show/NCT02200718

24. Safety and Efficacy of Fingolimod in Pediatric Patients With Multiple Sclerosis. https://clinicaltrials.gov/ct2/show/NCT01892722

25. Study to Evaluate the Efficacy and Safety of Dimethyl Fumarate (Tecfidera) and Peginterferon Beta-1a (Plegridy) for the Treatment of Relapsing-Remitting Multiple Sclerosis in Pediatric Participants. https://clinicaltrials.gov/ct2/show/NCT03870763

26. Phase 3 Efficacy and Safety Study of BG00012 in Pediatric Subjects With Relapsing-remitting Multiple Sclerosis (RRMS) (CONNECT). https://clinicaltrials.gov/ct2/show/NCT02283853

27. A Study to Evaluate Efficacy, Safety, and Tolerability of Alemtuzumab in Pediatric Patients With RRMS With Disease Activity on Prior DMT (LemKids). https://clinicaltrials.gov/ct2/show/NCT03368664

28. A Study of Ocrelizumab in Children and Adolescents with Relapsing-Remitting Multiple Sclerosis. https://clinicaltrials.gov/ct2/show/NCT04075266

29. Efficacy, Safety and Pharmacokinetics of Teriflunomide in Pediatric Patients with Relapsing Forms of Multiple Sclerosis (TERIKIDS). https://clinicaltrials.gov/ct2/show/NCT02201108

30. A Study to Evaluate the Safety, Tolerability, and Efficacy of BIIB017 (Peginterferon Beta-1a) in Pediatric Participants for the Treatment of Relapsing-Remitting Multiple Sclerosis. https://clinicaltrials.gov/ct2/show/NCT03958877

31. Thomsen MDT. Global Pediatric Drug Development. *Curr Ther Res Clin Exp* 2019; 90: 135-142. www.ncbi.nlm.nih.gov/pmc/articles/PMC6677570/pdf/main.pdf

Chapter 16: COVID-19

1. García LF. Immune Response, Inflammation, and the Clinical Spectrum of COVID-19. *Front Immunol* 2020; 11: 1441. www.ncbi.nlm.nih.gov/pmc/articles/PMC7308593/pdf/fimmu-11-01441.pdf

2. Pascarella G, Strumia A, Piliego C, et al. COVID-19 diagnosis and management: a comprehensive review. *J Intern Med* 2020; 288(2): 192-206. www.ncbi.nlm.nih.gov/pmc/articles/PMC7267177/pdf/JOIM-9999-na.pdf

3. Wikipedia: Coronavirus disease 2019. https://en.wikipedia.org/wiki/Coronavirus_disease_2019

4. Zimmermann P, Curtis N. Coronavirus Infections in Children Including COVID-19: An Overview of the Epidemiology, Clinical Features, Diagnosis, Treatment and Prevention Options in Children. *Pediatr Infect Dis J* 2020; 39(5): 355-368. www.ncbi.nlm.nih.gov/pmc/articles/PMC7158880/pdf/inf-39-355.pdf

5. Zimmermann P, Curtis N. COVID-19 in Children, Pregnancy and Neonates: A Review of Epidemiologic and Clinical Features. *Pediatr Infect Dis J* 2020; 39(6): 469-477. www.ncbi.nlm.nih.gov/pmc/articles/PMC7363381/pdf/inf-39-469.pdf

6. Naja M, Wedderburn L, Ciurtin C. COVID-19 infection in children and adolescents. *Br J Hosp Med* 2020; 81(8): 1-10. www.magonlinelibrary.com/doi/pdfplus/10.12968/hmed.2020.0321

7. Ciuca IM. COVID-19 in Children: An Ample Review. *Risk Manag Healthcare Policy* 2020; 13: 661-669. www.ncbi.nlm.nih.gov/pmc/articles/PMC7334563/pdf/rmhp-13-661.pdf

8. Zhou MY, Xie XL, Peng YG, et al. From SARS to COVID-19: What we have learned about children infected with COVID-19. *Int J Infect Dis* 2020; 96: 710-714. www.ncbi.nlm.nih.gov/pmc/articles/PMC7204709/pdf/main.pdf

9. Dhochak N, Singhal T, Kabra SK, et al. Pathophysiology of COVID-19: Why Children Fare Better than Adults? *Indian J Pediatr* 2020; 87(7): 537-546. www.ncbi.nlm.nih.gov/pmc/articles/PMC7221011/pdf/12098_2020_Article_3322.pdf

10. Balasubramanian S, Rao NM, Goenka A, et al. Coronavirus Disease 2019 (COVID-19) in Children – What We Know So Far and What We Do Not. *Indian Pediatr* 2020; 57(5): 435-442. www.ncbi.nlm.nih.gov/pmc/articles/PMC7240240/pdf/13312_2020_Article_1819.pdf

11. Riphagen S, Gomez X, Gonzalez-Martinez C, et al. Hyperinflammatory shock in children during COVID-19 pandemic. *Lancet* 2020; 395(10237): 1607-1608. www.ncbi.nlm.nih.gov/pmc/articles/PMC7204765/pdf/main.pdf

12. Verdoni L, Mazza A, Gervasoni A, et al. An outbreak of severe Kawasaki-like disease at the Italian epicentre of the SARS-CoV-2 epidemic: an observational cohort study. *Lancet* 2020; 395(10239): 1771-1778. www.ncbi.nlm.nih.gov/pmc/articles/PMC7220177/pdf/main.pdf

13. US Centers for Disease Control and Prevention (CDC) 2020: Kawasaki Syndrome www.cdc.gov/kawasaki/index.html

14. US Centers for Disease Control and Prevention (CDC) Health Alert Network (HAN) May 14, 2020: HAN00432. Multisystem Inflammatory Syndrome in Children (MIS-C) Associated with Coronavirus Disease 2019 (COVID-19). https://emergency.cdc.gov/han/2020/han00432.asp

15. American Academy of Pediatrics (AAP) 2020. Multisystem Inflammatory Syndrome in Children (MIS-C) Interim Guidance. https://services.aap.org/.en/pages/2019-novel-coronavirus-covid-19-infections/clinical-guidance/multisystem-inflammatory-syndrome-in-children-mis-c-interim-guidance/

16. US National Library of Medicine PubMed https://pubmed.ncbi.nlm.nih.gov/

17. Wikipedia PubMed https://en.wikipedia.org/wiki/PubMed

18. Morris SB, Schwartz NG, Patel P, et al. Case Series of Multisystem Inflammatory Syndrome in Adults Associated with SARS-CoV-2 Infection – United Kingdom and United States, March-August 2020. *MMWR Morb Mortal Wkly Rep* 2020; 69(40): 1450-1456.

19. Theoharides TC, Conti P. COVID-19 and Multisystem Inflammatory Syndrome, or is it Mast Cell Activation Syndrome? *J Biol Regul Homeost Agents* 2020; 34(5): 1633-1636.

20. CDC MIS-A website. www.cdc.gov/mis-c/mis-a.html

21. Icenogle T. COVID-19: Infection or Autoimmunity. *Front Immunol* 2020; 11: 2055. www.ncbi.nlm.nih.gov/pmc/articles/PMC7518086/pdf/fimmu-11-02055.pdf

22. Giamarellos-Bourboulis EJ, Netea MG, Rovina N, et al. Complex Immune Dysregulation in COVID-19 Patients with Severe Respiratory Failure. *Cell Host Microbe* 2020; 27(6): 992-1000.e3.

23. FDA 2020. Remdesivir prescribing information. www.accessdata.fda.gov/drugsatfda_docs/label/2020/214787Orig1s000lbl.pdf

24. FDA 2020: Fact Sheet For Healthcare Providers. Emergency Use Authorization (EUA) Of Veklury® (Remdesivir) For Hospitalized Pediatric Patients Weighing 3.5 Kg To Less Than 40 Kg or hospitalized Pediatric Patients Less Than 12 Years Of Age Weighing At Least 3.5 Kg. www.fda.gov/media/137566/download

25. FDA 2021: COVID-19 Vaccines. www.fda.gov/emergency-preparedness-and-response/coronavirus-disease-2019-covid-19/covid-19-vaccines

26. EMA COVID-19 vaccines. www.ema.europa.eu/en/human-regulatory/overview/public-health-threats/coronavirus-disease-covid-19/treatments-vaccines/covid-19-vaccines

27. Long B, Bridwell R, Gottlieb M. Thrombosis with thrombocytopenia syndrome associated with COVID-19 vaccines. *Am J Emerg Med* 2021; 49: 58-61. www.ncbi.nlm.nih.gov/pmc/articles/PMC8143907/pdf/main.pdf

28. Kantarcioglu B, Iqbal O, Walenga JM, et al. An Update on the Pathogenesis of COVID-19 and the Reportedly Rare Thrombotic Events Following Vaccination. *J Clin Appl Thromb Hemost* 2021; 27: 10760296211021498. www.ncbi.nlm.nih.gov/pmc/articles/PMC8173993/pdf/10.1177_10760296211021498.pdf

29. Makris M, Pavord S, Lester W, et al. Vaccine-induced Immune Thrombocytopenia and Thrombosis (VITT). *Res Pract Thromb Haemost* 2021; 5(5): e12529. www.ncbi.nlm.nih.gov/pmc/articles/PMC8178610/pdf/RTH2-5-e12529.pdf

30. Thakur KT, Tamborska A, Wood GK, et al. Clinical review of cerebral venous thrombosis in the context of COVID-19 vaccinations: Evaluation, management, and scientific questions. *J Neurol Sci* 2021; 427: 117532. www.ncbi.nlm.nih.gov/pmc/articles/PMC8178065/pdf/main.pdf

31. FDA Pfizer-BioNTech vaccine fact sheet www.fda.gov/media/144413/download

32. FDA Moderna vaccine fact sheet www.fda.gov/media/144637/download

33. FDA Janssen COVID-19 vaccine fact sheet. www.fda.gov/media/146304/download

34. Burckart GJ, Kim C. The Revolution in Pediatric Drug Development and Drug Use: Therapeutic Orphans No More. *J Pediatr Pharmacol Ther* 2020; 25(7): 565-573. www.ncbi.nlm.nih.gov/pmc/articles/PMC7541025/pdf/i1551-6776-25-7-565.pdf

35. Howard M, Barber J, Alizei N, et al. Dose adjustment in orphan disease populations: the quest to fulfill the requirements of physiologically based pharmacokinetics. *Expert Opin Drug Metab Toxicol* 2018; 14(12): 1315-1330.

36. FDA/EMA 2020: FDA / EMA Common Commentary on Submitting an initial Pediatric Study Plan (iPSP) and Paediatric Investigation Plan (PIP) for the Prevention and Treatment of COVID-19. www.fda.gov/media/138489/download and www.ema.europa.eu/en/documents/other/fda/ema-common-commentary-submitting-initial-pediatric-study-plan-ipsp-paediatric-investigation-plan-pip_en.pdf

37. EMA 2020. EMA initiatives for acceleration of development support and evaluation procedures for COVID-19 treatments and vaccines. www.ema.europa.eu/en/documents/other/ema-initiatives-acceleration-development-support-evaluation-procedures-covid-19-treatments-vaccines_en.pdf

38. EMA 2020: Remdesivir PIP EMEA-002826-PIP01-20. www.ema.europa.eu/en/documents/pip-decision/p/0046/2020-ema-decision-29-january-2020-agreement-paediatric-investigation-plan-granting-deferral-granting_en.pdf

39. SARS-CoV-2 spike protein (BNT162b2) PIP EMEA-002861-PIP02-20 www.ema.europa.eu/en/documents/pip-decision/

p/0480/2020-ema-decision-27-november-2020-agreement-
paediatric-investigation-plan-granting-deferral-highly_en.pdf

40. EMA 2020. Moderna Vaccine mRNA-1273 PIP EMEA-002893-
PIP01-20. www.ema.europa.eu/en/documents/pip-decision/
p/0481/2020-ema-decision-30-november-2020-agreement-
paediatric-investigation-plan-granting-deferral-mrna_en.pdf

41. Worldometer: Coronacases. www.worldometers.info/
coronavirus/?utm_campaign=homeAdvegas1?%22

Chapter 17: Infectious diseases, antibiotics and other antimicrobials

1. Hilts PJ. *Protecting America's Health: The FDA, Business, and One Hundred Years of Regulation.* New York, USA: Alfred A Knopf Publishers; 2003.

2. Simon AK, Hollander GA, McMichael A. Evolution of the immune system in humans from infancy to old age. *Proc Biol Sci* 2015; 282(1821): 20143085. www.ncbi.nlm.nih.gov/pmc/articles/PMC4707740/pdf/rspb20143085.pdf

3. Mostaghim M, McMullan BJ, Rowles G. Penicillin – getting prescribing right for children. *Aust Prescr* 2020; 43(3): 81-84. www.ncbi.nlm.nih.gov/pmc/articles/PMC7358052/pdf/austprescr-43-81.pdf

4. Kearns GL, Abdel-Rahman SM, Alander SW, Blowey DL, Leeder JS, Kauffman RE. Developmental pharmacology – drug disposition, action, and therapy in infants and children. *N Engl J Med* 2003; 349(12): 1157-1167. https://pdfs.semanticscholar.org/55f8/1745303e9aaec7f4cb85f0b5921eec14a9c0.pdf

5. Levels and Trends in Child Mortality. United Nations Inter-Agency Group for Child Mortality Estimation (UN IGME), Report 2020. https://data.unicef.org/resources/levels-and-trends-in-child-mortality/

6. Rose K. The Challenges of Pediatric Drug Development. *Curr Ther Res Clin Exp* 2019; 90: 128-134. https://doi.org/10.1016/j.curtheres.2019.01.007

7. Rose K, Neubauer D, Grant-Kels JM. Rational Use of Medicine in Children – The Conflict of Interests Story. A Review. *Rambam*

Maimonides Med J 2019; 10(3): e0018. Review. doi:10.5041/
RMMJ.10371. www.rmmj.org.il/userimages/928/2/
PublishFiles/953Article.pdf

8. Philip AG. The evolution of neonatology. *Pediatr Res* 2005; 58(4):
   799-815. www.nature.com/articles/pr2005743

9. Thompson G, Barker C, Folgori L, et al. Global shortage of
   neonatal and paediatric antibiotic trials: rapid review. *BMJ Open*
   2017; 7(10): e016293. www.ncbi.nlm.nih.gov/pmc/articles/
   PMC5652566/pdf/bmjopen-2017-016293.pdf

10. Garazzino S, Lutsar I, Bertaina C, et al. New Antibiotics for
    Paediatric Use: A Review of a Decade of Regulatory Trials
    Submitted to the European Medicines Agency From 2000--why
    Aren't We Doing Better? *Int J Antimicrob Agents* 2013; 42(2): 99-
    118. https://iris.unito.it/retrieve/handle/2318/140674/263834/
    New%20antibiotics%20for%20paediatric%20use_4aperto.pdf

11. FDA 1999. Moxifloxacin prescribing information. www.accessdata.
    fda.gov/drugsatfda_docs/label/2016/021085s063lbl.pdf

12. EMA 2009: Moxifloxacin PIP EMEA-000492-PIP01-08-M01 www.
    ema.europa.eu/en/documents/pip-decision/p/264/2009-
    european-medicines-agency-decision-23-december-2009-
    acceptance-modification-agreed-paediatric_en.pdf

13. Safety, Tolerability and Pharmacokinetics of Single Dose
    Intravenous Moxifloxacin in Pediatric Patients. NCT01049022
    www.clinicaltrials.gov/ct2/show/NCT01049022?term=
    moxifloxacin&age=0&fund=2&
    draw=3&rank=1

14. Moxifloxacin in Pediatric Subjects with Complicated Intra-
    abdominal Infection (MOXIPEDIA). NCT01069900
    www.clinicaltrials.gov/ct2/show/NCT01069900?
    term=moxifloxacin&age=0&fund=2&draw=2&rank=2

15. AAP 1995: Guidelines for the Ethical Conduct of Studies to
    Evaluate Drugs in Pediatric Populations, Committee on Drugs.
    Pediatrics 1995; 95(2): 286-294. https://pediatrics.aappublications.
    org/content/pediatrics/95/2/286.full.pdf

16. Rose K. *Considering the Patient in Pediatric Drug Development. How
    good intentions turned into harm.* Elsevier, London, 2020
    www.elsevier.com/books/considering-the-patient-in-pediatric-
    drug-development/rose/978-0-12-823888-2

17. FDA 2018. Baloxavir marboxil Label. www.accessdata.fda.gov/
    drugsatfda_docs/label/2018/210854s000lbl.pdf
18. EMA 2019: Baloxavil marboxil PIP EMEA-002440-PIP01-18
    www.ema.europa.eu/en/documents/pip-decision/
    p/0300/2019-ema-decision-2-september-2019-agreement-
    paediatric-investigation-plan-granting-deferral_en.pdf
19. FDA 2015: Voriconazole prescribing information.
    www.accessdata.fda.gov/drugsatfda_docs/
    label/2015/021266s038,021267s047,021630s028lbl.pdf
20. EMA 2013: Voriconazole PIP EMEA-000191-PIP01-08-M05.
    www.ema.europa.eu/en/documents/pip-decision/
    p/0151/2013-ema-decision-5-july-2013-acceptance-modification-
    agreed-paediatric-investigation-plan_en.pdf
21. FDA 2018: Ibalizumab prescribing information. www.accessdata.
    fda.gov/drugsatfda_docs/label/2018/761065lbl.pdf
22. EMA 2018: Ibalizumab PIP EMEA-002311-PIP01-17. www.ema.
    europa.eu/en/documents/pip-decision/p/0271/2018-ema-
    decision-17-august-2018-agreement-paediatric-investigation-
    plan-granting-deferral-granting_en.pdf

Chapter 18: Inflammatory bowel disease (IBD)

1. Kapoor A, Bhatia V, Sibal A. Pediatric Inflammatory Bowel Disease.
   Indian Pediatr 2016; 53(11): 993-1002.
   www.indianpediatrics.net/nov2016/993.pdf
2. Wehkamp J, Götz M, Herrlinger K, et al. Inflammatory Bowel
   Disease. *Dtsch Arztebl Int* 2016; 113(5): 72-82.
   www.ncbi.nlm.nih.gov/pmc/articles/PMC4782273/
3. Buderus S, Schulz D, Behrens R, et al. Inflammatory bowel disease
   in pediatric patients: Characteristics of newly diagnosed patients
   from the CEDATA-GPGE Registry. *Dtsch Arztebl Int* 2015; 112(8):
   121-127. www.ncbi.nlm.nih.gov/pmc/articles/PMC4361801/
   pdf/Dtsch_Arztebl_Int-112-0121.pdf
4. Däbritz J, Gerner P, Enninger A, et al. Inflammatory Bowel Disease
   in Childhood and Adolescence. *Dtsch Arztebl Int* 2017; 114(19):
   331-338. www.ncbi.nlm.nih.gov/pmc/articles/PMC5470346/
   pdf/Dtsch_Arztebl_Int-114-0331.pdf

5. Chams S, Badran R, Sayegh SE, et al. Inflammatory bowel disease: Looking beyond the tract. *Int J Immunopathol Pharmacol* 2019; 33: 2058738419866567. www.ncbi.nlm.nih.gov/pmc/articles/PMC6685113/pdf/10.1177_2058738419866567.pdf

6. Rosen MJ, Dhawan A, Saeed SA. Inflammatory Bowel Disease in Children and Adolescents. *JAMA Pediatr* 2015; 169(11): 1053-1060. www.ncbi.nlm.nih.gov/pmc/articles/PMC4702263/pdf/nihms-727007.pdf

7. Aardoom MA, Veereman G, de Ridder L. A Review on the Use of Anti-TNF in Children and Adolescents with Inflammatory Bowel Disease. *Int J Mol Sci* 2019; 20(10): 2529. www.ncbi.nlm.nih.gov/pmc/articles/PMC6566820/pdf/ijms-20-02529.pdf

8. Kelsen JR, Russo P, Sullivan KE. Early-Onset Inflammatory Bowel Disease. *Immunol Allergy Clin North Am* 2019; 39(1): 63-79. www.ncbi.nlm.nih.gov/pmc/articles/PMC6954002/pdf/nihms-1065525.pdf

9. Oliveira SB, Monteiro IM. Diagnosis and management of inflammatory bowel disease in children. *BMJ* 2017; 357: j2083. www.ncbi.nlm.nih.gov/pmc/articles/PMC6888256/

10. Corica D, Romano C. Biological Therapy in Pediatric Inflammatory Bowel Disease: A Systematic Review. *J Clin Gastroenterol* 2017; 51(2): 100-110.

11. Veereman G, Hauser B, De Greef E, et al. Reflections on treatment of IBD in children and adolescents. *Immunopharmacol Immunotoxicol* 2018; 40(6): 461-464.

12. EMA 2019: Adalimumab PIP ulcerative colitis EMEA-000366-PIP02-09-M06 www.ema.europa.eu/en/documents/pip-decision/p/0174/2019-ema-decision-15-may-2019-acceptance-modification-agreed-paediatric-investigation-plan_en.pdf

13. EMA 2018 Vedolizumab PIP EMEA-000645-PIP01-09-M06 ulcerative colitis and Crohn's disease. www.ema.europa.eu/en/documents/pip-decision/p/0109/2018-ema-decision-11-april-2018-acceptance-modification-agreed-paediatric-investigation-plan_en.pdf

14. EMA 2019: Tofacitinib PIP EMEA-000576-PIP03-12-M02 Ulcerative Colitis. www.ema.europa.eu/en/documents/pip-decision/p/0071/2019-ema-decision-22-march-2019-acceptance-modification-agreed-paediatric-investigation-plan_en.pdf

References

15. Momper JD, Mulugeta Y, Green DJ, et al. Adolescent dosing and labeling since the Food and Drug Administration Amendments Act of 2007. *JAMA Pediatr* 2013; 167(10): 926-932. https://jamanetwork.com/journals/jamapediatrics/fullarticle/10.1001/jamapediatrics.2013.465

Chapter 19: Rare and ultra-rare diseases

1. Hilts PJ. *Protecting America's Health: The FDA, Business, and One Hundred Years of Regulation.* New York, USA: Alfred A Knopf Publishers; 2003.
2. Wikipedia: Laparascopy. https://en.wikipedia.org/wiki/Laparoscopy
3. Wikipedia: National Organization for Rare Disorders. https://en.wikipedia.org/wiki/National_Organization_for_Rare_Disorders
4. Wikipedia: Tourette syndrome. https://en.wikipedia.org/wiki/Tourette_syndrome
5. Fagnan DE, Gromatzky AA, Stein RM, et al. Financing drug discovery for orphan diseases. *Drug Discov Today* 2014; 19(5): 533-538. www.sciencedirect.com/science/article/pii/S1359644613004030?via%3Dihub
6. Wiki Biosimilar https://en.wikipedia.org/wiki/Biosimilar
7. EMA 2015. European Medicines Agency decisionCW/0001/2015 of 23 July 2015 on class waivers. www.ema.europa.eu/en/documents/other/european-medicines-agency-decision-cw-0001-2015-23-july-2015-class-waivers-accordance-regulation-ec_en.pdf
8. Richter T, Janoudi G, Amegatse W, et al. Characteristics of drugs for ultra-rare diseases versus drugs for other rare diseases in HTA submissions made to the CADTH CDR. *Orphanet J Rare Dis* 2018; 13(1): 15. www.ncbi.nlm.nih.gov/pmc/articles/PMC5793441/pdf/13023_2018_Article_762.pdf
9. Penkov D, Tomasi P, Eichler I, et al. Pediatric Medicine Development: An Overview and Comparison of Regulatory Processes in the European Union and United States. *Therapeutic Innovation & Regulatory Science* 2017, 51(3):

271

360-371. https://europepmc.org/backend/ptpmcrender. fcgi?accid=PMC5493316&blobtype=pdf

10. Bucci-Rechtsweg C. Enhancing the Pediatric Drug Development Framework to Deliver Better Pediatric Therapies Tomorrow. *Clin Ther* 2017; 39(10): 1920-1932. www.clinicaltherapeutics.com/ action/showPdf?pii=S0149-2918%2817%2930832-9

11. Thomsen MDT. Global Pediatric Drug Development. *Curr Ther Res Clin Exp* 2019; 90: 135-142. www.ncbi.nlm.nih.gov/pmc/articles/ PMC6677570/pdf/main.pdf

12. De la Torre AJ, Luat AF, Juhász C, et al. A Multidisciplinary Consensus for Clinical Care and Research Needs for Sturge-Weber Syndrome. *Pediatr Neurol* 2018; 84: 11-20. www.ncbi.nlm. nih.gov/pmc/articles/PMC6317878/pdf/nihms961373.pdf

13. Wikipedia: Sturge-Weber syndrome https://en.wikipedia.org/ wiki/Sturge%E2%80%93Weber_syndrome

14. Happle R. *Mosaicism in Human Skin: Understanding Nevi, Nevoid Skin Disorders, and Cutaneous Neoplasia.* Springer, Heidelberg, Germany, 2016

15. Shirley MD, Tang H, Gallione CJ, et al. Sturge-Weber syndrome and port-wine stains caused by somatic mutation in GNAQ. *N Engl J Med* 2013; 368(21): 1971-1979. www.ncbi.nlm.nih.gov/pmc/ articles/PMC3749068/pdf/nihms491917.pdf

16. Higueros E, Roe E, Granell E, et al. Sturge-Weber Syndrome: A Review. *Actas Dermosifiliogr* 2017; 108(5): 407-417. www.actasdermo.org/en-pdf-S1578219017300975

17. Wikipedia: Periodic fever syndromes https://en.wikipedia.org/ wiki/Periodic_fever_syndrome

18. Wikipedia: Cryopyrin-associated periodic syndrome https://en.wikipedia.org/wiki/Cryopyrin-associated_periodic_ syndrome

19. Özen S, Batu ED, Demir S. Familial Mediterranean Fever: Recent Developments in Pathogenesis and New Recommendations for Management. *Front Immunol* 2017; 8: 253. www.ncbi.nlm.nih. gov/pmc/articles/PMC5362626/pdf/fimmu-08-00253.pdf

20. Gram H. The long and winding road in pharmaceutical development of canakinumab from rare genetic autoinflammatory syndromes to myocardial infarction and cancer. *Pharmacol Res* 2019: pii: S1043-6618(18)31983-

2. https://reader.elsevier.com/reader/sd/pii/S1043661818319832?token=A6994A4A9579EFFE8C5E11B4E735A08C61A1D579DEBDF679404CD19064C00F22E6A3213D99C400A4D3F1E106DF65EED2

21. Gurung P, Kanneganti TD. Autoinflammatory Skin Disorders: The Inflammasomme in Focus. *Trends Mol Med* 2016; 22(7): 545-564. www.ncbi.nlm.nih.gov/pmc/articles/PMC4925313/pdf/nihms793570.pdf

22. Wikipedia: Canakinumab https://en.wikipedia.org/wiki/Canakinumab

23. Cudrici C, Deuitch N, Aksentijevich I. Revisiting TNF Receptor-Associated Periodic Syndrome (TRAPS): Current Perspectives. *Int J Mol Sci* 2020; 21(9): 3263. www.ncbi.nlm.nih.gov/pmc/articles/PMC7246474/pdf/ijms-21-03263.pdf

24. Flume PA, Van Devanter DR. State of progress in treating cystic fibrosis respiratory disease. *BMC Med* 2012; 10: 88. www.ncbi.nlm.nih.gov/pmc/articles/PMC3425089/

25. Davis PB. Cystic Fibrosis since 1938. *Am J Respir Crit Care Med* 2006; 173(5): 475-482. www.ecfs.eu/society-details/about

26. Cystic Fibrosis Foundation. www.cff.org/

27. Cystic Fibrosis Foundation. Our history. www.cff.org/About-Us/About-the-Cystic-Fibrosis-Foundation/Our-History/

28. CF Foundation Venture Philanthropy Model. www.cff.org/About-Us/About-the-Cystic-Fibrosis-Foundation/CF-Foundation-Venture-Philanthropy-Model/

29. EMA 2019. Lumacaftor + Ivakafor PIP EMEA-001582-PIP01-13-M09. www.ema.europa.eu/en/documents/pip-decision/p/0431/2019-ema-decision-6-december-2019-acceptance-modification-agreed-paediatric-investigation-plan/ivacaftor-orkambi-emea-001582-pip01-13-m09_en.pdf

30. EMA 2017. elexacaftor + tezacaftor + ivacaftor PIP EMEA-002324-PIP01-17. www.ema.europa.eu/en/documents/pip-decision/p/0091/2019-ema-decision-22-march-2019-agreement-paediatric-investigation-plan-granting-deferral-n-13_en.pdf

31. Rose K. *Considering the Patient in Pediatric Drug Development. How good intentions turned into harm*. London, UK: Elsevier; 2021 www.elsevier.com/books/considering-the-patient-in-pediatric-drug-development/rose/978-0-12-823888-2

32. Korth-Bradley JM. The Path to Perfect Pediatric Posology – Drug Development in Pediatrics. *Clin Pharmacol* 2018; 58 Suppl 10: S48-S57. https://accp1.onlinelibrary.wiley.com/doi/pdf/10.1002/jcph.1081

33. Burckart GJ, Kim C. The Revolution in Pediatric Drug Development and Drug Use: Therapeutic Orphans No More. *J Pediatr Pharmacol Ther* 2020; 25(7): 565-573. www.ncbi.nlm.nih.gov/pmc/articles/PMC7541025/pdf/i1551-6776-25-7-565.pdf

34. Howard M, Barber J, Alizei N, et al. Dose adjustment in orphan disease populations: the quest to fulfill the requirements of physiologically based pharmacokinetics. *Expert Opin Drug Metab Toxicol* 2018; 14(12): 1315-1330.

Chapter 20: Cystic fibrosis

1. Newborn screening for CF. www.cff.org/What-is-CF/Testing/Newborn-Screening-for-CF/

2. Cystic Fibrosis Foundation. www.cff.org/

3. Cystic Fibrosis foundation. Our history. www.cff.org/About-Us/About-the-Cystic-Fibrosis-Foundation/Our-History/

4. CF Foundation Venture Philanthropy Model. www.cff.org/About-Us/About-the-Cystic-Fibrosis-Foundation/CF-Foundation-Venture-Philanthropy-Model/

5. Feuerstein A, Herper M. 'A game-changer': How Vertex delivered on cystic fibrosis. *Statnews* 2019. www.statnews.com/2019/10/23/we-conquered-a-disease-how-vertex-delivered-a-transformative-medicine-for-cystic-fibrosis/

6. Cystic Fibrosis Foundation Receives $3.3 Billion Royalty Pay Out. Philanthropynewdigest 2014. https://philanthropynewsdigest.org/news/cystic-fibrosis-foundation-receives-3.3-billion-royalty-pay-out

7. Gentzsch M, Mall MA. Ion Channel Modulators in Cystic Fibrosis. *Chest* 2018; 154(2): 383-393. www.ncbi.nlm.nih.gov/pmc/articles/PMC6113631/pdf/main.pdf

8. Joshi D, Ehrhardt A, Hong JS, Sorscher EJ. Cystic fibrosis precision therapeutics: Emerging considerations. *Pediatr Pulmonol* 2019;

54 Suppl 3: S13-S17. https://onlinelibrary.wiley.com/doi/epdf/10.1002/ppul.24547

9. FDA written requests issued. www.fda.gov/drugs/development-resources/written-requests-issued

10. FDA 2017. Kalydeco® (ivacaftor) label. www.accessdata.fda.gov/drugsatfda_docs/label/2017/203188s019lbl.pdf

11. Hilts PJ. *Protecting America's Health: The FDA, Business, and One Hundred Years of Regulation.* New York, USA, Alfred A Knopf Publishers; 2003.

12. Maude SL, Laetsch TW, Buechner J, Rives S, Boyer M, Bittencourt H, Tisagenlecleucel in Children and Young Adults with B-Cell Lymphoblastic Leukemia. *N Engl J Med* 2018; 378(5): 439-448 www.ncbi.nlm.nih.gov/pmc/articles/PMC5996391/pdf/nihms966186.pdf

13. Emily Whitehead: A Young Girl Beats Cancer with Immunotherapy. www.cancerresearch.org/immunotherapy/stories/patients/emily-whitehead

14. Rose K. *Considering the Patient in Pediatric Drug Development. How good intentions turned into harm.* Elsevier, London; 2020. www.elsevier.com/books/considering-the-patient-in-pediatric-drug-development/rose/978-0-12-823888-2 and www.sciencedirect.com/book/9780128238882/considering-the-patient-in-pediatric-drug-development

15. Cooney AL, McCray PB Jr, Sinn PL. Cystic Fibrosis Gene Therapy: Looking Back, Looking Forward. *Genes* 2018; 9(11): 538. www.ncbi.nlm.nih.gov/pmc/articles/PMC6266271/pdf/genes-09-00538.pdf

16. Irfan A, O'Hare E, Jelin E. Fetal interventions for congenital renal anomalies. *Transl Pediatr* 2021; 10(5): 1506-1517. www.ncbi.nlm.nih.gov/pmc/articles/PMC8192995/pdf/tp-10-05-1506.pdf

17. Sago H, Wada S. Fetal therapies as standard prenatal care in Japan. *Obstet Gynecol Sci* 2020; 63(2): 108-116. www.ncbi.nlm.nih.gov/pmc/articles/PMC7073354/pdf/ogs-63-108.pdf

Conclusion: How to restore public trust

1. Hilts PJ. *Protecting America's Health: The FDA, Business, and One Hundred Years of Regulation.* New York, USA: Alfred A Knopf Publishers; 2003.

2. George SL, Buyse M. Data fraud in clinical trials. *Clin Investig* 2015; 5(2): 161-173. www.ncbi.nlm.nih.gov/pmc/articles/PMC4340084/pdf/nihms662892.pdf

3. Hwang TJ, Tomasi PA, Bourgeois FT. Delays in completion and results reporting of clinical trials under the Paediatric Regulation in the European Union: A cohort study. *PLoS Med* 2018; 15(3): e1002520. https://journals.plos.org/plosmedicine/article/file?id=10.1371/journal.pmed.1002520&type=printable

4. Rose K. *Considering the Patient in Pediatric Drug Development. How good intentions turned into harm.* Elsevier, London, 2021 www.elsevier.com/books/considering-the-patient-in-pediatric-drug-development/rose/978-0-12-823888-2

5. EMA 2020: opinions and decisions on PIPs. www.ema.europa.eu/en/medicines/ema_group_types/ema_pip

6. EMA 2015: EMA 2015. Better medicines for children. www.ema.europa.eu/en/documents/leaflet/better-medicines-children_en.pdf

7. Rose K, Neubauer D, Grant-Kels JM. Rational Use of Medicine in Children – The Conflict of Interests Story. A Review. Rambam Maimonides Med J. 2019 Jul 18; 10(3): e0018. Review. doi:10.5041/RMMJ.10371. www.rmmj.org.il/userimages/928/2/PublishFiles/953Article.pdf

8. Penkov D, Tomasi P, Eichler I, et al. Pediatric Medicine Development: An Overview and Comparison of Regulatory Processes in the European Union and United States. *Therapeutic Innovation & Regulatory Science* 2017; 51(3): 360-371. https://europepmc.org/backend/ptpmcrender.fcgi?accid=PMC5493316&blobtype=pdf

9. Thomsen MDT. Global Pediatric Drug Development. *Curr Ther Res Clin Exp* 2019; 90: 135-142. www.ncbi.nlm.nih.gov/pmc/articles/PMC6677570/pdf/main.pdf

10. Executive Interview – Synteract: Advances in Pediatric Clinical Research & the Promise for the Future. Interview with Martine Dehlinger-Kremer. *Drug Development & Delivery* June 2019. https://drug-dev.com/executive-interview-synteract-advances-in-pediatric-clinical-research-the-promise-for-the-future/

11. Rocchi F, Paolucci P, Ceci A, et al. The european paediatric legislation: benefits and perspectives. *Ital J Pediatr* 2010; 36: 56. www.ncbi.nlm.nih.gov/pmc/articles/PMC2933611/pdf/1824-7288-36-56.pdf

12. Severin T, Corriol-Rohou S, Bucci-Rechtweg C, et al. How is the Pharmaceutical Industry Structured to Optimize Pediatric Drug Development? Existing Pediatric Structure Models and Proposed Recommendations for Structural Enhancement. *Ther Innov Regul Sci* 2020; 54: 1076-1084. https://link.springer.com/article/10.1007/s43441-020-00116-4

13. Ruperto N, Giannini EH, Pistorio A, et al. Is it time to move to active comparator trials in juvenile idiopathic arthritis?: a review of current study designs. *Arthritis Rheum* 2010; 62(11): 3131-3139. https://onlinelibrary.wiley.com/doi/epdf/10.1002/art.27670

14. Brunner HI, Rider LG, Kingsbury DJ, et al. Pediatric Rheumatology Collaborative Study Group - over four decades of pivotal clinical drug research in pediatric rheumatology. *Pediatr Rheumatol Online J* 2018; 16(1): 45. www.ncbi.nlm.nih.gov/pmc/articles/PMC6042275/pdf/12969_2018_Article_261.pdf

15. World Medical Association (WMA) Declaration of Helsinki – Ethical Principles for Medical Research Involving Human Subjects. Adopted by the 18th WMA General Assembly, Helsinki, Finland, June 1964, and amended by the 64th WMA General Assembly, Fortaleza, Brazil, October 2013. www.wma.net/policies-post/wma-declaration-of-helsinki-ethical-principles-for-medical-research-involving-human-subjects/

16. International Committee of Medical Journal Editors (ICMJE) Recommendations for the Conduct, Reporting, Editing, and Publication of Scholarly work in Medical Journals. www.icmje.org/recommendations/

17. Ollivier C, Mulugeta YL, Ruggieri L, et al. Paediatric extrapolation: A necessary paradigm shift. *Br J Clin Pharmacol* 2019; 85(4): 675-679.
www.ncbi.nlm.nih.gov/pmc/articles/PMC6422664/pdf/BCP-85-675.pdf

18. van Riet-Nales DA, Römkens EG, Saint-Raymond A, et al. Oral medicines for children in the European paediatric investigation plans. *PLoS One* 2014; 9(6): e98348.
www.ncbi.nlm.nih.gov/pmc/articles/PMC4045729/pdf/pone.0098348.pdf

19. Penazzato M, Gnanashanmugam D, Rojo P, et al. Optimizing Research to Speed Up Availability of Pediatric Antiretroviral Drugs and Formulations. *Clin Infect Dis* 2017; 64(11): 1597-1603.
www.ncbi.nlm.nih.gov/pmc/articles/PMC5927327/pdf/cix194.pdf

20. Collignon O, Koenig F, Koch A, et al. Adaptive designs in clinical trials: from scientific advice to marketing authorisation to the European Medicine Agency. *Trials* 2018; 19(1): 642.
www.ncbi.nlm.nih.gov/pmc/articles/PMC6245528/pdf/13063_2018_Article_3012.pdf

21. Waubant E, Banwell B, Wassmer E, Sormani MP, Amato MP, Hintzen R, et al. Clinical trials of disease-modifying agents in pediatric MS: Opportunities, challenges, and recommendations from the IPMSSG. *Neurology* 2019; 92: e2538-e2549.
www.ncbi.nlm.nih.gov/pmc/articles/PMC6556085/pdf/NEUROLOGY2018940742.pdf

22. Auvin S, French J, Dlugos D, et al. Novel study design to assess the efficacy and tolerability of antiseizure medications for focal-onset seizures in infants and young children: A consensus document from the regulatory task force and the pediatric commission of the International League against Epilepsy (ILAE), in collaboration with the Pediatric Epilepsy Research Consortium (PERC). *Epilepsia Open* 2019; 4(4): 537-543.
www.ncbi.nlm.nih.gov/pmc/articles/PMC6885693/pdf/EPI4-4-0.pdf

23. Pellock JM, Carman WJ, Thyagarajan V, Daniels T, Morris DL, D'Cruz O. Efficacy of antiepileptic drugs in adults predicts efficacy in children: a systematic review. *Neurology* 2012; 79(14): 1482-1489.

References

www.ncbi.nlm.nih.gov/pmc/articles/PMC4098824/pdf/znl1482.pdf

24. Pellock JM, Arzimanoglu A, D'Cruz O, et al. Extrapolating evidence of antiepileptic drug efficacy in adults to children ≥2 years of age with focal seizures: The case for disease similarity. *Epilepsia* 2017; 58(10): 1686-1696.
https://onlinelibrary.wiley.com/doi/epdf/10.1111/epi.13859

25. Wadsworth I, Jaki T, Sills GJ, et al. Clinical Drug Development in Epilepsy Revisited: A Proposal for a New Paradigm Streamlined Using Extrapolation. *CNS Drugs* 2016; 30(11): 1011–1017
www.ncbi.nlm.nih.gov/pmc/articles/PMC5078157/pdf/40263_2016_Article_383.pdf

26. Rennie 2004 Trial Registration. A Great Idea Switches From Ignored to Irresistible. *JAMA* 2004; 292(11): 1359-1362.
www.researchgate.net/publication/8357963_Trial_Registration_A_Great_Idea_Switches_From_Ignored_to_Irresistible/link/5797dec708aeb0ffcd06e58a/download

27. Gasparyan AY, Yessirkepov M, Voronov AA, et al. Comprehensive Approach to Open Access Publishing: Platforms and Tools. *J Korean Med Sci* 2019; 34(27): e184.
www.ncbi.nlm.nih.gov/pmc/articles/PMC6624413/pdf/jkms-34-e184.pdf

28. Benson T. Open Source Paradigm: A Synopsis of The Cathedral and the Bazaar for Health and Social Care. *J Innov Health Inform* 2016; 23(2): 488-492.
https://informatics.bmj.com/content/bmjhci/23/2/488.full.pdf

29. Pediatric Rheumatology Collaborative Study Group (PRCSG).
www.prcsg.org

30. Paediatric Rheumatology International Trials Organization (PRINTO).
www.printo.it

31. Wikipedia: Charity (Practice)
https://en.wikipedia.org/wiki/Charity_(practice)

32. Wikipedia: Charitable organization
https://en.wikipedia.org/wiki/Charitable_organization

33. Wikipedia: Philanthropy
https://en.wikipedia.org/wiki/Philanthropy

34. Charity Navigator – About us
www.charitynavigator.org/index.cfm?bay=content.
view&cpid=8658

35. Charity Navigator
www.charitynavigator.org/index.cfm?bay=search.
categories&categoryid=5

36. Charity Navigator – Giving Statistics
www.charitynavigator.org/index.cfm?bay=content.
view&cpid=42

37. Wikipedia: Tuskegee Syphilis Study.
https://en.wikipedia.org/wiki/Tuskegee_Syphilis_Study

38. Beecher HK. Ethics and clinical research. *N Engl J Med* 1966;
274(24): 1354-1360.
www.observatoriobioetica.org/wp-content/uploads/2016/09/
Beecher_Ethics_and_Clinical_Research_1966.pdf

39. Rose CD. Ethical Conduct of Research in Children: Pediatricians
and Their IRB (Part 1 of 2). *Pediatrics* 2017; 139(5): e20163648.
https://pediatrics.aappublications.org/content/
pediatrics/139/5/e20163648.full.pdf

40. Adashi EY, Walters LB, Menikoff JA. The Belmont Report at 40:
Reckoning With Time. *Am J Public Health* 2018; 108(10): 1345-1348.
www.ncbi.nlm.nih.gov/pmc/articles/PMC6137767/pdf/
AJPH.2018.304580.pdf

41. Washington HA. *Medical Apartheid: The Dark History of Medical
Experimentation on Black Americans from Colonial Times to the
Present.* New York, NY, USA: Doubleday Publishing Group; 2006.

Index

Index

Index

immune system
  adaptive/acquired (specific), 168, 187
  babies and infants, 168
  cancer and, 62
  infections and, 167
  innate (non-specific), 132, 135, 169, 187
  intestine and, 176
  skin and, 132
individuals (role)
  clinicians, 208
  readers, 210
infants *see* babies and infants; neonates
infections, 167–173
  arthritis and, 143
  drugs used *see* antimicrobials
  vaccination *see* vaccines
inflammatory bowel disease (IBD), 175–181
  extraintestinal manifestations, 175
  gastrointestinal tract/gut in, 175, 176
inflammatory joint disease *see* arthritis
inflammatory skin disorders, 132–140
inflammatory systemic diseases, 143
infliximab, 177, 178, 179
influenza (flu), 23–24, 171–172
informed consent, 56
injury, knee, 57, 106
innate immunity, 132, 135, 169, 187
institutional review boards and ethics committees (IRBs/ECs), 197, 201, 205, 208
  moxifloxacin and, 171
  multiple sclerosis and, 156
insulin, 89–90
  treatment with (including synthetic analogues), 90–91, 91, 93, 95
interferon beta-1a, 153
  see also peginterferon beta-1a
interleukin-1-beta, (biologics (incl. monoclonal antibodies to), 149, 188
International Committee of Medical Journal Editors (ICMJE), 201, 203–204
International League of Associations for Rheumatology, 143
International Paediatric Multiple Sclerosis Study Group (IPMSSG), 154, 155

international studies, 15
intestine *see* gut; inflammatory bowel disease
intra-abdominal infections, 170–171
iron lung, 6
ivacaftor, 188, 189, 194, 195
ixekizumab, 139

Janssen vaccine, 160
joint inflammation *see* arthritis
juvenile idiopathic (chronic) arthritis (JIA), 41–50, 189

Kawasaki disease, 158
keyhole knee surgery, 106–107
knee surgery, 57, 105–112

law *see* regulation
lawyers, 209
legislation *see* regulation
leukaemia, 30, 55, 62, 67, 75
  acute lymphoblastic (ALL), 30–32, 52, 66, 68, 75, 196
  chronic myelogenous, 75
lifestyle and diabetes, 92
liraglutide, 21–22, 91, 92–93
Lisbon Strategy, 111
low birth weight babies, 41, 44
lumakaftor, 188, 189
lung surfactant, 41–42
lymphoblastic leukaemia, acute (ALL), 30–32, 52, 66, 68, 75, 196

macrophage activation syndrome (MAS), 159
malignancies *see* cancer
matrix-assisted autologous chondrocyte implantation (MACI), 107, 109
maturation (child's body), 6, 36, 37, 39–40, 109, 200
  perinatal depression and, 114
medical (academic/scientific) publications, 20, 45, 50, 202–204
  see also research
medicines *see* drugs
Medicines and Healthcare Regulatory Agency (MHRA), 11, 32, 50
Mediterranean fever, familial, 149, 187, 189
melancholia, 81, 82
melanoma, 31, 57, 70–71
mental disorders
  children, 79–83, 125–130

Also from Hammersmith Health Books

The New Alchemists

The rise of deceptive healthcare

By Bernie Garrett

'a well-written, informative, critical, and evidence-based text that I can recommend wholeheartedly. .. it is good to have another splendid book that will help us in our struggle to inform the public responsibly.'

Edzard Ernst, Emeritus Professor of Complementary Medicine, University of Exeter

Also from Hammersmith Health Books

No Pills, No Needles

How to reverse diabetes and hypertension by finding out what works for you

By Dr Eugene Kongnyuy

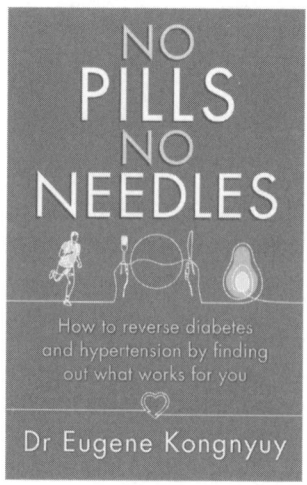

Based on Dr Kongnyuy's successful search for ways to reverse his own type 2 diabetes and hypertension, this clear account of the factors that can improve health and those that hold us back from change provides inspiration and practical guidance. Find out what works for you using the author's '3 Ts': Try, Track and Tell.

Also from Hammersmith Health Books

Crypto-infections

Denial, censorship and suppression – the truth about what lies behind chronic disease

By Dr Christian Perronne

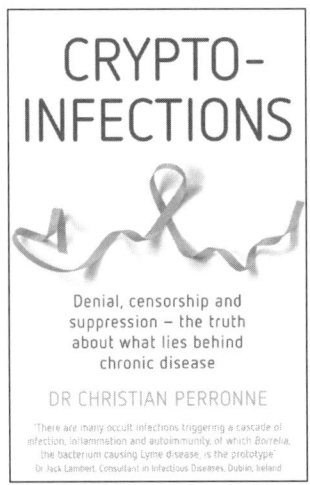

Evidence is growing that many of our modern 'diseases of civilisation' are the result of hidden ('crypto')chronic infections. As an exemplar of how the organisms responsible can hide in plain sight, causing devastation while the medical world is in denial, *Borrelia burgdorferi* – the bacterium responsible for Lyme disease – has led Dr Perronne to clash with his fellow specialists in infectious disease (ID) and challenge the status quo. From his experience as one of France's – and the world's – leading ID specialists, he examines the threats that both Lyme in particular and crypto-infections in general pose and how we can rise to the challenge.

A note about the cover image

The cover shows a scene from the fairy tale of Hansel and Gretel. Hungry and abandoned in a forest, the brother and sister have arrived at a house made of gingerbread. It looks so tempting Hansel cannot resist breaking off a piece and beginning to eat it and when the owner of the house appears she at first seems kindly and caring, welcoming the children in. However, in reality she is a witch who likes to eat children; she imprisons Hansel to fatten him for the pot and puts Gretel to work doing all the chores – the children are far worse off than they were before despite the outward appearance of kindness. Finally, Gretel outwits the witch and kills her; they find her treasure, escape and return home, so the story has a happy ending as do most fairy tales.

The picture symbolises temptation in the face of great pressure and apparent good will. One such modern tempatation is the lure for parents to consent to their sick child's participation in a clinical study. This will advance treatments for all children and give the individual young person the chance to try a new solution, or so parents often assume. However, after thalidomide caused malformations in thousands of babies, today we face a new global disaster called 'paediatric drug development', disguised as benevolence and justified by pseudoscience. Read this book and you will find out how a flawed concept of treatment for children pervades every specialty in children's medicine, how to distinguish useful research from useless, and what – as a parent, health professional, academic or business person – you can do.